The Doctorate Worldwide

SRHE and Open University Press Imprint

General Editor: Heather Eggins

Current titles include:

The Doctorate Worldwide

Stuart Powell and Howard Green

Society for Research into Higher Education
& Open University Press

Open University Press
McGraw-Hill Education
McGraw-Hill House
Shoppenhangers Road
Maidenhead
Berkshire
England
SL6 2QL

email: enquiries@openup.co.uk
world wide web: www.openup.co.uk

and Two Penn Plaza, New York, NY 10121-2289, USA

First published 2007

Copyright © Stuart Powell and Howard Green 2007

A catalogue record of this book is available from the British Library

ISBN-10: 0 335 22020 7 (pb)   0 335 22021 5 (hb)
ISBN-13: 978 0 335 22020 5 (pb)   978 0 335 22021 2 (hb)

Library of Congress Cataloging-in-Publication Data
CIP data has been applied for

Typeset by RefineCatch Limited, Bungay, Suffolk
Printed in Poland by OZ Graf S.A.
www.polskabook.pl

The *McGraw·Hill* Companies

Contents

The contributors

Dr Sakari Ahola, Vice Director of The Research Unit for the Sociology of Education, (RUSE), University of Turku, Finland

Dr. Jeroen A. Bartelse, Center for Higher Education Policy Studies (CHEPS), University of Twente Enschede, Netherlands

Professor Ahmed Bawa, Deputy Vice Chancellor – Research, University of Kwazulu-Natal, South Africa

Professor Sudhanshu Bhushan, Senior Fellow & Head, Higher Education Unit, National Institute of Educational Planning and Administration (NIEPA), 17-B, Sri Aurobindo Marg, New Delhi - 110 016, sudhanshu@niepa.org

Dr Paul Biaudet, Institute of Doctoral Training, University Pierre et Marie Curie (UPMC), Paris, France, paule.biaudet@upmc.fr

Professor Jean Chambaz, Institute of Doctoral Training, University Pierre et Marie Curie (UPMC), Paris, France, jean.chambaz@upmc.f

Professor Dr Soottiporn Chittmittrapap, MD, FACS, Professor of Paediatric Surgery, Vice-President for Research and International Affairs, Chulalong-korn University, Thailand

Dr Sylvain Collonge, Institute of Doctoral Training, University Pierre et Marie Curie (UPMC), Paris, France, svlvain.collonge@upmc.fr

Professor Barbara Evans, Convenor Australian Deans & Directors of Graduate Studies, Pro-Vice Chancellor (Research Training) and Dean of Graduate Studies, The University of Melbourne, Australia

Howard Green Ph.D., Emeritus Professor of Urban Planning, Staffordshire University, and Senior Partner, Postgraduate Directions, UK

Dr Hans Siggaard Jensen, Professor, Head of Department, The Danish University of Education, Learning Lab Denmark, Denmark

Dr Piotr W. Juchacz, Faculty of Philosophy, Poznan University, Poznan, Poland

Dr Barbara M. Kehm, Professor of Higher Education Research, Director of the International Centre for Higher Education Research, University of Kassel, Germany

Professor Marek Kwiek Ph.D., Director of the Center for Public Policy, Department of Philosophy, Poznan University, Poznan, Poland

Dr Sudaporn Luksaneeyanawin Ph.D., Deputy President for Research Affairs, Chulalongkorn University, Thailand

Louis Maheu, FRSC, Full Professor, Sociology Department, Université de Montréal, Canada

Dr Salvador Malo, Director General, Centre for the Assessment of Higher Education (CENEVAL), San Angel, DF, Mexico

Maresi Nerad Ph.D., Associate Graduate Dean, Associate Professor and Director, Center for Innovation and Research in Graduate Education (CIRGE), University of Washington, Seattle, WA, USA

Dr H.A. (Heinze) Oost, Nederlands Centrum voor de Promotieopleiding, Netherlands Centre for Research Schools and Graduate Schools, p/a IVLOS / Universiteit Utrecht, Netherlands

Dr Stuart Powell, Professor of Educational Psychology, Research Professor at the University of Hertfordshire, UK

Dr Renato Janine Ribeiro, Professor of Ethics and Political Philosophy, University of São Paulo, Brazil (and Evaluation Director of Brazilian Federal Agency for Support and Evaluation of Graduate Education, Brasilia, Brazil)

Dr J.F.M. (Hans) Sonneveld, Nederlands Centrum voor de Promotieopleiding, Netherlands Centre for Research Schools and Graduate Schools, p/a IVLOS / Universiteit Utrecht, Netherlands

Shinichi Yamamoto Ph.D., Professor, Research Institute for Higher

Education, Hiroshima University, Kagamiyama 1-2-2, Higashi-Hiroshima, Japan, yamamoto-rihe@hiroshima-u.ac.ip

Lee Zhuang Ph.D., Director of International Activities, Business School, Staffordshire University, UK

Foreword

It might be assumed that the Ph.D. is an academic award that can be attained in many countries across the world and that there is some common understanding of what such attainment would mean, i.e. that 'having a doctorate' has some common meaning. However, the editors of this book reveal, through their survey of 17 countries from across the globe, that such common understandings are elusive. They show that there are significant differences in such things as the typical amount of time spent studying for a doctorate, the ways in which such study is funded and the way in which the doctorate itself is described (in terms of nomenclature), valued and examined. Similarly, there are differences in the way in which countries treat the doctorate in relation to national aspirations for technological advancement and societal gain more generally.

The editors have searched far and wide to produce this rich collection of international facts and figures relating to doctoral study and the doctoral award. The result is a book that goes beyond existing analyses of the doctorate that have tended to focus on concerns within country borders or within areas such as the European Union. Here the reader is exposed to both information and self-reflection from a selection of international authors who report on the situation in their own countries with regard to the doctorate. The upshot of this review for the reader is a chance to set one's own (national) concerns within a wider context.

By considering doctoral study in this worldwide context the authors challenge us to reconsider just what it is that we engage in when educating students towards the Ph.D. and the various other doctoral awards that now exist. Their conclusions and suggestions of ways forward make an important contribution to the current critical debate about doctoral study and how it should be organized, managed and developed.

Professor Malcolm McCrae
University of Warwick, UK
Chairman of the UK Council for Graduate Education

Preface

This book is about doctoral study. The context is a disparate group of countries from around the world and the purpose is to better understand the way in which postgraduate research is organized and delivered. We intended the better understanding to arise from informed descriptions of doctoral processes and procedures in the various countries sampled.

To achieve our aims we asked a group of international contributors to address a template of common questions relating to, for example, numbers of doctoral students, kinds of institutions offering doctoral programmes and ways of examining doctoral outcomes. We also gave the contributors scope to address other issues, important to them in their own countries, which we here in the UK may not have considered.

What we found were some areas of common understanding (e.g. that the doctoral award signifies an ability to contribute to the relevant discipline or professional area), other areas where there was a significant difference in emphasis (e.g. in terms of the relationship between postgraduate education and national research, and development spend and gain) and a number of areas where there were common issues being addressed in wholly or subtly different ways (e.g. the focusing of research degree education in selected institutions or selected parts of some institutions).

In our summarizing chapter we discuss this range of findings and draw out conclusions relating to the purposes of doctoral awards and doctoral study. We set out a framework for discussing the issues that face many countries, albeit in differing forms and with differing emphases. By considering the multi-faceted nature of doctoral study and doctoral awards worldwide, our intention is to highlight various idiosyncrasies within national systems and point to a need for a critical re-evaluation of purposes and their pursuit within national and institutional practices.

Stuart Powell and Howard Green

Part 1

Origins and Structure

In Part 1 we describe the origins of this book and the structure set up for collecting information. We sketch out in broad terms the way in which the doctorate has developed to the present time and some of the key issues that face doctoral study worldwide.

Our aim is to begin to map out some of the issues we deem to be of importance when considering the way in which doctoral study has developed and may continue to develop, taking perspectives from a sample of countries across the globe.

The dangers of seeking to establish comparative data are discussed and it is stressed that the intention here is that the information and discussions in this book should be treated as reflective tools for those planning and organizing doctoral study worldwide. We argue that seeing one's own system within the perspective of the wider international scene enables understanding of just why systems operate as they do and what may be the possibilities for change.

1

Introduction

Howard Green and Stuart Powell

Overview

There have been significant changes in the nature of doctoral education across the world in the 13 years since Noble (1994: 1) observed that 'essentially the same process, which was conceived and propagated in Europe and later spread first to North America then around the world, continues unchanged today'. Many countries are re-examining the doctorate (or Ph.D.), its role and purpose. Some, such as Canada, are looking internationally when they make their analyses, others are largely inward-looking. Many seem to be operating on the basis of assumed commonalities of approach – even of 'givens' in respect of what a doctorate means and how it can be attained.

In our earlier book about doctoral study in contemporary higher education (Green and Powell 2005) we noted that the UK is developing its approach to the doctorate in a fragmented manner without any clear understanding of its character and purpose as between institution, discipline or constituent country within the UK. Equally we observed that the wider discussion of the doctorate at a European level was based similarly on a limited understanding of the interests or activities of member states. The work reported by the European Universities Association (EUA 2005) on the doctorate is partial in that it was undertaken by a network of individual institutions reflecting institutional rather that national views.

When we come to investigate the extent to which our thinking is based on an even broader understanding of what is going on in countries worldwide, we find ourselves in even more difficulty. For while there are some excellent works on the doctorate in individual countries (see e.g. Golde and Dore 2001; Academy of Finland 2003), there is little that brings these discussions together to provide a framework or a baseline on which to build our understanding. Comparative study seems to be almost completely lacking at the level of the doctorate. Even the volume entitled *Research and Higher Education, The United Kingdom and the United States* (Whiston and Geiger

1992) devoted only 13 pages of rather high level discussion to graduate education in the two countries (Clark 1992).

It is to rectify this omission that this book has been written. Put more specifically, our objectives are to inform the sector, and those interested in the international development of the doctorate more widely, about the current state of the full range of doctoral awards worldwide in order to:

- allow international comparisons to be made more easily;
- provide some baseline evidence for the international development of the doctorate;
- draw together themes of common concern into a framework for development;
- help identify aspects of good practice.

The choice of countries and contributing authors

A range of imperatives driving research degree study

To achieve our objectives we have brought together colleagues from across the globe who are involved in doctoral education at a senior level in their own countries. Their contributions form the content of the respective country chapters. In selecting the countries and authors we were concerned to capture different imperatives of importance to our understanding of the global position of the doctorate and its relationship with the UK.

Several of these imperatives form the basis of our synthesis. At this stage we wish simply to identify our reasoning behind the countries selected and what we hoped to achieve from the accounts.

Spectrum of countries relating to the percentage of GDP spent on research

We were concerned to involve countries across a wide spectrum of commitment to research. For this purpose we worked in the context of the Organization for Economic Cooperation and Development (OECD) data on the importance of research as reflected in the percentage of gross domestic product (GDP) spend on research as indicated in Table 1.1. The final selection from the OECD countries is highlighted in the table and reflects our hope to investigate countries in the top, middle and bottom of the ranges.

Countries chosen for inclusion in this book

Clearly, we could have chosen a number of different combinations of countries to fulfil our aim of sampling countries from across the range with

Table 1.1 Rank order % GDP expenditure on research and development

Country	Rank	Country	Rank	Country	Rank
Sweden	1	Austria	11	New Zealand	21
Finland	**2**	**France**	**12**	Ireland	22
Japan	**3**	**Canada**	**13**	Spain	23
Iceland	4	**UK**	**14**	Hungary	24
USA	**5**	**Netherlands**	**15**	Portugal	25
Germany	**6**	Norway	16	Turkey	26
Denmark	**7**	Luxembourg	17	Greece	27
Korea	8	**Australia**	**18**	Slovak Republic	28
Switzerland	9	Czech Republic	19	**Poland**	**29**
Belgium	10	Italy	20	**Mexico**	**30**

Source: OECD in Figures (2005), www.oecd.org/infigures

regard to 'GDP spend on research'. However, pragmatic concerns and some anecdotal observations played their part in our choice.

The USA has been held up by the UK government (see Department for Education and Skills 2003) as a model of concentration of awards within a small group of 'elite' institutions. Equally, the particular approach to the Ph.D., with the inclusion of a significant element of taught programmes, is regarded by many as something to emulate. The Australians, while adopting a predominantly Anglo-Saxon model have made significant strides in the professional doctorate.

Perhaps most importantly, both the USA and Australia are seen by many countries worldwide as competitor destinations for students wishing to undertake doctoral studies. An understanding of their approaches will be important to estimating the relative comparative advantages in the international market for doctoral students.

The choice of Germany and France stems in part from the significance of those two counties in the development of the European higher education area and indeed the very different approaches that they each display towards doctoral studies (Green and Powell 2005). We were aware of the importance of state and central control in France and that of the federal *lander* structure in Germany. From these two aspects it was anticipated that there would be much to learn.

Poland was selected because of its significance as a new and important player on the European stage following accession to the European Union (EU). We were anxious to see how it would develop and change its doctoral provision. Poland comes near the bottom of the OECD league table with a lot to develop if it is to achieve the EU aspiration of investment in research.

The Nordic countries (and hence here Finland and Denmark) are of special interest because they are countries with relatively small populations that have placed great emphasis on the development of a highly qualified labour force as part of their economic development strategies. This is reflected in their positioning in the OECD table. Finland in particular has made great strides in the link between doctoral education, knowledge transfer and industrial growth and, as we have already noted elsewhere (Green and Powell 2005), has developed a series of innovative approaches towards the organization and management of doctoral education.

Finally, we wanted to capture what was happening in those countries that have traditionally been seen as 'purchasers' rather than providers of research degree programmes. Brazil, Mexico, Thailand and in particular India and China were selected from this perspective. Issues of the quality of the student experience highlighted by the Brazilian government is often suggested as one of the underlying reasons for the establishment of the Harris review of postgraduate education in the UK. In the Indian and Chinese cases we were anxious to investigate the extent to which they were developing their own production of doctorates to service their rapidly growing economies. Mexico is also at the bottom of the OECD table.

South Africa is our only contribution from the African sub-continent. Our experience suggested that most African countries continued to have systems which heavily depended on colonialist traditions. South Africa on the other hand provides us with a discourse which could illustrate the approach in a country which is in the process of transition.

The approach taken in eliciting contributions

Unstructured and structured approaches

In asking colleagues to write about research degree study in their own countries there is an inherent tension: should they (i) be requested to write as they feel appropriate and hence highlight what is important to them (or treated by others as important within their own national debates), or (ii) be provided with a specification, posing selected issues to which they should respond? In short, should contributing authors be free to address the topic or asked to follow a template addressing pre-specified issues?

There are problems inherent in both approaches. In the former, the discourse may be anecdotal and partial, thus making comparison or synthesis problematic. Such discourse might however be meaningful in identifying what is important within individual countries and will not be led by the perceptions and values of the editors. The latter approach is, of course, led by those perceptions. It does therefore beg the question about the validity and relevance of the comparisons as the issues themselves may not be of mutual significance. However, it does provide a model which allows comparison to be made more readily.

The imposition of specified issues to be addressed

The second approach was adopted for the purposes of this book. Each contributing author was asked to respond to a series of questions and complete a template which essentially provided numerical data. The questions themselves cover only a part of the doctoral process and we acknowledge that the information contained in this book is partial. To do more would have been to produce a chapter of book length for each country. However, the questions posed are those which we concluded were of basic importance for our global understanding and are ones which our previous research suggested were of importance.

In an attempt to redress the balance somewhat towards a less partial approach we did incorporate a section of 'any other issues', thus enabling contributors to comment on aspects of doctoral study that were not included in our template. Interestingly there is no clear pattern of responses to that section – indicating perhaps that there was no glaring omission from the template. Similarly, in an attempt to avoid a purely descriptive text that merely listed information, we included a section for critical comment on the situation in the specific country.

Questions asked of contributors

We replicate in Table 1.2 the questions that were asked of contributors.

In addition we asked each of the contributors to provide some basic data which would give us an indication of the magnitude of the doctoral process in their country. We were aware from the UK experience that there may be difficulties in locating some of these data and that in some cases it might have to be estimated. Nevertheless we thought it vital that volume of activity was reflected in our study. A template was provided to the authors that included the following data requirements:

- number of doctoral students studying;
- number of institutions offering doctoral programmes;
- number of doctoral students studying who are nationals of other countries;
- completion rates;
- age profiles of doctoral candidates;
- destinations;
- historical period over which doctorates offered;
- number of different doctoral awards (e.g. including professional doctorates);
- organizational structure (e.g. existence of graduate schools).

Table 1.2 Questions asked of contributors

---

1 The place of doctoral study in the national/international context

- What is the role of the doctorate in relation to national research policy?

2 Funding issues

- How are candidates funded?
- How are institutions funded?

3 Kinds of institution

- What kinds of institution offer the award(s)?
- How are those awarding institutions organized (e.g. are there 'graduate schools)?

4 Forms of doctoral study

- What are the different forms of doctoral study and different doctoral qualifications (if more than one) (e.g. are there professional doctorates)?

5 Students and their programmes of study

- What qualifications are required of candidates?
- What are the periods of study?
- Can study be undertaken in part-time and full-time modes?
- What kinds of employment do they go to (destinations)?
- Are there identifiable gender issues in relation to doctoral study?
- Are there identifiable race issues in relation to doctoral study?
- Are there issues of religion that relate specifically to doctoral study?

6 Supervision

- How are candidates supervised (e.g. in teams or by one supervisor continuously)?

7 Examination

- How are candidates examined (e.g. can you describe briefly the typical examination procedure)?

8 Any other issues

- Contributors were asked here to add text in relation to any issues they deemed to be of importance but which had not been included in the above and to add reference to any statistical information that had not been included in the statistical table.

9 Critical comment

- In this section we asked contributors to offer some critical evaluation of some of the key issues in their country in relation to doctoral education. In so doing they might have been commenting on any of the items from the template above.

Aims underpinning the book

A reflective tool with regard to doctoral study worldwide

The purposes of the book are set out above; in short we aim to map out some of the issues that seem to us to be of importance when considering the way in which doctoral study may develop, taking perspectives from a sample of countries across the globe. In so doing we intend the information and discussions in the book to be useful reflective tools for those planning and organizing doctoral study worldwide.

In the section below we use the UK's experience of the doctorate as a starting point for consideration of developments in this respect worldwide. Our intention here is not to be overly centred on the UK but rather to use it as an example to pursue the wider considerations.

Countries as providers of PGR and as suppliers of students to other countries

Our immediate goal is to understand aspects of the doctoral process from the perspective of understanding how the doctoral market within which each country's postgraduate research (PGR) operates – all of the countries sampled here act both as providers of PGR education and as suppliers of students to the PGR production of other countries. Of course, the deviation across countries comes from the way in which provision and supply are balanced. In some countries where PGR is not long-established there may be a strong imbalance towards being a supplier of students to other, sometimes neighbouring, countries with established provision.

Increasing demand for PGR and adjustments in the way in which that demand is met are key themes in the world scene. The demand for doctoral research programmes in the UK has risen considerably over the past ten years, illustrating the attractive nature of the 'British Ph.D.', although there is some evidence that this has now levelled off (see Figure 1.1). However, this increasing demand is mirrored in many, if not all, of the countries sampled in this book. All have their own initiatives and their own tensions with regard to supply and demand of PGR. The spread of English as the language of research and academia, the drive towards technological advancement in a globally competitive market and the increasing mobility of students and workers, not just in Europe, are just some of the factors that have brought about adjustments – in some cases quite radical – in the balance between being a supplier of students on the one hand and a provider of PGR on the other. These balances are no longer solely a matter of tradition, experience and expertise. Knowledge and skills are readily transferred in the twenty-first century and this applies to the sphere of PGR as it does in other aspects of life.

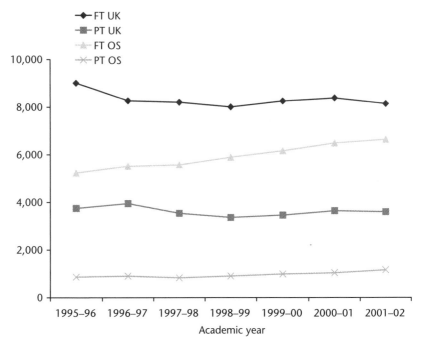

Figure 1.1 First year doctoral research students by domicile and mode, 1995–96 to 2001–02

Quality assurance

There are several reasons for the changes illustrated in Figure 1.1, which relate to nature of the award and the doctoral process itself which historically have given the UK an international comparative advantage. From the pre-Harris days of the early 1990s there has been a significant change in the way in which the doctorate is delivered and quality assured. In the UK, the Quality Assurance Agency's (QAA) *Code of Practice for Postgraduate Research Awards*, and the associated institutional audit of process is a major factor in reassuring international students and sponsors of the quality of the doctorate. Such concern with quality assurance is increasingly a feature of PGR provision internationally – with a difference often at the level of the degree to which such assurance functions at a central, national level as opposed to the more local regional or institutional level.

The status of individual institutions

The status of individual institutions is important for international students and for the UK there is a degree of good fortune in that several of its universities occupy world positions. As in many areas of higher education, rankings are now commonplace, and such is the case with the international status of universities. In 2005, twenty US universities ranked in the top 50, followed by eight UK institutions, six Australian, three Canadian, three Chinese/Hong Kong and three French. Status is, then, not confined to any single country or group of countries; it is spread, not evenly but widely and it seems likely that this spread will increase over the coming years.

The language of academic delivery

The language of delivery in academia is significant, particularly in the sciences where English is now the common international language of the scientific community. Clearly the UK is not the only English language speaking country offering doctorates, with Australia, Canada and the USA all competing for students.

We should note however that research undertaken in the English language is increasingly observed in countries in which English is not the first or predominate language. The Nordic countries as well as Germany and Holland undertake much of their research in English. In China, research students are required to study a second language and the evidence is that many choose English (see Chapter 13). Clearly the progress of a dominating scientific language, whether for better or for worse, impacts on PGR provision and on the supply of PGR students.

Time to completion

Expected time to completion is a further significant factor in attracting out of country students. Recent evidence in the UK suggests that 'overseas' students (as well as home students) complete in significantly shorter periods than is the case in many other countries. This is particularly important for overseas candidates who are paying significant tuition fees and charges for accommodation.

The balance between 'out of country' and home students

While many countries would suggest that there are significant advantages for international students to study with them, the growth of 'out of country' students relative to the overall student body needs to be treated with care.

Lack of joined up thinking can have a major effect on the student experience and recruitment. For example, in the UK the recent changes in the 'right to work' regulations have had some influence on the financial situation of students from overseas. The regulations now allow overseas students to work up to 20 hours per week during term-time and any number of hours during vacations without additional visa requirements. There is some anecdotal evidence that this increased opportunity is directing students away from their research work to the detriment of time to completion. This is exacerbated by the relative earning power of many students in the UK relative to that which exists in their home country. Some it seems use the additional earnings to support families back home.

Additionally the charge for renewal of students' visas in the UK has impacted on the budget of many students and hence may impact on future recruitment. Similar issues face other countries and are dealt with by greater or lesser degrees of joined up thinking.

The traditional view concerning the recruitment of out of country students has in part revolved around income to institutions. In the UK (as well as in many other countries), the number of home students willing and able to enter PGR programmes, particularly in the sciences, engineering and technology, has been problematic over recent years. Many institutions have been keen to recruit overseas students as a lucrative source of supplementary income. Interestingly, recent work in the UK by the Higher Education Policy Institute (HEPI) (2005), building on the costing work of JMConsulting, has shown that over the life of a doctoral programme even overseas students fail to cover the full costs of provision for the university concerned. Assuming the HEPI analysis to be correct, the impact on institutions, and potential future recruitment patterns will depend on the significance of overseas students to the overall student mix. This impact may well generalize to a greater or lesser extent to other countries as well as to the UK. By way of exemplar, Table 1.3

Table 1.3 Proportion of postgraduate students in ten UK Institutions

	Overseas postgraduates as % of student body	All overseas student fees as % of revenue
London School of Economics	42.2	33.6
Cranfield	31.9	3.5
Essex	22.6	17.2
UMIST	18.3	11.6
Surrey	16.9	10.7
Oxford	16.1	4.5
Cambridge	15.4	5.4
Imperial	14.7	6.7
Institute of Education	13.7	3.6
UCL	13.6	7.1
England overall	6.2	7.5

Source: HEPI (2004)

illustrates the impact of overseas postgraduates in relation to all overseas students in some UK universities.

Making comparisons and transferring ideas

All contributors to this book indicate in their writings an awareness that we are all working in a global market and hence need to appreciate the changing nature of comparative advantages which operate within the PGR market internationally. Given a completely free market there are several aspects of PGR which we would wish to take into account and these will become apparent as the book develops; they are also spelt out in the concluding chapter. However, there are inherent problems in a project of this nature, in part because it is tempting to make comparisons and transfer ideas that are derived from too general an understanding. Also, we have only allowed 4000 words for each country, clearly not enough for an exhaustive account. More importantly, there are limitations in what can be derived from comparative study of the kind upon which we are engaged here. Wolman (1993) has described these and pointed to what he saw as the major strengths and weaknesses of comparative study in terms of policy learning, policy transfer and systems understanding.

In our context, the country chapters will allow us to learn about how the doctorate is developing, the pressures and opportunities, according to the questions which we noted above. We will also learn about the systems which are operating in each of the countries, whether these are those associated with, or predominantly driven by, funding on the one hand or by quality assurance on the other. Our limitations however will be in terms of transferability, as this is so dependent on context: administrative, socioeconomic, historical and cultural. We would argue however, that our purpose is not diminished by this limitation. Indeed it is probably enhanced as one of our own personal objectives was to couch developments in the UK in an understanding of circumstances elsewhere rather than to transfer ideas from other contexts. We wanted to understand the UK situation more fully by considering it in the light of what is happening elsewhere.

The presentational structure of the book

Each contributing author was asked to address the issues in the template within a limit of 4000 words. In ordering these chapters we considered following our original selection process and grouping chapters according to expenditure on research as a proportion of GDP. In the end we decided on a more geographically-based taxonomy simply for ease of use by readers. The country chapters are therefore grouped in the following order.

- The chapters in Part 2 deal with Europe. The UK, France and Germany as the major European producers of doctorates are followed by the Netherlands and then the Nordic countries of Finland and Denmark. Finally in this European section comes Poland, a new accession country to the European Union. The country chapters are presented in alphabetical order.

• Part 3 includes the USA, Canada and Australia, major international competitors for research students.
• Part 4 includes countries with emerging potential both as suppliers of PGR students and provision of PGR programmes: Brazil, Mexico, Thailand, India, China, South Africa and Japan.

Conclusion

The final chapter presents a concluding synthesis of what we have learned from the country chapters. At this stage we do not want to anticipate the messages which will come from our country contributions. After all, that is the purpose of the book.

However, it is interesting to anticipate whether or not some of the concerns that are present in the UK are similarly found elsewhere. For example, to what extent have quality, organizational structure and change, completion rates, funding and diversification concerned individual countries from our sample, and what can we learn about how these issues have been approached? Each country may wish to learn about, and take into account in their planning, the issues that may ultimately affect their own comparative advantage and global position.

Many countries are concerned by the problems of the so-called 'brain drain': the haemorrhaging of talented students to other countries for the short or long term. Consideration needs to be made then of the problems that are created for some countries when their students remain in the (other) country of study to continue their contribution to the advancement of knowledge – particularly perhaps in the sciences and in technology. Clearly, continuing to contribute 'elsewhere' may impact on the technological advance of both involved countries. We will return to these and other matters in our final chapter.

References

Clark, B.R. (1992) Graduate education and research training, in T.G. Whiston and R.L. Geiger (eds) *Research and Higher Education, The United Kingdom and the United States*. Buckingham: The Society for Research into Higher Education and Open University Press.

Department for Education and Skills (DFES) (2003) *The Future of Higher Education*. London: DFES.

EUA (2005) *Doctoral Programmes for the European Knowledge Society*. Report of the EUA Doctoral programmes Project 2004–5. Brussels: European University Association.

Green, D.H. and Powell, S.D. (2005) *The Doctorate in Contemporary Higher Education.* Buckingham: The Society for Research into Higher Education and Open University Press.

Higher Education Policy Institute (HEPI) (2004) *Postgraduate Education in the United Kingdom.* Oxford: HEPI.

Higher Education Policy Institute (HEPI) (2005) *Postgraduate Research Degree Programmes in English Universities.* Oxford: HEPI.

Noble, K. (1994) *Changing Doctoral Degrees: An International Perspective.* Buckingham: The Society for Research into Higher Education and Open University Press.

Whiston, T.G. and Geiger, R.L. (1992) *Research and Higher Education, The United Kingdom and the United States.* Buckingham: The Society for Research into Higher Education and Open University Press.

Wolman, H. (1993) Cross-national comparisons of urban economic programmes: is the policy transfer possible? in D. Fasenfest (ed.) *Community Economic Development Formations in the US and the UK.* London: Macmillan.

Part 2

Europe

As noted in the introductory chapter our original selection process involved grouping chapters according to expenditure on research as a proportion of GDP. But we decided to group the chapters for presentational reasons on a more geographically-based taxonomy.

In Part 2 we focus on seven European countries. Here we include France, Germany and the UK as major European producers of doctorates as well as the Netherlands and then the Nordic countries of Finland and Denmark. Finally in this European section, we include the new accession country (that is: accession to the EU) of Poland.

Clearly, the EU brings about some sense of common ground with regard to quality issues and general purposes. But the differences across this group are nevertheless significant, perhaps most markedly in terms of examination and of the use of varied nomenclature for the so-called professional doctorates, where the UK stands apart.

We present these countries in alphabetical order.

2

Doctoral education in Denmark

Hans Siggaard Jensen

Introduction

Denmark has a long history in doctoral education going back to the late fifteenth century; the University of Copenhagen was founded in 1479 and offered the medieval doctoral degree. In terms of the modern Ph.D., Denmark started using the award in 1989 with the present system being initiated in 1993. There are now almost 5000 students studying at doctoral level in 15 universities in Denmark. In a recent governmental report it was suggested that the number of Danish doctoral students should be doubled in the next few years.

The questionnaire

Table 2.1 The questionnaire

Question	Number	Comment
1 Total number of doctoral students studying	4,815	Year 2003
2 Number of institutions offering doctoral programmes	15	12 universities under the Ministry of Science, Technology and Innovation and 3 institutions under the Ministry of Culture (Schools of Architecture and Library Studies)
3 Number of different doctoral awards (e.g. including professional doctorates)	2	The Ph.D. degree and the 'old' Dr degree, ex. Dr.tech. etc.
4 Number of years over which doctorates have been offered in the country	**527/13**	The University of Copenhagen was founded in 1479 and could offer the medieval doctoral degrees; the

(Continued overleaf)

Table 2.1 (Continued)

Question	Number	Comment
		present system was initiated in 1993. The awarding of a degree named 'Ph.D.' started in 1989
5 Proportion of full-time to part-time students	2:1	There are around 5000 doctoral students, and around 2500 have full-time fellowships; a fairly large amount of doctoral students in the medical field do the Ph.D. part-time
6 Average time to completion (in years)	3–5	3 years is the norm
7 Success rates	80%	The fully- funded complete at a very high rate
8 Typical age range of doctoral candidates	29–38	
9 Proportion of male/female students	6:4	
10 Proportion of doctoral students studying who are nationals of other countries?	1:20	Few nationals of other countries complete a doctorate in Denmark; there is a certain number of other Scandinavians who do, because of the Scandinavian system of transfer of rights in the educational field

The place of doctoral study in the national/international context

At present doctoral education in Denmark is an important focus for research policy. In a recent report from the Globalization Council in 2005, the suggestion is to double the number of Danish doctoral students in the next few years. This would mean going from awarding around 1000 degrees per year to around 2000, and thus aiming for a situation of 400 degrees awarded per million inhabitants per year. Funding for doctoral education has been growing, and now all major strategic research initiatives should contain a component relating to doctoral education. Also, funding should be used for attracting foreign doctoral students to Denmark. A sufficient number of people trained at the highest level for research is seen as an important factor in making Denmark a competitive society with a well-functioning economy.

The production of doctorates is seen not only as essential for the quality of higher education, but also for business and industry in general, related to the trend towards a private sector more focused on knowledge and knowledge-intensive organization. Furthermore, the quality development of the tertiary education sector is also seen as partly dependent upon a higher proportion of its teachers having a doctorate. It has of course for a long time in Denmark been a condition of a career in universities that one has a doctorate. So the necessary qualification for a post as assistant professor is a Ph.D. degree. The research policy of the Danish government stresses the relevance and usability of research and thus the importance of an increase in both the number of 'traditional' Ph.D. degrees that will be awarded, but also in the number of so-called 'industrial' Ph.D. degrees, where the doctorate education is in collaboration with a private company.

Funding issues

Doctoral students in Denmark are funded for the most part according to an agreement between the Danish Ministry of Finance and the Danish Association of Academic Workers. This provides a salary of €40,000 per year to the student. The student is thus both an enrolled student and an employee of the university. The industrial Ph.D. students are enrolled students but are employed by a private company, and the company receives fixed support from the government per student. It is possible for employees of institutions to be enrolled as doctoral students, and have a research project, based on an agreement between the student and their employer. A fairly large number of young medical doctors do a Ph.D. while employed at a hospital and/or in combination with taking a postgraduate training programme. Funding for the 'regular' doctoral students comes from the basic allocation to the Danish universities given under contract from the government and from public research funding typically through the research councils. All publicly-funded research training has to abide by the above-mentioned agreement governing the position as a Ph.D. student.

The degree-awarding institutions – the Danish universities and a few institutions under the Ministry of Culture – receive basic funding for research training. That funding is part of the basic allocation that is given to the universities to perform research. When a university receives funding for the salary of a doctoral student, it also receives funding for covering the costs of having the student *per se*. The amount is typically in the range of €20,000 to €25,000. The student does not pay for tuition, but the university receives support for having a doctoral programme. The costs covered are typically those for supervision, courses, travel, office and equipment, administration and costs directly related to the research project itself.

Kinds of institution

All Danish universities have the right to award doctoral degrees. Denmark has five general universities and seven more specialized universities such as the Danish Technical University and the Copenhagen Business School. Up until the end of the 1980s the degree awarded was named a licentiate and was given with reference to a specific scientific field. It was then decided to use the 'international' Ph.D. degree and name all degrees the same. Thus doctoral candidates in theology, engineering or business are all named 'Ph.D.'. A few institutions under the Ministry of Culture that do research have lately been given the right to award doctoral degrees, for example in architecture and design and in information sciences. The rules under which they do so are the same as those for the universities. The ministerial order governing doctoral studies is detailed, long and specific, and is binding for all Danish degree-awarding institutions (see www.videnskabsministeriet.dk/cgi-bin/doc-show.cgi?doc_id=130951&leftmenu=LOVSTOF).

Danish universities can have sub-parts called *fakultet*, such as 'The Faculty of Natural Sciences'. Some cover only one area of scientific study and thus have no sub-parts, except individual departments. The degree-granting power lies with a *fakultet* if such is present and if not, then with the university. The typically broad university will have three or more *fakultets*. The doctoral student is thus enrolled in a doctoral programme at a university or a *fakultet*. As an employee the student is a member of a department. The doctoral programme is run by a study board, which is responsible for setting up an individual programme for each student. The study board has an equal representation of faculty and doctoral students, elected from among the respective groups. A university and/or a *fakultet* can itself decide how the organization of study boards should be. Thus the doctoral student is part of a fairly complex contract. As a student they are under the authority of a study board with a chairperson. The study board decides who is going to be the supervisor for the student, and decides on a programme of study for the student. As an employee the student is under the authority of the head of department, in the department where the student is located. If the student is an industrial Ph.D. student, the employer is the company.

In recent years a number of research schools have been created. These can be local at a university, covering only one or maybe several scientific fields or they can be inter-university organizations, providing a forum for cooperation among several research environments. Thus in various ways non-university-based research groups from, for example, national research institutes, museums, archives, scientific libraries and research departments of private companies can be involved. The research school will then take over some of the responsibilities of the study boards. They are formed with the purpose of improving the quality of doctoral education through a higher degree of cooperation and focus. Thus a doctoral school could provide a programme of doctoral courses, a venue for international cooperation and an active environment of doctoral students. Around 90 such doctoral schools have been formed with various forms of support from research councils. The focus of the doctoral school is a scientific field defined through a discipline, an interdisciplinary problem area, a specific methodological approach or relevance for a specific social sector. Some are small – 15–20 doctoral students – and some are very large, providing training and education for several hundred doctoral students.

Forms of doctoral study

Doctoral education in Denmark is found in two forms. The traditional Ph.D. where the student is enrolled at and employed by the university and the industrial Ph.D. where the student is enrolled at a university but employed by a private company (defined as an organization that receives less than 50 per cent of its income from public sources). The rules governing the two forms are the same, but the organization of the study programme is a little different. The number of students in the industrial Ph.D. scheme is less than 10 per cent of the total number of doctoral students. In all cases a student has to take a number of doctoral courses equivalent to 30 European Credit Transfer and Accumulation System (ECTS) credits and to do a research project under supervision resulting in a thesis that has to be publicly defended. A student should gain experience of communicating about the research project to different audiences and should also be part of another research environment, typically through a stay at a foreign university or research institution. Traditional students are additionally obliged to provide 840 hours of work to the university.

Traditional students have supervisors that come from research institutions, whereas the industrial students have two supervisors, one from the institution where the student is enrolled and the other from the employing company. The traditional student is throughout the whole process under the authority of the study board and the institution where that is located, for example, in respect of selection of who should get a publicly-offered fellowship, whereas the industrial students are partly dependent on a board governing the industrial Ph.D. scheme that awards grants to the private companies that are willing to employ doctoral students. Their programme of study has to be approved by the study board. Both types of doctoral students can be part of research schools.

Universities can also award a doctoral degree based on individual research work done without supervision and without any formal requirements. This is the old medieval doctoral degree. This comes in various forms such as a doctor of law, a doctor of science or a doctor of arts. This was the normal requirement for a professorship until the 'modern' Ph.D. took over in the 1980s. This again was based on a licentiate degree that was typically used in the more professionally-oriented universities such as those specializing in technology, agriculture and business. The professional schools could also offer their own old doctoral degrees. In the last decades the number of such old doctoral degrees awarded has declined and the Ph.D. has taken over. A Ph.D. is required for university employment at the entry level of assistant professor.

Students and their programmes of study

Enrolling on a doctoral programme

To enrol in a doctoral programme an applicant has to have a masters degree or equivalent. This means that the student has to have written a long essay or report in which they show familiarity with the research area through presentation and discussion of a particular subject or problem. This typically means four or five years of university study. Furthermore the student has to present a proposal for a project and have acceptance of this from a department or research school, which is willing to take responsibility, and acceptance from a potential and qualified supervisor. Finally the applicant has to present a financial plan.

Typically, if research fellowships are offered, the selection is in two parts. First the institution decides who will get fellowships and they will then apply for enrolment in the doctoral programme that is relevant. In that case, of course, having got the fellowship automatically secures the presence of a financial plan. The proposed project and a proposed study plan outlining courses and stays abroad have to be approved by the study board. It is also essential that the programme of study conforms to specific regulations for doctoral study at the university or faculty or in the research school in which the student wants to enrol. So the programme of study is a mix of a general programme and a programme specific to the student. The supervisor has the responsibility for the programme and for making sure that the student adheres to it.

The format of a doctoral programme

The general format for a doctoral study programme is that it has a length of three years. The relevant study board can prolong the period, but not if the student has a fellowship. The actual length of study is often more than three years and other forms of financing then have to be found. The three years comprises a workload of a half year (30 ECTS) taking courses. This can be spread over the first years of study. Alongside this the student has to do independent research under supervision. Doctoral education is considered to be learning by doing in the framework of a master–apprentice relationship. The student has to get some experience communicating about the research done, and has to have experience of another research environment. This is typically done through a half-year stay in a foreign university with which the research group where the student is working has good relations. As a result of the rules governing the employment of doctoral students – the conditions, for example, of having a research fellowship – the student can be asked to do what amounts to a half year of work for the university. This is often done by being a teaching assistant or by being a research assistant on a project run in the department where the student is employed. Thus out of the three years, one year has to be used for activities that are not specifically doing research. In specific cases applicants with a couple of years of research experience – employed as research assistants – can be enrolled on fellowship conditions that give only two and a half years of employment, and there are no further work obligations.

There is no formal way of undertaking doctoral study part-time, and if one has a fellowship this should not be necessary. Some students have different conditions, and they are then de facto part-time students. If a teacher in a tertiary education institution wants to obtain a doctoral degree, they can negotiate a situation with reduced working obligations, and then enrol in a doctoral programme and take five years to complete the degree. Such arrangements can be made but have to be approved by the study board involved. In the ministerial order the period of study is defined by the amount of work that has to be done, equivalent to three years of full-time work. Most universities limit period of study to five years.

Different subject areas

The number of doctoral students in different subjects varies considerably. In some fields – for example, natural science and engineering – a substantial percentage of those getting masters degrees go on to doctoral study. In the social sciences and the humanities the percentage is much smaller – typically less than 10 per cent. The distribution of male and female students also varies according to subject area. In general the number of female doctoral students is only a little smaller than the number of males. The average age of completion also varies across subjects, being highest in the humanities. Completion rates are high but relate strongly to the financial situation of the student. Students with fellowships complete at much higher rates than those without.

Cultural issues

Denmark has a very homogenous population in terms of race and religion. It is a white Protestant country. Only in the last few decades has there been a significant immigration of people with a different cultural background. So at the present time there are around 200,000 Muslims in Denmark. They started entering Denmark around 1970 and have been coming both to get work, through rules for family transfers, and as refugees. The educational situation of this group of Danes is not good. A high proportion receives only a little education and they are under-represented in higher education. Denmark tries to attract potential doctoral students from abroad. The research institutions where they will be working and studying are international in outlook, but the students also have to be able to live a good life outside the institutions. Typically, foreign doctoral students will come from countries where English is an important foreign language – such as India or China.

Supervision

The central person for a doctoral student is the supervisor. Each doctoral student has a main supervisor and it is possible to have more than one, but there is always one that has the prime responsibility for the progress of the student. Every half year a report has to be sent to the study board detailing the progress of the student in relation to the agreed study plan. If things are not going to plan, in the worst case the study can be terminated. The supervisor has a significant role here. Students may be enrolled at a university but be working at another location, such as a government research institution. If that is the case the student can have a main supervisor who is a professor at the university and a project supervisor at the place of work. The supervisor is responsible for documenting that the student has done what was planned and has fulfilled the requirements in the programme. Supervision is often a critical factor in the programme. Some students are very independent and can do things on their own, and require only talks with their supervisor a few times per term, others require nearly daily contact. That of course also depends on the project the student is doing. The research schools have been established in part to provide better conditions for supervision and more focus on it and its quality. Most doctoral schools have some form of training for their supervisors. Only associate and full professors can be supervisors and typically doctoral students cluster around certain supervisors. These are typically highly research-active professors, who also have a good status as teachers and are thus able to get in touch with the best and brightest students when they are in their masters years. Most doctoral students get their fellowships through application based on open calls. This is a condition for all fellowships financed through the government grant to universities and through research councils.

For industrial doctoral students the company applies for a fellowship based on recommendations of a specific candidate for the position. The call is typically based on research projects being done in research groups, and will mention the professors involved in the group, who become the supervisors later on. On average the number of doctoral students in relation to the number of professors available as supervisors is around 1:1. A recent international evaluation of doctoral education in Denmark has pointed out that this is significantly lower than at the best universities with which the Danish universities normally wish to be compared.

Examination

The main result of a period of doctoral study is the dissertation. This can be a monograph – typically of between 150 and 250 pages – or a collection of published or accepted papers plus a summary that provides a synthesis. The dissertation has to be published and to be defended publicly. It is assessed by a committee consisting of three members. They have to come from research groups outside the group where the research work has been done, and specifically two members have to come from another institution. The supervisor cannot be a member of the committee. The committee has to come forward with a preliminary evaluation of the dissertation, stating whether it can be accepted for defence. If that is the case the defence will take place. The defence typically consists of comments and questions from the members of the committee and the response of the candidate. Others can be allowed to take part. On the basis of the defence the committee submits a recommendation to the institution about the awarding of the degree.

The selection of the committee is done by the relevant academic council of the institution involved. Each faculty or institution has an academic council responsible for the awarding of degrees. Typically the committee writes a fairly extensive evaluation of the dissertation giving a summary of results obtained and stating criticisms. On the basis of this evaluation the defence can then proceed. In cases where the committee finds the dissertation not acceptable it can be recommended that it should be reworked and then evaluated by the same committee, or if revisions are more substantial it would have to be evaluated by a new committee. The committee can also simply reject the dissertation. If the dissertation is accepted for defence, the defence typically has the purpose of providing an opportunity for ensuring that the candidate who has submitted the thesis is actually knowledgeable and responsible for the text, and has done the work reported. Typically, the work is presented in a short lecture by the candidate. The defence typically lasts two to three hours. Each university has to make specific guidelines and can have different traditions in the different scientific fields. The essential quality system is based on the evaluation of the dissertation by a committee of highly qualified and independent peers.

Other issues

In March 2006 an international evaluation panel published a report on Ph.D. education in Denmark called *A Public Good* (see www.vidensk absministeriet.dk/fsk/publ/2006/International_evaluering_af_ph_d_uddan nelsen_Marts2006.pdf). It followed an international evaluation that was published in 2000 and had the title *A Good Start – Evaluation of Research Training in Denmark*. Danish doctoral education has been under close scrutiny. The process of creating a modern system of doctoral education in Denmark started with a reform in 1993, which essentially created the present system described above. It was followed by massive new investment in fellowships and the creation of new agencies responsible for advising and deciding in the field. In the mid-1990s initiatives were taken to develop new forms of doctoral training – what became research schools. This mirrored a more general European trend. The 2000 evaluation wanted more focus on doctoral training, clearer goals and a system of research schools. This indicated that there was a certain scepticism about the existing research infrastructure, where the individual university department was the nucleus. There had to be a new focus on critical mass, on internationalization, on quality in courses and on supervision.

The Danish Parliament was also concerned about doctoral education and focused on the establishment of research schools. The concept of a research school was in no way precise. A process of experimentation was initiated and a system of research schools established with many different forms from close-knit centres to networks of cooperating departments and research groups. The 2006 evaluation focused on this diversity of research schools and recommended that a refocus take place, and that Denmark develop an innovative new form of research school that blends the best of what has already been done with inspiration from the best US universities and their graduate schools. They are typically cross-disciplinary intraorganizations responsible for quality and research focus in all the departments of the university that offer doctoral training. Both the 2000 and the 2006 evaluation look at the principle that all Danish universities can offer and award doctoral degrees in all the areas they cover irrespective of the quality of the research groups working there. Both evaluations focus on and stress the principle that doctoral education has to go on in research groups of the highest standard. The basic premise of research training is the availability of highly competent researchers. The 2006 report concludes that Denmark has the potential to increase the number of doctoral students considerably, and ought to develop and take advantage of the experience gained from more than ten years of working at improving the quality of doctoral education.

3

Doctoral education in Finland: between traditionalism and modernity

Sakari Ahola

The role of doctoral study in Finland

Investment in doctoral education, both its volume and quality, has been a key issue in Finnish higher education and science policy since the beginning of the 1990s (MoE 2000). The increased interest in doctoral training relates to the national innovation strategy and the strong commitment of the Finnish government to fulfil the international standards regarding the level of research and development (R&D) investments. Finland is, indeed, one of the top countries in this respect. In 2004 Finnish R&D investments amounted to 3.5 per cent of gross domestic product (GDP) (www.research.fi).

Substantial investments and the restructuring of postgraduate training, especially graduate school reform, has led to a rapid expansion of doctoral degrees. During the 1980s the number of doctoral degrees increased by 50 per cent; during the 1990s the increase was 120 per cent. In 2004, 1399 doctoral candidates graduated. According to its current development plan[1] for 2003–8 the Ministry of Education (MoE) envisages a further increase to 1600 doctoral degrees.

In order to understand Finnish postgraduate training, and its particular structural dualism, it is useful to briefly describe the history of graduate school reform. In the Finnish system the graduate schools (hereafter GS) are collaborative doctoral programmes based on competitive scientific evaluation and financing. Thus, if we take the US system as a point of comparison, the Finnish concept clearly deviates from it.

The history of the GSs in Finland goes back to the 1980s and the Europe-wide changes in higher education policy emphasizing accountability and efficiency. The historical situation where 'decisions can no longer be fobbed off' (Neave 1998: 268) emerged in Finland in 1987 when the Organization for Economic Cooperation and Development's (OECD) evaluation of Finnish national science and technology policies concluded bluntly that our postgraduate training was poorly organized or even totally disorganized

(OECD 1987). It was obvious that something had to be done (Ahola and Kivinen 2001).

At the beginning of the 1990s, during the years of recession, a special policy of 'structural development' was launched in order to reform the higher education system to survive considerable budget cuts. Enormous amounts of resources were redirected to compensate for unemployment using education as an instrument. Higher education had its share, which enabled rapid decisions concerning the new GSs. Thus, the GS reform was partly launched as protection against graduate unemployment. The first application round was announced by the Academy of Finland in 1994 and the first graduate schools started working in 1995 (Ahola *et al.* 1999).

Referring to data sources

The main data source for Table 3.1 is the KOTA online database of the Ministry of Education (www.csc.fi/kota/kota.html). Additional online data sources are Statistics Finland (www.stat.fi/index_en.html), the Finnish Science and Technology Information Service (www.research.fi/index_en.html) and the MoE's annual report (www.minedu.fi/julkaisut/koulutus/2005/Universities%202004.pdf).

Institutional landscape

There are 20 university-level institutions in Finland,[2] ten multi-faculty universities, three universities of technology, three schools of economics and business administration, and the remaining four are art academies. Importantly in the context of this book, all these institutions combine teaching and research functions, and have the right to confer doctoral degrees. There are basically two types of doctoral award in Finland. The art academies have their own degree with special requirements. The science universities have a uniform award although the names are field-specific, such as Doctor of Social Sciences. They will be hereafter referred to simply as Ph.D. There is also an optional intermediate postgraduate degree called the licentiate (Government Decree on University Degrees 2004).

Table 3.2 gives the basic figures concerning postgraduate activities in the university sector. The University of Helsinki is clearly the largest university in Finland with nearly 5500 postgraduate students and 400 Ph.D. degrees per year. Medium-sized institutions include the universities of Turku, Oulu, Tampere and Jyväskylä, and the two technology universities in Helsinki and Tampere. The remaining institutions are relatively small with a few hundred postgraduate students each.

In 2004 558 licentiate degrees and 1399 Ph.D. degrees were completed altogether, and the total number of postgraduate students was 22,105. A special feature of Finnish postgraduate education is the relatively large

Table 3.1 The questionnaire

Question	Number	Comment
		In the Finnish case it is difficult to give even an approximate figure here because of the optional intermediate licentiate degree. In 2004 the total number of postgraduate students was 22,105
1 Total number of doctoral students studying		
2 Number of institutions offering doctoral programmes	20	
3 Number of different doctoral awards	2	
4 Number of years over which doctorates have been offered in the country	365	
5 Proportion of full-time to part-time students	Not applicable	
6 Average time to completion (in years)		The are no accurate statistics but some occasional information exists
7 Success rate		The are no accurate statistics but some occasional information exists
8 Typical age range of doctoral candidates		The age range of all postgraduate students in 2004 was from 18–70. Half of the students were between 30 and 44
9 Proportion of male/female students	55/44	
10 Proportion of doctoral students who are nationals of other countries	1,580	

number of postgraduate students as compared to the number of postgraduate degrees.

Table 3.3 offers basic figures in selected fields of study, illustrating the fast expansion since the beginning of the 1990s. The numbers show that the expansion is particularly concentrated on fields of study where the tradition of postgraduate education has been weak. The notion of weak tradition, taking a longer historical perspective, also applies to women's participation. Between 1990 and 2004, the number of female Ph.D.s in Finland increased four times, while the increase of male Ph.D.s was 129 per cent. In the fields of economics and education, for instance, where the tradition to embark on postgraduate studies has been generally low, the number of female Ph.D.s increased ten times.

Table 3.2 Number of postgraduate students and degrees in 2004, and number of graduate schools and graduate school students in 2006 by coordinating university

	All postgraduate students 2004	Licentiate degrees 2004	Doctoral degrees 2004	Graduate schools 2006	Graduate school students 2006
Univ. of Helsinki	5,488	137	395	30	346
Univ. of Turku	2,038	37	144	14	153
Univ. of Oulu	1,783	43	130	6	87
Univ. of Tampere	1,779	51	105	11	112
Univ. of Jyväskylä	1,616	65	113	8	66
Åbo Akademi Univ.	844	29	66	6	109
Univ. of Joensuu	763	35	57	8	124
Univ. of Kuopio	647	11	76	8	67
Univ. of Vaasa	422	15	10		
Univ. of Lapland	378	5	19	3	23
Helsinki Univ. of Tech.	2,762	72	130	17	221
Tampere Univ. of Tech.	1,838	31	61	5	71
Lappeenranta Univ. of Tech.	556	12	29	2	22
Helsinki School of Econ.	393	6	18	2	35
Turku School of Econ.	252	4	15	1	4
Swedish School of Econ.	179	4	18		
Univ. of Art and Design	185	0	8	1	6
Sibelius Academy	133	1	5	2	12
Theatre Academy	35	0	0		
Academy of Fine Arts	14	0	0		
All	**22,105**	**558**	**1,399**	**124**	**1,458[1]**

[1] In addition to student places financed by the MoE, there are other postgraduate students working in or with close connection to the graduate schools. The total number of students is estimated to be 4500 (Dill *et al.* 2006: 27).

Forms and funding

Finnish doctoral education is based on certain founding principles rooted in the Humboldtian tradition and the Nordic social-democratic welfare state model. These include substantial freedom in both access and involvement, as well as free tuition, diversified funding opportunities and high overall emphasis on equality. In addition, a strong belief in common research standards among the universities prevails. Another feature is the dissertation-centred model of doctoral education. All these features also mean that in Finland the postgraduate student body is relatively heterogeneous.

Table 3.3 Number of Ph.D.s in 2004, growth between 1990–2004 and masters/Ph.D. ratio in 1990 and 2004 in selected fields of study

	Number of Ph.D. degrees in 2004		Growth index 1990–2004		Masters/Ph.D. ratio	
	Males	Females	Males	Females	1990	2004
Humanities	53	66	378.6	366.7	35.4	15.1
Education	29	50	414.3	1,000	81.5	19.7
Social sciences	58	43	223.1	430	26.4	12.1
Law	15	8	500	400	83.6	19.3
Economics	54	28	600	933.3	99.3	20.3
Natural sciences	180	126	178.2	420	6.3	4.6
Engineering	208	48	495.2	800	28.8	9.4
Medicine	101	144	117.4	293.9	3.3	1.7
All	**762**	**623**	**228.8**	**401.9**	**16.9**	**8.8**

Note: art education excluded

After the introduction of the GSs, Finnish doctoral education has consisted of three 'realms'. The GSs are specific, usually inter-university and interdisciplinary or subject-oriented programmes. Students work full time, receive full pay and are expected to complete in four years. GSs usually offer taught courses, and tutoring is well organized.

In addition to the GSs, institutions and departments organize traditional forms of postgraduate training as part of their general research and teaching tasks; it is financed mainly from the regular higher education budget. The students in this system can be divided in two overlapping groups. In the first place, there are assistants, researchers and other university employees in departments and working on various projects, who study for a postgraduate degree. For them studying is to varying degrees mixed with their normal duties. The other group works typically outside the university full-time or receive small grants from various independent foundations. From an individual point of view, a postgraduate research career is in most cases a mix of different posts and varying funding sources.

On the whole, the GS is a special 'funding instrument' of the MoE. The Academy of Finland is responsible for the scientific evaluation of the proposed GSs. According to these evaluations, the MoE makes the final funding decisions. The total amount of funding for 2006 equalled €39.9 million, which will be used to hire 1458 full-time doctoral students and 23 research coordinators. The usual salary for doctoral students at the time of writing is €2235 per month. In addition, separate funding is available from the Academy for postgraduate courses and other activities.

Students and studying

Access

In the Finnish system access to postgraduate studies is relatively open. All those who have the basic degree (masters) can seek permission to carry out postgraduate studies. Also other degrees, including foreign ones, which are comparable to the second cycle degree give general eligibility. In line with the principles of open access and lifelong learning, the university can also accept candidates who have in other ways acquired the necessary aptitude for postgraduate studies. Universities themselves decide on their admissions, and faculties and departments have various recruitment policies and procedures (Universities Act 1997).

In a typical situation a person wishing to carry out postgraduate studies has to consult their professor on the proposed research topic, in some cases write a research plan, and present a study plan for the relevant administrative body, faculty board, GS management team etc. In some cases there are fixed dates for application and special application forms. In other cases, application is continuous and more informal. In addition to the formal eligibility criteria, admission is based on various criteria including success in graduate studies, and the relevance and quality of the proposed research plan.

Despite the long tradition of educational policy emphasizing equal opportunity, higher education in Finland, as elsewhere, is socially quite selective. Parents' socioeconomic status and education affect their children's probability of participating in higher education (Kivinen *et al.* 2001). In 2000, from a cohort of 33–65-year-olds a total of 0.8 per cent had a postgraduate degree. However, if their fathers had acquired postgraduate education, the probability of them gaining a postgraduate degree was 14 times greater.[3]

In the field of postgraduate education, gender questions are also still on the policy agenda. The higher up the academic ladder we look, the fewer women there are. In the early 1990s, women's share of basic university degrees was 54 per cent, but only 31 per cent of new Ph.D.s and 13 per cent of professors were women. In 2004 the corresponding figures were 61, 45 and 22 per cent (MoE 2005).

Modes of study

Due to the different traditions, postgraduate studies take different forms. As pointed out before, in the GSs, students work full-time and are expected to complete in four years. GSs offer taught courses and well-organized and efficient supervision and tutoring. In large research groups peer support is also important. However, competition may also be tough.

The MoE administered a survey for the first graduate school students in 1996 (MoE 2000). At that time, 55 per cent evaluated their overall experience of the new system as good or excellent and 25 per cent as satisfactory. The remaining fifth had unsatisfactory or even bad experiences. As regards the quality of tutoring, 25 per cent claimed that their experience was below satisfactory.

According to a second survey conducted in 1999 at the end of the first graduate school period, the majority (67 per cent) of respondents wanted more tutoring and support. One out of four thought that the supervision they had received for their dissertation was unsatisfactory or even poor. At that time 15 per cent had completed their doctoral degree.

There is very little up-to-date information on the lives and studies of regular postgraduate students. There is also inadequate statistical information on the completion and duration of postgraduate studies. If we look at the median ages of graduates, we can estimate the average time from the masters degree to the doctoral degree. In 2001, the median age of masters degree graduates was 27 in comparison with 36.3 for Ph.D. graduates (Statistics Finland 2004). This means that the average gross time between these two degrees is 9.3 years. Considering the actual duration of studies, we have to take into account that not everyone embarks on postgraduate studies immediately after graduation. It is clear, however, that the postgraduate student body includes a large group of relatively old students whose probability of completion is low. In 2001 over half (54 per cent) of all postgraduate students were older than 34 (Statistics Finland 2004).

In the aforementioned GS survey, it was estimated that 58 per cent of all the students who were participating in the schools would graduate within the required four years. This corresponds well to students' own estimation in the 1999 survey. Half of them said that they would manage within four years and the other half estimated that it would probably take a longer time for them to graduate.

The results also illustrate the typical routes to postgraduate studies. In the 1996 survey 6 per cent of students were unemployed prior to enrolling at the school. The majority of GS students (69 per cent) came from another university or research institute posts, and 18 per cent were employed in other sectors; 7 per cent had student status while enrolling.

In 1999 the share of those with student status had increased to 29 per cent, and only 9 per cent came from outside the field of research. In other words, during their first four-year period, the GSs were distinctively a new financing opportunity for postgraduate students already holding different research and student positions in universities or research institutes. There is no up-to-date information on the current situation, but an informed guess would be that there have been no notable changes.

Examination

Finnish doctoral education was recently evaluated by an international expert group. Their report describes the examination procedure as follows:

In its ideal form . . . the completed dissertation manuscript is reviewed prior to publication by a faculty-appointed team that includes outside reviewers, copies of the published dissertation are made available to members of the relevant faculty and to others prior to the defense, and the published dissertation is defended in a public meeting involving faculty-appointed 'opponents' from other universities, who are also expected to submit a written evaluation of the dissertation. Anyone who has concerns about the quality of the dissertation can also express her or his critical comments during the public defense. As described this ideal process is at least as rigorous if not more rigorous than the quality assurance process for dissertations in other countries.

(Dill *et al.* 2006: 56)

The report points to the various weaknesses that can creep into the process, starting from the selection of the reviewers. This can, indeed, be a problem in a small country like Finland, especially because the academic field is scattered among relatively small departments. These kinds of problems naturally take different shape depending on the field in question. In recent years, in fields like the social sciences or education, the number of theses written in English has grown, which has broadened the pool of reviewers and increased the credibility of the system. The crucial point is that there is no systematic evaluation or monitoring of the whole process by the university.

The rapid growth of the number of dissertations in recent years has initiated a debate over their quality. Both the MoE and the Academy of Finland, who run the GS system, are constantly advocating the persistent quality of the output. Messages from the field, however, are quite different. Because under the current funding model every new Ph.D. brings a considerable amount of money to the university's coffers, the fear is genuine, highlighting the need for a quality assurance system.

Employment

Expansive postgraduate policies have evoked serious questions concerning the employment of doctoral degree holders. The MoE maintains the 'education always pays' position, referring to the overall unemployment statistics. For instance, from those who completed their doctoral degree in 2001 only 1 per cent was unemployed at the end of 2002. Corresponding unemployment rates for licentiate and masters degree holders are presented in Table 3.4.

Overt unemployment is not, however, the entire picture. Table 3.4 also shows other ways to be flexible in the competitive job market. Out of doctoral degree holders, 7.5 per cent were outside the labour market and 2.1 per cent were still studying full-time. Women seem to be continuing full-time studies more often than men (3.4/1 per cent). Women are also

Table 3.4 Main activity of university graduates in 2001 at the end of year 2002 by level of degree

	Number of graduates	Employed (%)		Full-time students (%)	Unemployed (%)	Other activity (%)
			Of which studying			
Masters	11,370	87.6	16.8	5.3	3.8	3.3
Licentiate	575	85.9	44.7	9.9	2.6	1.6
Doctorate	1,106	89.4	7.8	2.1	1.0	7.5

more often unemployed than men (1.2 / 0.8 per cent). There is, however, no gender difference in the probability of ending up outside the labour market (Statistics Finland 2004).

There are clear differences between different fields of study as regards unemployment. The humanities and the social sciences, in particular, have been suffering from the expansion. On the other hand, in fields like engineering, economics, law and medicine, unemployment is almost non-existent. What has been especially worrying for policy-makers is the relatively high doctoral unemployment in the field of natural sciences.

During the years of expansion, technology-driven higher education policy has emphasized the need to increase the number of Ph.D.s in the private sector, industry and especially information and communication technology (ICT). Since the late 1980s, the objective has been that more than half of university graduates would be able to find employment outside the public sector. This situation has changed, however, at an agonizingly slow pace. In 2002, of the newly graduated, still less than 50 per cent were working in the private sector. For doctoral degree holders, the share was only 24 per cent.

Graduates in the field of technology seem to go into the private sector more often than others. In 1999 the share was 38 per cent. From engineering Ph.D.s working in the private sector 52 per cent was employed in industry and 47 per cent in services. In the fields of humanities and social sciences, about 80 per cent worked in the public sector in 1999, most of them in the universities (Husso 2005).

Concluding remarks

The international evaluation report gives several recommendations to enhance and revise Finnish doctoral education (Dill *et al.* 2006). It shows a green light to the continuation of the GS system but proposes changes in the evaluation and selection of new postgraduate programmes. According to the report, the primary criterion for the selection of future GSs should be the existence of a strong research programme. Second, GSs should apply effective quality assurance procedures. In addition to the development of the structures and processes of doctoral education, the evaluation report also proposes a national code of conduct for doctoral education.

There has been criticism in Finnish discussions directed towards the Academy of Finland, claiming that the selection process is not transparent enough. The guidelines for applications are either very broad or non-existent, and review results and selection criteria are not made public. In the eighth application round in 2005, selection criteria included the internationalization of GSs, mobility of researchers and doctoral employment. In addition, GSs should be connected to the areas of strength in each university, their centres of excellence, or existing strong research networks. The scope and composition of accepted GSs give the impression that these criteria are not uniform and consistent. Taking this into consideration, it is no surprise that the evaluation team would like to transform the present collaborative doctoral programmes towards US-style graduate schools with strong leadership and a university-wide graduate faculty.

The evaluation report also addresses the 'passive participation' problem, listing some of the policies and solutions other countries have been adopting to tackle similar problems. These include fees, developing professional doctorates, residency requirements and time limits. At the moment it seems that in Finland fees are out of the question. What the MoE and the universities should seriously consider is the application of time limits coupled with a total reform of current postgraduate statistics. In addition, there should also be clear policy regulations defining the terms of re-entry.

The evaluation report is not all that explicit when dealing with the related questions of the volume of postgraduate education and doctoral employment. This is, however, an important problem that policy-makers should solve, especially if they follow the recommendations that stipulate new resources in order to maximize four-year funding to doctoral students. Finally, the question of whether or not the current bipolar postgraduate education system compromises on principles of equity and equality should be addressed.

Notes

1 The development plan is one of the most important higher education policy documents in Finland stating, among other things, the quantitative objectives and the necessary resources. See www.minedu.fi/julkaisut/koulutus/2004/opm08/opm08.pdf.

2 In addition, there is one military academy under the Ministry of Defence which is excluded from this analysis.

3 Based on a sample from the Finnish longitudinal census dataset (see Kivinen *et al.* 2001).

References

Ahola, S. and Kivinen, O. (2001) Postgraduate education in Europe: harmonising with a dissonance? Paper presented at the conference 'Postgraduate education in Europe – past, present and future', University of Linköping, Sweden, 4–5 May.

Ahola, S., Kivinen, O. and Kokko, A. (1999) PhD Training in Finland: problems and prospects, in O. Kivinen, S. Ahola and P. Kaipainen (eds) *Towards the European Model of Postgraduate Training*, Research Unit for the Sociology of Education, Research Report 50, University of Turku, Finland.

Dill, D. *et al.* (2006) *PhD Training and the Knowledge-Based Society. An Evaluation of Doctoral Education in Finland*. Tampere: Finnish Higher Education Evaluation Council, Tampere: Tammer-Paino Oy. www.kka.fi/pdf/julkaisut/KKA_106.pdf (accessed 24 February 2006).

Government Decree on University Degrees (2004) www.finlex.fi/fi/laki/kaannokset/2004/en20040794.pdf (accessed 24 February 2006).

Husso, K. (2005) *Tohtorit, tiedepolitiikka ja työmarkkinat. Tutkijakoulutus Suomessa 1950-luvulta tutkijakoulujen aikaan.* Opetusministeriön julkaisuja 2005:21. Helsinki: Yliopistopaino.

Kivinen, O., Ahola, S. and Hedman, J. (2001) Expanding education and improving odds? Participation in higher education in Finland in the 1980s and 1990s, *Acta Sociologica*, 44(2): 171–81.

MoE (2000) *The Graduate School System in Finland. Survey of Functioning, Results and Efficiency by 2000*. Helsinki: Ministry of Education, Department for Education and Science Policy.

MoE (2005) *OECD Thematic Review of Tertiary Education. Country Background Report for Finland.* www.minedu.fi/julkaisut/koulutus/2005/opm38/opm38.pdf (accessed 24 February 2006).

Neave, G. (1998) The evaluative state reconsidered, *European Journal of Education*, 33(3): 265–84.

OECD (1987) *Reviews of National Science and Technology Policies: Finland.* Paris: OECD.

Statistics Finland (2004) *Oppilaitostilastot 2004. Koulutus 2004.* Helsinki: Yliopistopaino Oy.

Universities Act (1997) www.finlex.fi/fi/laki/kaannokset/1997/en19970645.pdf (accessed 24 February 2006).

4

Doctoral education in France

Jean Chambaz, Paule Biaudet and Sylvain Collonge

Introduction

France has a strong tradition in doctoral education. As with many other European countries its system of higher education is developing within the frameworks of the European Union (EU). In that context doctoral education in France has undergone some significant changes – particularly since the reforms of 2000. This chapter highlights these changes and indicates some of the ongoing issues that face universities, supervisors and doctoral students in France today.

The questionnaire

Table 4.1 The questionnaire

Question	Number	Comment
1 Total number of doctoral candidates	Approximately 70,000	Source: French Ministry of Research (2005), www.recherche.gouv.fr
2 Number of institutions offering doctoral programmes	124/311	124 institutions entitled to deliver the doctoral level through 311 doctoral schools
3 Number of different doctoral awards	1	Doctorate of University
4 Number of years over which doctorates have been offered in the country	Approximately 1,000 years 23 years in the current form	The current form of doctorate has existed since 1984

5 Proportion of part-time to full-time doctoral candidates	Approximately 10%	This figure is not directly available, and most likely undervalued in humanities
6 Average time to completion (in years)	4 years	From 3.2 to 4.9 years according to the different scientific fields. The duration is fixed at 3 years by the official regulation
7 Success rates		Very dependent on the scientific field (from approximately 80% to less than 50%)
8 Typical age range of doctoral candidates	24–30	
9 Proportion of male/female doctoral candidates	60/40	
10 Proportion of doctoral candidates who are nationals of other countries	Approximately 25%	The figure is probably higher in 2007

Source: French Ministry of Research (2000), www.recherche.gouv.fr

Data source

The source, except where mentioned, is the French Ministry of Research. A new survey is expected soon.

The place of doctoral training in the national/ international context

The reforms of 2000

The 2000 French reforms considered doctoral training as a critical tool and a true contribution to improve research in France and its readability abroad. The set-up of doctoral schools aimed to focus on the high-quality scientific environment required for efficient training by research, i.e. a site-based critical mass of research teams organized in laboratories or scientific milieus, according to the research field.

This reform brought the doctorate out of the one-to-one relationship between the candidate and their professor, and embedded doctoral training at the institutional level. Standards were defined concerning management of the doctoral project, for example, (a) funding, (b) follow-up of the scientific project as well as the professional project, and (c) relative complementary courses and workshops on scientific and employability issues. Once the doctoral candidates graduated, their integration in the job market is followed to provide data on scientific and doctorate careers. All these tasks were assigned to doctoral schools.

After five years, one can already notice the role played by the setting up of doctoral schools in the organization of research on site, through instigation of interactions between universities and research and higher education institutions in their surrounding. This move should develop in the next few years, assuming sustainable support to be guaranteed by the government. Even in the region of Paris, which concentrates more than 40 per cent of the research potential in France and where the organization of research lacks clarity, doctoral schools contribute to networking, complementarity and simplification of the map.

Most interestingly, the setting up of doctoral schools has sped up the crucial and beneficial debate in human and social sciences about the necessary structuring of research in these fields, as well as about the running of doctorate education and its supervision – with pioneering actions of some doctoral schools acting as a catalyst.

Doctoral training as a first professional experience

Finally, the new prospect of doctoral training as a first professional experience, and the emphasis put on information and training in generic transferable skills contribute to modify the perception of doctors, mostly seen in France until recently as the self-reproduction of the old-fashioned scholar and/or as a leading-edge expert in a highly narrow speciality.

A new government regulation, based on the experience since 2000 and a consultation run by the ministry, is about to be enacted and will reinforce this new vision of the organization of doctoral training in France, in accordance with the new *European Charter for Researchers*.

Funding issues

Grant allocations

The new regulation expressly recommends the funding of candidates. The ministry in charge of higher education and research grants 4000 allocations, which are attributed by doctoral schools after evaluation of the research project and the corresponding scientific qualification of the candidate. This funding corresponds to the French minimum salary, but the ministry has recently announced an objective to revalue this funding of 50 per cent to ensure the attractiveness of the doctorate. About 2000 benefit from a complementary allocation for teaching in universities; this 'monitorat' is alleged to be generalized in the future. Another governmental program, CIFRE fellowships, allows the recruitment of more than 1000 candidates each year, in partnership with companies. Other sources of funding are different ministries in their specific domains, especially the Ministry of Foreign Affairs for candidates from abroad. These different financial sources cover the full funding of less than half the doctoral candidates and provide partial support to others. Still, a significant fraction of candidates are not funded, especially in human and social sciences. Consequently, candidates can only dedicate part of their time to their research project, having to work for their living as well. This situation is a major obstacle to the dissemination of the new vision of the doctorate in these fields, the reality being closer to the previous conception of a personal achievement than of a professional experience.

Funding and doctoral schools

Doctoral schools are light structures without walls. They receive funding from the ministry, through universities, for a total amount of €8.6 million. Some complementary funding is proposed by the ministry or regions through specific programmes for the organization of summer schools and workshops. The administrative staff of doctoral schools is very limited and depends on the means and policy of the university. Some universities have developed structures to mutualize complementary training in generic skills and optimize dedicated staff.

Kinds of institution

The doctorate is awarded by universities and some other higher education institutions, the list of which is fixed by ministerial decree. From 1984, the third cycle was organized in France on the basis of the diploma of advanced studies (the fifth year at university), which consisted of highly specialized courses, discipline-oriented, associated with a short research project run under the supervision of a senior scientist. The students pursuing a thesis were followed up by the director of the diploma, in a so-called 'formation doctorale'. Diploma proposals were the result of professors' initiatives rather than being based on an institutional policy.

With the prospect of the Bologna process, a governmental reform established doctoral schools in 2000. The schools were associated with training teams based on the existing DEA and a group of research teams on site on a disciplinary or interdisciplinary basis, according to the critical mass present (a university or a group of universities and research and higher education institutions). In order to build doctoral schools as scientific milieus, a research team is allowed to participate only within one doctoral school. Doctoral schools were assigned the organization of doctoral training in scientific and general skills, the follow-up of the thesis and the early career of the doctors. Most doctoral schools are inter-institutional, but depend on a university for their administration. The doctorate diploma is delivered at the university level, under the control of a university thesis committee.

The hybrid nature of doctoral schools was simplified in 2004 by the shift of most universities to the 'LMD' organization: i.e. a three-year *l*icence (bachelor), a two-year *m*asters and a three-years *d*octorate. In this scheme, doctoral schools are now focusing on doctoral training, the pre-doctoral DEA being included as the second year of the masters level.

The main strength of French doctoral schools is to emphasize that 'doctorate' means training by research, i.e. performing an original research project under the supervision of a senior scientist, and that this training is favoured in a high-quality research environment ensured by a critical mass in a scientific field or in interdisciplinary domains. In such conditions, doctoral education is not only a training period during which the student enhances their scientific expertise but also a real professional experience, as far as the young scientist has to manage an original research project in a competitive context. In this case, the so-called 'doctoral student' turns to a 'junior (early stage) researcher'.

Consequently, another major point in the reform is the statement that the doctorate should be considered as leading to various professional careers in all socioeconomic fields and not only be training for research-linked jobs. From this perspective, doctoral programmes must include specific training dealing with knowledge of the job market and the added value of training by research. These specific courses and/or workshops must help the candidate to discover the wide range of opportunities open to young doctors and to be aware of the generic transferable skills they develop during their development of a thesis.

Indicators such as funding, employment training, follow-up of the doctoral project and of the careers of the young doctors are alleged to be taken into account in the accreditation of doctoral schools and in the allocation of state funding.

Forms of doctoral study

Doctorate of university

From 1984, there is only one doctoral qualification, named doctorate of university, which acknowledges three years of training by running an original research project under the supervision of a senior scientist. Some professional programmes lead to doctorates (of practice), to allow the practice of professions such as medical doctor, dentist, pharmacist or veterinary surgeon. Such programmes do not include training by research, and candidates trained in these programmes and willing to be trained by research should apply for a doctorate in a doctoral school. 'Professional doctorates' do not exist in France, unlike the UK.

Doctorate of state and 'habilitation to supervise research'

Before 1984, two doctoral qualifications coexisted: a third-cycle thesis, prepared in two years, and the doctorate of state, considered as a sum of research work, the establishment of a scientific career and the gateway to professorship. In place of the doctorate of state, a 'habilitation to supervise research' was established in 1984 as a prerequisite for professorship and for autonomous supervision of doctoral candidates. This 'habilitation' is achieved on average, after about five years of research work after the doctorate.

Doctoral training is organized in different ways, according to the doctoral school policy. The major part of the programme is the running of an original research project. For this reason, training is evaluated as a whole, at the occasion of the submission of the report and of the defence, and the European Credit Transfer and Accumulation System (ECTS) does not apply at the doctoral level. However, doctoral candidates have to attend complementary training in sciences as well as in generic skills proposed by doctoral schools. Doctoral schools are also in charge of the follow-up of the professional insertion of doctorates in the job market. To harmonize training actions and follow-up of the professional project of candidates, large universities or consortia of institutions on the same campus have created colleges of doctoral schools or institutes of doctoral training.

Candidates and their programmes of study

Requisite qualification

The qualification required to enter a doctoral school is a masters degree, or an equivalent diploma obtained in another country. Dispensation can be given, based on the experience of the candidate in research.

The duration of doctoral training

The duration of doctoral training is officially three years, as is the duration of governmental granting of candidates. Initiation to the running of an original research project is performed during the second year of a research masters programme. Three years of training by research appears to be a good scheme for a full-time research project, which requires funding of candidates. Obviously, in many cases, candidates need more than three years, due to the management of a research activity being highly dependent on the subject. In these cases, the director of a doctoral school could accept the continuation of the thesis, with yearly approval of extra enrolment. Theses longer than three or four years could be avoided by close follow-up of work progress by the doctoral school (tutor, mid-term committee, etc.) and by an incentive for candidates and supervisors (too often the latter still consider doctoral candidates as their workforce).

Part-time and full-time modes of study

A doctorate can be prepared part-time, but the doctoral school should ensure that the time dedicated to the doctorate is sufficient to guarantee efficient training via research and work. This is the case for candidates already involved in a professional activity they cannot interrupt but who can organize their work part-time on a regular basis over several years. Candidates not involved in professional activity and forced to take unqualified jobs should be discouraged. Since a doctorate is a professional experience and candidates actually contribute to the production of knowledge or devices, research teams must always do their best to obtain funding to pay their doctoral candidates.

Doctoral schools are firmly encouraged to offer candidates a large range of complementary training such as disciplinary and interdisciplinary courses, seminar series, workshops or summer schools, annual seminars during which candidates of the school present their work and share their experience and professional/personal training. Seminars, workshops and summer schools introduce candidates to business organization and management, intellectual property rights and the development of personal skills such as self-evaluation, communication, team-working and building, and project management. Such training is crucial to awaken candidates' awareness of their job opportunities and to make them active in the building of their professional projects.

Issues of gender, race and religion

Gender issues are slowly being recognized; indicators are required by the ministry, but no direct action is planned. Race or religious issues are not taken into account in France, and collecting data on them is hopefully forbidden, but this does not prevent discriminatory attitudes.

Supervision

Charter of thesis

Supervision modes are formally determined by the 'charter of thesis' established by each university according to a national legal framework. This charter defines the rights and duties of the different partners involved in the doctorate, who sign the charter: the candidate, the supervisor, the head of the research team, the director of the doctoral school and the president of the university.

Of course, the supervision of the research project is the direct responsibility of the supervisor. The regulation states that a supervisor must not supervise more than two candidates at a time, and the ratio is taken into account in the four-year accreditation of doctoral schools. Nevertheless, the figures are still often (much) higher, especially in humanities and social sciences. A 'habilitation to supervise research' must be awarded to a supervisor. The applicant has to compose a presentation of their research results and a research project, which is reviewed by three experts and defended before a board. Junior researchers may start to supervise doctorates in collaboration (and under the control) of the supervisor. At this time, there is no regular assessment of supervisors, but assessment is easy to perform regularly each time a doctorate candidate's training is assessed by the doctoral programme, through the regular follow-up of the doctoral project progression, and through indicators of doctorate achievement rate and doctors' employment rate.

Critical mass

The emphasis on the need to organize doctoral schools as a critical mass of research teams, organized in laboratories or scientific milieus, points out the complementary responsibilities of the research team in which the project is developed and those of the doctoral school in the follow-up of the project's progress. Some doctoral schools ensure the follow-up of the thesis by tutorship of each candidate by a senior scientist outside the lab, and/or the appointment of a mid-term thesis committee, which provides scientific advice on the progress of the work. Such follow-up is taken to be very beneficial for all parties.

The follow-up of the professional project of candidates is mostly a matter for the institution, i.e. the doctoral school and the university. Indeed, the main responsibility of the supervisor and of the lab is training by research. Of course supervisors must be aware of the importance of the working out of the professional project. For this purpose, some universities and doctoral schools develop information and seminars for supervisors to make them aware of their responsibilities, not only for the supervision of the research project but also in the choice of complementary courses and the working out of the professional project.

Examination

Submission of the dissertation and its defence

Since the core of the doctorate is the running of an original research project, the doctorate is evaluated as a whole, at the occasion of the submission of the dissertation and of the defence. For these reasons, in France, credit transfer schemes do not apply at the doctoral level.

A 1992 government regulation sets common guidelines for the examination procedure, and a new regulation is about to be enacted. A 2005 regulation relaxes the conditions for the defence of theses in *co-tutelle*, allowing universities to adapt their procedure to that of the partner.

The modalities of application are defined at the university level. The authorization to defend is given by the president of grading at the university, often after advice from a committee of theses, on the proposition of the supervisor, confirmed by the director of the doctoral school.

The dissertation is a dedicated text, written in French. For foreign candidates, a text written in their home language is accepted, but an abstract has to be written in French. In experimental sciences, most often the dissertation consists of a dedicated bibliographic introduction, the presentation and discussion of the results – in some disciplines as a bunch of research papers – and a dedicated general discussion of the prospects. In humanities and social sciences, most often the dissertation is conceived as a book. The general discussion and prospects are the most important part to evaluate the personal scientific skills of the defendant.

Referees

Two referees, senior scientists awarded a 'habilitation to supervise research' or equivalent outside the doctoral school and the grading university, are designated by the committee of theses, on the proposition of the candidate and the supervisor, after approval by the director of the doctoral school. On the basis of the referees' reports, the committee allows the defence.

Public defence

The defence is public, in front of a jury composed of the two referees, the supervisor and other experts. The applicant gives a talk on their research results followed by a discussion with the jury about the results, justification of the research strategy, possible alternatives, the scientific context and the literature, further developments and prospects. The quality of the discussion greatly varies from one jury to another; there are no formal guidelines for the organization of the defence. At the end of the defence, the jury may award the candidate the grade of doctor of the university, after in camera deliberation.

No examination or assessment is planned for complementary training at this time. Complementary training is regarded as an opportunity for candidates to gain extra knowledge on scientific matters and to build their professional project. Attendance is required, but there is no need for formal assessment at the doctoral level.

Other issues: the added value of training by research

The added value of doctoral training is a key issue. The objective of the Lisbon communiqué is to train more researchers for academic and private research. The building of Europe as a knowledge-based economy and society also requires more doctors at executive managerial level in all sectors. This means that the ultimate goal of training by research is not only the acquisition of scientific and technical skills, but also to prepare candidates for a wide range of jobs in the various socioeconomic sectors.

The social and economic value of a doctorate degree is not sufficiently recognized in France at present. Traditionally, executive manager positions are offered to students trained in engineering-, trade- and administration-oriented *Grandes Ecoles*, a parallel system to universities set up by Napoleon and expanded over recent decades. Conversely, for most policy-makers and media, as for lots of academics and candidates entering a doctoral programme, the doctorate is still most often acknowledged as leading to research. This old-fashioned conception contributes to undervaluing the doctorate in sectors other than academic and private research. As a consequence, a doctor is usually not even regarded as an asset in private research, because they are presumed to lack sufficient knowledge of the business world.

However, progress has been made recently. The doctorate, as defined above, allows candidates to acquire a double competence in the specialized field of the thesis and in generic personal and managerial skills. Such skills include the following: facing the unknown, quickly extracting and synthesizing knowledge, discovering innovative solutions, solving complex problems, developing strategies by combining multiple perspectives, creativity, networking, communication and quality assessment, time and resource management, as well as failure management. Obviously, these skills will allow candidates to successfully perform in executive manager positions in a wide range of corporate areas.

Furthermore, candidates entering a doctoral programme are highly motivated people, devoted to a personal project. This project might involve participating in the development and the diffusion of knowledge, being useful to society by protecting the environment, discovering medicines, inventing new products or materials, fighting and/or preventing natural disasters, producing a better comprehension of human societies, helping policy-makers to arbitrate decisions in complex environments, etc. These candidates must permanently cope with very high competition and pressure from the selection to enter the programme as well as publish the results of their research work.

It is therefore the responsibility of universities to make others aware that hiring people with doctoral degrees for executive managerial positions represents a valuable input for companies, services and organizations to build a European knowledge-based economy and society.

Critical comments

Though the set-up of doctoral schools dramatically changed in a few years the way of thinking about and organizing a doctorate in France, their vague structure combined with their loose relation to universities represents a major weakness. Indeed, they are mostly accountable only to the ministry in charge of research and higher education, but do not have real autonomy to develop complementary training and follow-up of young doctors. It is therefore very difficult for any doctoral school to develop interdisciplinary programmes, interdisciplinary-based international cooperation and training in general skills to the required extent. On the contrary, these actions challenge universities and fully justify a tight association of doctoral schools to a university, breaking the traditionally suspicious governmental policy towards universities and establishing a strict a posteriori control of a clear contract.

Another difficulty is that the doctorate is still perceived as training *for* research rather than *by* research. Clearly, the number of doctors exceeds the positions offered in research, academic and private, even if policies of EU and European countries reached the ambitious figures of the Lisbon communiqué! The 'hidden market' for doctors requires full awareness and motivation and a greater open-mindedness in most French recruiters, who still are stuck in the old way of considering the doctorate. In this context, taking a job is difficult, and too many doctors choose postdoctoral work instead.

Still, a significant number of candidates are not funded or are funded without basic social protection, especially in human and social sciences and, to a lesser extent, in life sciences. Consequently, candidates can only dedicate part of their time to their research project, having in addition to work for their living. This situation is a major obstacle to the dissemination of the new vision of the doctorate, the reality being closer to the previous conception of a personal achievement than a professional experience.

To overcome these difficulties, French universities need to develop a better quality assessment policy, based on well-defined indicators, in order to ensure the acknowledgement by all the actors involved – and especially by the recruiters – of the large range of skills that doctors are able to impart.

The development of interdisciplinary and multicultural sessions and of small-scale workshops on generic transferable skills is one of the keys to success but requires a larger funding effort from different sources, including the EU, to complement the excellent research-based discipline-oriented Marie Curie programme.

5

Doctoral education in Germany: between tradition and reform

Barbara M. Kehm

Introduction

Germany has been engaged in doctoral education since the Middle Ages and led its development in Europe. It produces one of the highest proportions of doctorates in relation to number of graduates worldwide with more than 10 per cent of all examinations being at doctoral level. However, reforms to the German system of doctoral education are gathering momentum, with increasing concerns about the time taken to gain a doctorate, the supervision process and ultimately the attractiveness of the German doctorate within the global market-place. This chapter explores the tension between a robust tradition on the one hand and increasing pressures for reform on the other.

An overview of current data

The following overview intends to provide a snapshot of the most important statistical data on doctoral education and training in Germany. As the number of doctoral students studying provides the basis for the questions in the generic table used in this book many of the questions cannot be answered directly for Germany because no information is available. The basis for statistical data of doctoral education and training in Germany is the number of doctoral degrees awarded in a given year rather than the number studying.

Compared to the total student population Germany is the country among the Organization for Economic Cooperation and Development (OECD) member states, and possibly worldwide, in which the highest number of doctoral degrees are awarded annually. For example, about 80 per cent of all graduates in medicine get a doctoral degree, 69 per cent of all graduates in chemistry, 44 per cent of all graduates in biology and 42 per cent of all graduates in physics. The proportion is clearly lower in the other main subject groups: 12.8 per cent of all graduates in engineering, 11.7 per cent of all graduates in the humanities and 9.3 per cent of all graduates in the social

Table 5.1 The questionnaire (figures from 2000 and 2003)

Question	Number	Comment
1 Total number of doctoral students studying	Not known	Professors at universities are free to accept (or reject) doctoral students. There is still a considerable number of them being registered as regular students or not registered at all. What is known is the number of doctoral degrees awarded annually which was 23,043 in 2003
2 Number of institutions offering doctoral programmes	100	All German universities have the right to award doctoral degrees and all university professors have the right to act as supervisors of doctoral candidates. There is no complete statistical overview of the number of actual programmes. The majority of doctoral students in Germany get their degree outside doctoral programmes
3 Number of different doctoral awards	47	In Germany there is no distinction between professional and research doctorates. The different awards rather indicate the subject or subject group in which the doctorate was awarded by using abbreviated Latin titles, e.g. Dr. phil., Dr. med., Dr. iur., Dr. rer.nat., Dr. rer. pol., Dr. ing. etc.
4 Number of years over which doctorates have been offered in Germany	Since the Middle Ages	Ever since the doctorate was introduced as a degree awarded by universities in Europe
5 Proportion of full-time to part-time students	Not known	The majority of German doctoral students are *(Continued overleaf)*

Table 5.1 (Continued)

Question	Number	Comment
		working on their thesis outside of programmes, either in their spare time, or with a scholarship, or as a part-time research assistant. There is no official status of part-time doctoral student
6 Average time to completion	Estimated to be between 3 and 6 years	The average age upon completion and award of the degree was 32.7 years in 2000 including medicine and 33.0 without medicine. There are large differences among subject groups: 31.8 years in mathematics and science, 36.1 years in the humanities, 41.0 years in education
7 Success rates	Not known	The actual failure rate is relatively low but there is a high estimated dropout rate which might be up to 80% in some subjects and as low as 10% in others
8 Typical age range of doctoral candidates	Between 31.8 and 41.0 years upon completion	The figure refers to the average age upon completion and award of the degree
9 Proportion of male/female students	Not known	8724 of all doctoral degrees were awarded to women in 2003 (37.9%)
10 Proportion of doctoral students who are nationals of other countries	Not known	In 2003 2308 doctoral degrees were awarded to nationals of other countries (10%)

sciences (including law) (figures from 2000). Altogether 21.4 per cent of all graduates from German universities get a doctorate; if medicine is excluded the figure is still 15.4 per cent. About a third of all doctorates awarded annually in Germany are in medicine.

The place of the doctorate in the national context

German postgraduate research is basically divided into three fields: basic and applied research being carried out at universities, in extra-university research institutions like the Fraunhofer Society or the Max-Planck Society, and finally in the more applied fields in large private sector companies.

Higher education is the responsibility of the 16 German states. Doctoral education and training is considered to be an academic affair, i.e. it is part of the traditional academic freedom of individual professors who act as supervisors and are free in their decision to accept as many or as few doctoral students as they want.

With the change to more managerial approaches in higher education governance in recent years, most of the German states have switched to performance-based funding contracts with the universities based on output rather than paying per student enrolled. The output of doctoral degree holders is a key indicator in this framework and most university presidents provide incentives to departments to increase their output of doctoral degree holders and support candidates to complete in a timely manner.

The majority of doctoral candidates are not considered to be students, being either employed as research assistants or receiving scholarships from the state or a private foundation. Those working within the university as research assistants have an important function to support the teaching and research tasks of the professor who employs them and who normally acts as their supervisor.

Institutionally and at the level of the individual professor, the number of doctoral degrees awarded is seen as an indicator of reputation. Accepting doctoral 'students' is part of academic freedom and each professor can decide individually whom they want to accept and how many doctoral students to supervise.

There has been concern for quite some time about the quality of supervision and time to completion. The German Research Association (the equivalent of a research council) has since the late 1980s funded so-called *Graduiertenkollegs*. The idea is to introduce more structure into the doctoral process thus reducing the time to completion, improving the quality of supervision and providing some taught elements. Since the inclusion of the doctorate as a third cycle of study into the Bologna reforms the idea of establishing doctoral programmes is taking hold in Germany and many such programmes are currently developed.

Issues of funding

There are basically three forms of funding which are available to doctoral candidates.

Research assistant of a chairholder

The first and dominant is a position as a research assistant of a chairholder that can take two forms. Either it is a budgeted position of the university paid from state money or it is a position within an externally funded research project or projects. As a rule most of the full professors (chairholders) have one or two positions for research assistants of this type which are provided to them by the university as part of the infrastructure for research. However, there are also chairs that do not have any funding for infrastructure attached to them. These are called 'naked' professorships. For the first type of position the duration of the contract used to be three plus two years. This has in recent times been reduced to two plus two or even two plus one. The second type of position is dependent on the duration of the research project and a doctoral candidate might be given several employment contracts in sequence, moving from one funded project to the next and writing the dissertation in their free time. Contracts for doctoral candidates are generally limited to 50 per cent of the regular workload.

A scholarship from a foundation

The second form of funding is a scholarship from a foundation. This normally requires a good relationship and good communication between the doctoral candidate and their supervisor because work on the doctoral thesis is basically done independently apart from meetings with the supervisor and possibly participation in a colloquium upon invitation. The new trend to establish *Graduiertenkollegs* or doctoral programmes should improve contact between supervisor and doctoral candidate and provide better integration. Most of these graduate schools have a limited number of scholarships attached to them.

Part-time study funded by employment outside the university

There is no official part-time study in doctoral programmes, although in fact most doctoral candidates are not able to devote all of their working time to their research. However, the third form of funding is having a regular full-time or part-time job outside the university and researching in one's spare time. This form of doctorate takes the longest time to complete and regularly results in high dropout rates. It is also the form which is least integrated into any kind of research context. Many professors have one or two, sometimes even more, candidates of this type.

The institutional context

All German universities have the right to award doctoral degrees. Since doctoral education and training is considered to be an academic affair it is regulated autonomously by each university, which for each subject formulates a *Promotionsordnung*, i.e. regulations and requirements for doctoral education. These regulations determine the requirements a candidate has to meet before they can be accepted as a doctoral 'student'. They also determine the rules for the submission of the thesis, for the final examination and for the conditions that need to be fulfilled before being allowed to officially carry a doctoral title. The actual doctoral degree is awarded by the respective department or faculty.

The introduction of contract management working, with performance indicators, between universities and the state on the one hand and institutional leadership and departments or faculties on the other hand has led to more systematic monitoring of output in recent years. The production of doctoral degrees is one of the indicators being monitored at the institutional level and this has led to a shift in institutional policies. The production of doctoral degree holders is no longer seen as an academic matter, and part of academic freedom alone, but has become an object of strategic policy and decision-making.

Forms of doctoral education and training

The traditional way of getting a doctoral degree in Germany was, and still dominantly is, that the candidate and the supervisor agree on a topic for the dissertation and the candidate then starts their research work. Periodically there will be a meeting between the two to discuss parts of the thesis and the doctoral candidate might be invited to their supervisor's research colloquiums. Upon submission of the finished thesis the supervisor acts as the main referee and selects (often together with the candidate) a second referee. The submitted thesis is publicly accessible for a limited period of time so that others can comment on it. After the reviews have been written and a grade for the thesis determined there is a public defence in front of a commission consisting of four or five people often including an external examiner. The commission has to agree on a final grade. The candidate is normally allowed to carry the title officially only after the thesis has been published.

In recent years more and more doctoral programmes and graduate schools have been set up to improve supervision, reduce dependency on the supervisor and provide more structure. Such programmes often include taught elements and offer a higher degree of integration of the doctoral candidates into the research work of a department.

Status of students and programmes of study

As a rule a doctoral candidate has to have a masters degree from a university before they are accepted by a professor and by the department. It is possible for older and employed persons to become doctoral candidates if they find a professor who will supervise the thesis. Graduates from *Fachhochschulen* (universities of applied sciences) will be accepted only in very few cases because their degrees are considered not to be equivalent to a university degree.

There has been much concern in Germany over time-to-degree in doctoral education and training. Most doctoral candidates used to take between four and six years in order to successfully complete. This is currently changing with the Bologna reforms and the intention is to reduce time-to-degree to three years. In order to achieve this, more structured doctoral programmes are being established.

The full-time or part-time mode of doctoral education is a matter for the candidate and the supervisor. There is no official part-time status. As long as the candidate continues to signal that they are still intending to finish the thesis and defend it, they are considered to be a doctoral candidate. Where a candidate is in a *Graduiertenkolleg*, within the framework of a doctoral programme, depending on a scholarship or a position as a research assistant, the time is usually limited to three to four years. After that period a university will not renew a contract for a research assistant. The candidate can continue to write the thesis, however, and eventually submit it.

Traditionally the German doctorate was, and is still considered to be, a research doctorate. There is no distinction between professional and research doctorates. While universities train their doctoral 'students' according to the disciplinary culture and thus form a pool for the recruitment of junior academic staff, both the public and the private sector often recruit doctoral degree holders.

The transition into the non-university labour market might vary somewhat according to the subject, i.e. transition is longer and more difficult in the humanities and social sciences, but generally opportunities to find adequate employment are good.

Race and religion are not issues in doctoral education in Germany. Gender used to be and still is, in particular in the natural sciences and engineering subjects. However, over the last 15 to 20 years the position has changed and it has become normal to take gender issues into account.

Supervision: a question of quality

The quality of supervision has been of considerable concern in Germany. The most critical points in this respect have been a high level of dependency on supervisors, some of whom may have tended to exploit their doctoral candidates for their own research and teaching tasks and thus did not provide sufficient and regular feedback on the research work. In such cases there was insufficient monitoring of progress and time-to-degree. With the establishment of doctoral programmes and *Graduiertenkollegs* this is changing. In both forms of doctoral education and training candidates are given the opportunity to have more than one supervisor or at least to have more than one person to address for feedback and critical comment. In addition, there is more organized exchange among doctoral candidates through self-organized colloquiums and working groups or regular meetings of several doctoral candidates to present draft versions of their work, discuss methodological approaches and problems and generally support each other. Most programmes also include taught elements in which generic skills and key qualifications are conveyed.

Defending the thesis

As noted above, typically the (main) supervisor of the thesis also acts as main referee and main examiner. Each thesis must be refereed by two persons, one of whom can be from another university in Germany or even from abroad. The two referees submit their assessment of the thesis in written form and also propose a grade.

A date for the defence is then set up. A defence is always a public affair to which anyone interested can come. However, interaction is only between the candidate and the commission members. A defence commission is normally a group of four professors, two of whom are from the department in which the thesis has been submitted while the other two can be from another department, another university or from abroad. Usually they are all from the same subject or a closely related field. Among the four are always the two referees of the thesis.

In the first part of the examination the candidate will present their thesis: research question, methodology, results. Then a question and answer 'game' starts in which the candidate who was given the reviews of the two referees beforehand defends the thesis with regard to the criticism offered in the reviews. The whole procedure lasts about one and a half to two hours. Towards the end the examiners will also comment on the aspect of publication. They may make recommendations or formulate conditions for publication of the thesis that the candidate has to take into account before publishing.

Then the public as well as the candidate will be sent out of the room while the examiners agree on a final grade. All doctoral degrees are awarded with a grade attached. Grades are in the old Latin form ranging from *summa cum laude* to *rite*.

The candidate is informed about the grade immediately.

The issue of statistics

German statistical data on doctoral education and training do not lend themselves easily to international comparison. In most countries records and overviews about the number of doctoral students are gathered. For Germany these figures do not exist. Instead, the basis for all statistical information is the annual number of doctoral degrees awarded and from this basis detailed information according to university, subject group, average age upon completion, gender and proportion of international students.

This is related to the fact that doctoral education until very recently has been considered to be a matter of academic freedom. Hardly any structured programmes, no tuition fees and the possibility of getting a doctoral degree from a university where a candidate has never studied added to the fact that this phase of qualification used to be a rather individual relationship between the doctoral candidate and supervisor. Sporadic contacts and the consent of the professor were sufficient to remain a doctoral candidate. This relationship became formalized only at a very late stage in the process of getting the degree, when the thesis was officially submitted with all the necessary papers to prove required qualifications to the department and the process of reviewing and determining a second referee was set in motion. At that stage, however, the risk of failure was very low. A professor would not allow their doctoral candidate to officially submit an inadequate thesis because failure of a candidate had a repercussion on the reputation of the professor.

Thus, an unknown but relatively high level of drop-out occurred between the first acceptance of a person as a doctoral candidate and final submission of the thesis. Whenever the transition of graduates from certain subjects into the labour market became difficult due to economic conditions the number of doctoral candidates in that subject tended to increase. In fact, this phase of qualification in many of the social sciences and humanities was considered frequently as a holding position until adequate employment could be found. For a person freshly graduated with a masters degree it tended to be preferable to being unemployed. It provided some sort of status. However, to continue looking for employment and dropping the doctorate when employment was found was a widespread practice.

This is about to change. Most universities now have central offices or units monitoring the number of doctoral candidates and their time-to-degree. Professors are requested to provide information to this central unit as soon as they agree to become the supervisor of a thesis. In addition, the number of doctoral degrees awarded is part of the performance of a department on the basis of which funding is allocated. In many universities it is still an incentive structure, i.e. a department receives additional money for every doctoral candidate successfully completing the degree. But an increase in output of doctoral degrees awarded has also become an object of contract negotiations between a department and the central level.

Conclusions

Current reforms

The fact that the German university system produces one of the highest proportion of doctorates in relation to the number of graduates worldwide could be seen as an indicator that the system of doctoral education and training is working well. However, apart from particular national concerns like time-to-degree and quality of supervision there have also been increasing concerns about the attractiveness of the German university system and its degrees for international students. Increasing international competition for the best talent among young researchers has challenged the German system. Major reforms are currently taking place that include doctoral education and training. For the medium term it is expected that there will exist several ways of getting a doctoral degree, ranging from the traditional individual relationship between doctoral candidate and supervisor, to doctoral programmes and graduate schools. But there will also be clusters of excellence and elite universities aiming to become global players in the market. First steps have been taken to introduce a kind of ranking of institutions by the 'initiative for excellence' in the framework, for which a number of universities have been selected on the basis of competitive bidding to receive considerable amounts of extra funding for the establishment of graduate school clusters of excellence and institutional development concepts.

The disinterested pursuit of knowledge

In terms of the traditional principles of doctoral education and training in Germany the most profound shift, however, is that doctoral education and research training is no longer regarded exclusively as curiosity driven and as the disinterested pursuit of knowledge. Instead the generation of new knowledge has become an important strategic resource and economic factor. It thus becomes a commodity and its shape acquires a more utilitarian approach. Policy-makers have begun to scrutinize research training and universities have been requested to develop institutional strategies to improve it. In addition, it is deemed so important a resource that it is no longer left in the hands of professors and departments alone but has become an object of policy-making and has moved to the institutional and national, even supra-national level.

Further reading

Bartelse, J. (1999) *Concentrating the Minds. The Institutionalisation of the Graduate School Innovation in Dutch and German Higher Education.* Enschede: CHEPS and Utrecht, Lemma.

Berlin Communiqué (2003): www.aic.lv/ace/ace_disk/Bologna/maindoc (accessed 7 October 2005).

Berning, E. and Falk, S. (2005) Das Promotionswesen im Umbruch (Changes in the shape of the doctorate), in *Beiträge zur Hochschulforschung (Contributions to Higher Education Research)*, 27(1): 48–72.

Bologna Declaration (1999) www.aic.lv/ace/ace_disk/Bologna/maindoc (accessed 7 October 2005).

Bourner, T., Bowden, R. and Laing, S. (2000) Professional doctorates: the development of researching professionals, in T. Bourner, T. Katz and D. Watson (eds) *New Directions in Professional Higher Education*. Buckingham: SRHE and Open University Press.

CHEPS (ed.) (2002) *Science, Training and Career. Changing Modes of Knowledge Production and Labour Markets*. Proceedings of an international workshop organized by the Centre for Higher education Policy Studies (CHEPS), University of Twente, October 2002, www.utwente.nl/cheps/documenten/engreportproceedings1 (accessed 22 June 2004).

Commission of the European Communities (2003a) *Communication from the Commission: The Role of Universities in the Europe of Knowledge*. Brussels: COM(2003) 58 final.

Commission of the European Communities (2003b) *Communication for the Commission to the Council and the European Parliament: Researchers in the European Research Area: One Profession, Multiple Careers*. Brussels: COM(2003) 436 final.

DAAD (German Academic Exchange Service) (2004) *50 Select International Postgraduate Programmes at Universities in Germany*. Bonn: DAAD.

Enders, J. (1996) *Die wissenschaftlichen Mitarbeiter. Ausbildung, Beschäftigung und Karriere der Nachwuchswissenschaftler und Mittelbauangehörigen an den Universitäten (The Academic Assistants. Training, Employment and Career of Junior Researchers and Middle Level Research and Teaching Staff at Universities)*. New York: Campus.

Enders, J. (2005a) Brauchen die Universitäten in Deutschland ein neues Paradigma der Nachwuchsausbildung? (Do German universities need a new paradigm for training future researchers?), *Beiträge zur Hochschulforschung (Contributions to Higher Education Research)*, 27(1): 34–47.

Enders, J. (2005b) Wissenschaftlicher Nachwuchs in Europa (Junior academic staff in Europe), in *Zeitschrift für Pädagogik. 50. Beiheft: Hochschullandschaft im Wandel (Changes in the Higher Education Landscape)*. Weinheim und Basel: Beltz.

Enders, J. and Bornmann, L. (2001) *Karriere mit Doktortitel? Ausbildung, Berufsverlauf und Berufserfolg von Promovierten (Careers of Doctoral Degree Holders. Education, Careers, and Professional Success of Doctoral Degree Holders)*. New York: Campus.

Green, H. and Powell, S. (2005) *Doctoral Education in Contemporary Higher Education*. Maidenhead: Society for Research into Higher Education and Open University Press.

Hochschulrektorenkonferenz (HRK) (2003) *Zur Organisation des Promotionsstudiums (About the Organization of Doctoral Studies)*. Entschließung des 199. Plenums vom 17/18. February. www.hrk.de/de/beschluesse/109_253.php (accessed 25 July 2005).

Hüfner, K. (2004) Doctoral degrees in Germany, in J. Sadlak (ed.) *Doctoral Studies and Qualifications in Europe and the United States: Status and Prospects*. Bucharest: UNESCO-CEPES.

Hüttl, R.F. (2005) Kernelemente für eine Neugestaltung der Promotionslandschaft (Core elements for a new structure of doctoral education), in *Hochschule Innovativ*, 14: 12–13.

Kehm, B.M. (1999) *Higher Education in Germany. Developments, Problems and Perspectives*. Bucharest: UNESCO-CEPES and Wittenberg: Institute for Higher Education Research.

Kehm, B.M. (2004 and 2005a) Developing doctoral degrees and qualifications in Europe. Good practice and Issues of concern, in J. Sadlak (ed.) *Doctoral Studies and Qualifications in Europe and the United States: Status and Prospects*. Bucharest: UNESCO-CEPES. Reprinted under the same title in *Beiträge zur Hochschulforschung (Contributions to Higher Education Research)*, 27(1): 10–33.

Kehm, B.M. (2005b) Promovieren in Europa: Strukturen und Konzepte im Vergleich (Getting a doctoral degree in Europe: a comparison of structures and concepts), in *Hochschule Innovativ*, 14: 2–3.

Kupfer, A. and Moes, J. (2003) *Promovieren in Europa. Ein internationaler Vergleich von Promotionsbedingungen* (Getting a doctoral degree in Europe. An international comparison of conditions). Frankfurt: GEW and Hans Böckler Foundation.

Lisbon Summit (2000) www.bologna-berlin2003.de/pdf/PRESIDENCY_CONCLU-SIONS_ Lissabon.pdf.

OECD (2002) *Science, Technology and Industry Outlook*. Paris: OECD.

Prömel, H.J. (2005) Promovieren an der Humboldt-Universität (Getting a doctoral degree at Humboldt University), *Hochschule Innovativ*, 14: 6.

Recotillet, I. (2003) Availability and characteristics of surveys on the destination of doctorate recipients in OECD countries, *OECD Science, Technology and Industry Working Papers, 2003/9*. Paris: OECD.

Reichert, S. and Tauch, C. (2005) *Trends IV: European Universities Implementing Bologna*. Brussels: EUA.

Sadlak, J. (ed.) (2004) *Doctoral Studies and Qualifications in Europe and the United States: Status and Prospects*. Bucharest: UNESCO-CEPES.

Scott, D., Brown, A., Lunt, I. and Thorne, L. (2004) *Professional Doctorates. Integrating Professional and Academic Knowledge*. Buckingham: Society for Research into Higher Education and Open University Press.

Senger, U. (2003) *Internationale Doktorandenstudien. Ein Modell für die Internationalisierung der Doktorandenausbildung an deutschen Hochschulen und Forschungseinrichtungen (International doctoral studies. A model for the internationalisation of doctoral education at German universities and research institutes)*. Bielefeld: Bertelsmann.

Sorbonne Declaration (1998) www.aic.lv/ace/ace_disk/Bologna/maindoc (accessed 7 October 2005).

Statistisches Bundesamt (2003) *Bildung und Kultur. Prüfungen an Hochschulen (Education and Culture. Examinations at Higher Education Institutions)*. Wiesbaden.

Wissenschaftsrat (1995) *Empfehlungen zur Neustrukturierung der Doktorandenausbildung und-förderung (Recommendations for a New Structure of Doctoral Education and Financial Support of Doctoral Students)*. Köln.

Wissenschaftsrat (2002) *Empfehlungen zur Doktorandenausbildung (Recommendations for the Education and Training of Doctoral Students)*. www.wissenschaftsrat.de/texte/5459–02.pdf (accessed 25 July 2005).

6

Doctoral education in the Netherlands

Jeroen Bartelse, Heinze Oost and Hans Sonneveld

Introduction

Doctoral education in the Netherlands has a long and distinguished history dating back to the seventeenth century. Indeed some of the traditions of those times survive in the practices of today, albeit in ceremonial form rather than in the detail of doctoral study. Almost four centuries later the doctorate remains alive with some 7443 students studying. As in many other countries however it is subject to significant change, with an increasing focus on purposes and costs and is now set within a European dimension.

The questionnaire

Table 6.1 The questionnaire[1]

Question	Number	Comment
1 Total number of doctoral students studying	7,443	VSNU (2004)
2 Number of institutions offering doctoral programmes	14	
3 Number of different doctoral awards (e.g. including professional doctorates)	1	
4 Number of years over which doctorates have been offered in the country	362	
5 Proportion of full-time to part-time students	No data	

6 Average time to completion (in years)	5.2	VSNU (2002)
7 Success rates	70%	VSNU (2002)
8 Typical age range of doctoral candidates	23–30	This typical age range applies for doctoral candidates within the so-called AiO system (see text below)
9 Proportion of male/female students	Male 58%, Female 42%	VSNU (2002)
10 Proportion of doctoral students studying who are nationals of other countries	No data	

1 The authors would like to thank Renee Westenbrink for his help in putting together this table.

Data sources

VSNU (2002, 2004a). See references.

The place of doctoral study in the national/international context

Origins of doctoral education in the Netherlands

The University of Utrecht awarded the first doctorate in the Netherlands in 1644. In those days the doctorate was a 'vocational' degree, rather than a research degree. The degree holder was entitled to teach. Little has been recorded about the process of acquiring the degree in this era, but Hesseling (1986: 26) describes, on the basis of seventeenth-century law and statutes of the University of Leiden, a picture of the lively rituals that took place during the public defence: 'a long procession of professors in black gowns, the promovendus also in gown with two secondants (paranymphs) . . . a prescribed promotion formula and a "laudation" on the qualities of the new doctor by the promotor following detailed regulations, and after an equally solemn return, the day was completed with a promotion dinner'. Nowadays, many of these rituals are still part of the ceremonies that accompany the doctoral graduation day. But the role and function of the doctorate has changed considerably.

Developments in the nineteenth and twentieth centuries

In the course of the nineteenth and twentieth centuries a research ethos developed at the Dutch universities (Wachelder 1992). The nature of the doctoral degree changed under the influence of the research imperative of the German universities and laboratories. The doctorate became proof of the ability to carry out independent scientific research. Particularly in the sciences, renowned professors formed research groups in which they trained their apprentices in research methods and techniques. The doctoral process was an informal endeavour, pretty much shaped within this master–apprentice relationship. There was no standardized process regulated by university or government.

The first Dutch higher education laws of 1815 and 1875 codified the doctorate as a formal university degree. However, serious policy reflections of the idea of the doctorate and the organization of doctoral education emerged much later. Until the 1980s, doctoral education typically fell between the domains of education and research policies. It was only marginally addressed during discussions on higher education reforms. In 1985, a new act regulated the doctoral process. A distinct academic position, the so-called 'assistant in training' – *assistent in opleiding* (AiO) – was created for the doctoral candidate. The objective of the AiO system is to provide advanced research training by way of active participation in university research and, to a limited extent (< 25 per cent), in teaching. All AiOs are supposed to have an instruction and supervision plan drawn up. The AiO is employed by the universities and receives remuneration. These AiO positions attract mainly candidates who have just finished a masters degree and wish to continue university training leading to the Ph.D. Although many doctoral theses are prepared in positions outside the AiO system, the introduction of the AiO position did lead to a sharp increase in doctoral candidates and doctoral degrees awarded in the 1990s.

Research schools

Pressed by increasing numbers of doctoral candidates and calls for more structured research training, the Dutch government stimulated the development of a system of research schools. The idea of the research school was formally launched in 1991. Research schools were envisioned to be organizations of adequate size that provide (1) a scientifically stimulating environment for carrying out high-quality research and (2) a curriculum for the doctoral candidate tuned to specific subjects fields. By creating a procedure for the establishment of 'recognized' research schools, these schools would share a number of common characteristics. The Royal Academy of Sciences (KNAW) is responsible for this procedure and established an independent committee to review the performance of research schools. The most important recognition criteria are: (1) a thorough and institutionalized, collective as well as individual training programme for doctoral candidates; (2) a well-defined scientific mission; (3) autonomy with respect to financial and administrative responsibilities; (4) the utilization of possibilities for national cooperation; (5) critical mass (KNAW 2005: 8–9).

European influences

The Bologna process is the next important impetus to change. In the Netherlands, this European-wide endeavour to create a coherent and cohesive higher education area did not merely change the degree labels. The introduction of the bachelor–master structure (this was regulated by law in 2002 and most universities started their first bachelor programmes under the new law in September 2002) is leading to far-reaching reforms in higher education programmes – and the doctorate seems to follow suit. In 2004, the Netherlands Association of Universities proposed a number of reforms in the doctoral system (VSNU 2004a). Among these proposals are the definition of general qualifications of the Ph.D., the incorporation of doctoral training in the national system of quality assurance and proposals for the further development of research schools/graduate schools. This shift may be summarized as follows:

* The introduction of the AiO system, the development of research schools and the implications of the Bologna process mark a gradual shift in thinking about the role of the doctorate and research training.
* As society is dependent on knowledge-related processes and work, the function of the doctorate should be more than replenishing the professoriate. It is increasingly seen as the ultimate phase of university education, aiming to train people to have the competencies to work in highly complex and knowledge intensive environments.
* As transferable skills gain importance in the training process, more coursework is introduced. There is a shift from the master–apprentice model to the professional model of doctoral education.
* Universities (re)discover doctoral training as an integral part of their institutional strategies. Institutional policies to organize doctoral training are being developed.

Funding issues

The funding of candidates

Dutch doctoral candidates are funded by three different sources, called first, second, and third stream money. The first source is supplied by the Ministry of Education, Science, and Culture. Universities use a part of this money stream to hire AiOs. The second flow of funds is allocated through the Netherlands Foundation for Scientific Research (NWO). From these funds, AiO positions can be acquired in a peer-reviewed competition. The third flow of funds is acquired through contracts with governments (both national and European), non-profit organizations, private companies and charitable boards. There are no precise data available on the proportions of doctoral candidates funded by these sources. However, the research carried out by Oost and Sonneveld (2005) on research schools provides rough indications (see Table 6.2).

Doctoral candidates that have acquired an AiO position receive a four-year contract on the basis of a special remuneration system. In this system the candidate receives training and education and carries out scientific work. In the first three years of the AiO appointment, salaries are significantly lower than academic staff salaries to compensate for the training that is provided. Table 6.3 indicates the monthly incomes for each year of their appointment (as of April 2006).

Table 6.2 Percentage of Ph.D. research in Dutch research schools with direct and indirect government funding, and funded as contract research

Sector		Direct government funding: first stream money	Indirect government funding: second stream money	Funded as contract research: third stream money
Humanities	Mean	77.7	13.3	9.0
	N	3	3	3
Natural sciences	Mean	39.4	39.2	19.8
	N	20	18	18
Social sciences	Mean	62.0	23.7	14.3
	N	12	13	12
Medicine	Mean	43.7	17.8	33.0
	N	6	5	5
Engineering	Mean	30.3	19.4	48.4
	N	6	5	5
Total	Mean	47.0	28.2	22.4
	N	47	44	43

Source: Ooost and Sonneveld (2006)

Table 6.3 Monthly income in € (before taxation) for AiOs, April 2006

Sector	1st year	2nd year	3rd year	4th year
Income	1,933	2,252	2,359	2,472

Source: VSNU (2006), www.vsnu.nl/web/show/id=58937/langid=42

The funding of institutions

Since the 1990s, a number of Dutch universities admit doctoral candidates with the support of a grant instead of offering them employment in an AiO position. Three reasons underlie this development. First, universities would like to accommodate candidates from abroad who seek (or have found) a stipend rather than employment. Second, the provision of grants saves a university the employer costs that go with regular labour positions. Third, universities acknowledge that a heterogeneous population of doctoral candidates will require alternative ways of financial support that AiO–employment alone. The introduction of doctoral stipends is however strongly contested by (associations of) doctoral candidates, which illustrates the ambiguity that exists around the status of doctoral candidates. On the one hand, they are students who receive training and supervision but on the other hand they are considered the engine of scientific work. The financial support structure that was introduced in the framework of the AiO system basically reflects this hybrid position. But external forces, such as the labour market and the internationalization of postgraduate training, are increasingly putting pressure on this situation.

Types of institution

Types of institution awarding doctorate degrees

The only type of institution authorized to award Ph.D. degrees in the Netherlands is the university. At present, there are 14 universities in the Netherlands. The higher education law provides a very general framework for doctoral education. Basically, the law charges the so-called *College van Promoties* (Doctoral Boards) of each university to regulate the award of doctoral degrees. The Doctoral Board, which is chaired by the *Rector Magnificus*, formulates rules and regulations regarding the process of obtaining the doctoral degree at that university. Formally, this includes the assignment of a supervisor and the appointment of doctoral committee. In practice, this authority may be delegated to the faculty deans, who in turn may delegate it to the chairs of the faculty departments.

The organizaton of institutions

The primary location of doctoral training is the research schools. At present, there are 105 research schools covering virtually all scientific fields. The main characteristics of research schools are the accommodation of research and research training within a single organization, the provision of course-work modules for doctoral candidates and frequent inter-institutional cooperation aimed at creating sufficient critical mass.

The system of research schools is entering a period of transition. The Netherlands Association of Universities (VSNU 2004b) acknowledges the value of the system of research schools, but points out that more flexible organizational models for research training should be developed that host *all* doctoral candidates in the Netherlands. At several universities doctoral training is now being organized under the internationally recognizable name of 'graduate school'. It is expected that these, predominantly locally-organized graduate schools will gradually merge or closely cooperate with the predominantly nationally-operating research schools. Although the formation of graduate schools at universities only started in 2005, the main characteristics of graduate schools in the Netherlands are likely to be that (VSNU 2004b: 25):

- the graduate school is responsible for the training and supervision of affiliated doctoral students and for the teaching programmes and the masters level;
- the graduate school is responsible for assuring the quality of its doctoral and masters programmes;
- the graduate school oversees the recruitment and selection of doctoral (and masters) students;
- the graduate school monitors progress of its affiliated students, and takes action in the event of failings on the part of supervisors, doctoral candidates or students;
- the graduate school must have sufficient critical mass and has to be large enough to provide proper interaction and efficiency, but not so big that it fails to provide a stimulating and personal environment.

Types of doctoral study

At present, there is only one type of doctoral study in the Netherlands. The successful candidate is awarded the degree of 'doctor' (dr.). Currently, the universities and the institutions for higher professional education (*hoge-scholen*) are exploring the options of introducing other programmes and degrees in the third cycle, including the professional doctorate.

Students and their programmes of study

Admission

The admission requirement for a doctoral position is a masters degree or a degree comparable to the level of a Dutch masters degree. The Doctoral Board is authorized to accept candidates on the basis of earlier acquired competences.

Requirements for obtaining the doctoral degree

In virtually all cases, writing and successfully defending the Ph.D. thesis is sufficient to complete the Ph.D. curriculum. Although the Ph.D. coursework is a compulsory section of the Ph.D. programme, only a few Ph.D. candidates receive a certificate for this work. To our knowledge, only one research school requires that such coursework be completed before allowing Ph.D. candidates to defend their thesis. In practice, the coursework in the Ph.D. programme is voluntary. Peer review committees of research schools have urged that the Ph.D. coursework programme be compulsory.

Periods of study

The nominal duration of the process of acquiring the doctorate is four years. The actual length will of course be dependent on factors such as a candidate's talents, ambitions, previously acquired competences and on the training and supervision provided. The periods of study of the AiO will differ from those who work on their dissertation while having another job. Typically, the study programme of the AiO and the scholarship recipients is structured as follows. The first year is primarily dedicated to the compulsory sections of the programme. While the candidates may attend courses in subsequent years, the coursework component is predominantly provided in this first year. The coursework components do not culminate in an examination. At virtually all research schools, the candidates are already fully involved in their Ph.D. research. They either design a research plan to be pursued in the next three years, or elaborate the provisional proposal provided by the supervisor or research group. In the second and third year, candidates carry out the research, while the fourth year is generally dedicated to the writing, revision and editing of the thesis.

The recent introduction of research programmes at masters level (socalled 'research masters') may lead to changes in the periods of doctoral study. We anticipate that during these research studies students will have the opportunity to prepare for a Ph.D. by drafting a research proposal or by taking preparatory courses. For these students the duration of doctoral study might be shortened. However, we do not expect a structural reduction of the nominal duration of the doctoral degree.

Can the study be undertaken either part-time or full-time?

Part-time appointments for AiOs do exist, but nearly always amount to 0.8 FTE (full-time equivalent). An exception is medicine, where the pursuit of a Ph.D. is often combined with clinical practice. Candidates that are not appointed on an AiO contract work on their dissertation in very different circumstances. In this group of candidates part-time study is probably very common.

Career destinations

Labour market data about Ph.D. candidates are incomplete. It is for this reason that the Minister of Education, Culture and Science (OCW 2005) announced an annual labour market monitor for Ph.D.-holders. Sonneveld and Oost (2006) present several preliminary observations reflecting on this issue. They base their observations on a review of the records of 32 Dutch research schools from different fields of scholarship. The research schools report favourable to very favourable labour market opportunities. This is illustrated in Table 6.4, which presents the 32 research schools surveyed by discipline. Two schools of history express concerns about employment opportunities for Ph.D.-holders, while two other schools of humanities do not address the matter. Twenty-eight schools (over 85 per cent) report that their Ph.D. candidates have good employment prospects.

Despite these impressions provided by the research schools, Ph.D. candidates and postdocs often express concerns about career prospects (PNN 2006). The Ministry of Education, Culture and Science recently stated (OCW 2005: 8) that 'In academia they often face inadequate career policies and a lack of advancement opportunities. Outside academia, the minimal demand for people with Ph.D.s is their main problem'. A clearer understanding of this issue will require additional research.

Table 6.4 Employment prospects in the different disciplines in general, based on the records of 32 research schools (N = 102)

Discipline	N	Prospects
Biology, oceanography and earth sciences	3	Good
Natural sciences	4	Good
Behavioural sciences	3	Good
Humanities, except for history	2	Unlisted
History	4	Mixed reports*
Agriculture	2	Good
Social sciences	4	Good
Medicine	6	Good
Law	2	Good
Technical sciences	2	Good

* Two schools report problems and concerns; two other schools are optimistic

Gender issues in relation to doctoral study

Women are under-represented in senior academic positions. Only 8 per cent of full professors are women. This alarming figure is subject of discussion and of a number of policy measures which focus on the stimulation of an academic career after the doctoral stage. At the doctoral level itself, the representation of women is not overly out of balance (see Table 6.1).

Race issues in relation to doctoral study?

There are concerns that the participation of ethnic minorities lags behind. In 2002, the Netherlands Organization for Scientific Research (NWO) commissioned an investigation into the causes of under-representation of ethnic minorities (Information can be accessed at www.nwo.nc/english). It was pointed out that, although the proportion of ethnic minorities successfully completing a university degree is increasing, these groups do not enter the doctoral system and are sparsely hired as academic staff. The report mentions two causes: academic institutions do not properly identify potential Ph.D. candidates from these groups and the potential doctoral students are often not aware of the opportunities. Recently, funds were made available to start a support programme (the Mozaiek programme) aimed to attract more ethnic minority graduates into academic research.

Supervision

Each Ph.D. candidate has a thesis supervisor (*promotor*) and, in many cases, a *co-promotor*. The *co-promotor* works under the responsibility of the *promotor* and must have a Ph.D. degree. Depending on the situation, this involvement may lead to a formal second supervisorship. At the last stage of the doctoral process a doctoral committee is composed (consisting of six to ten members) to evaluate the dissertation of the candidate.

Examination

The doctoral degree is granted to those who have proved themselves capable of the independent pursuit of scholarship. The proof of this capability is the doctoral thesis. It is the evaluation of this final product of the doctoral process that determines whether the candidate is granted the doctor's title.

The Doctoral Board has the formal power to award the doctorate. The examination procedure starts with the composition of a doctoral committee, whose task it is to evaluate the thesis. In consultation with the supervisor, the dean of the faculty submits a proposal for this composition to the Doctorate Board. If the supervisor approves the manuscript, they send copies to the members of the doctoral committee. Within six weeks of receiving the manuscript, the members of the committee should decide whether the candidate be permitted to defend the thesis. In a public meeting and ceremony, the candidate will then defend the thesis. After exactly one hour, the debates come to an (abrupt) end as the ceremonial host speaks up the words '*hora est*'. The doctoral committee withdraws to evaluate the quality of the thesis and the defence. Upon return of the committee the Ph.D. degree is awarded to the candidate and a *laudatium* is presented by the supervisor.

Critical observation

The Bologna process

Currently doctoral education is gracing the policy agendas in the Netherlands. The reason for this lies not primarily in attempts to meet the long-standing challenges that doctoral education faces, i.e. the long time to degrees, problematic career outlooks and the supervision process; rather, the debate on the third cycle picks up in the slipstream of the Bologna process and the ambition to stimulate a knowledge-based economy. In the Netherlands, the introduction of the bachelor–master structure inevitably raises questions about the relationship between the second and the third cycle. As universities develop (research) master programmes, they immediately address the organization of doctoral studies as well. The realization of a knowledge economy is dependent on advanced competencies and skills. The full potential of doctoral education is being (re)discovered as an important vehicle to deliver these highly educated people.

In our view, the debates revolve around three key questions. What is the nature of the doctorate? How should doctoral education be funded? And how should doctoral education be organized?

What is the nature of the doctorate?

Doctoral education is now considered to go beyond the training of new scientific researchers (see also VSNU 2004b; AWT 2005). Doctoral training is, more than ever, brought into the realm of higher education policies. The inclusion of research training in the Bologna process reinforces this development (Berlin Communiqué 2002; Bergen Communiqué 2005). Doctoral education is positioned in a straight 'education path' from the bachelor, to the master to the doctor's degree. Of course, the main component of doctoral education will remain the close link to research. However, if the doctorate is to meet the expectation of a broader and highly knowledge-based labour market, then the changes loom large. We anticipate an ongoing increase of enrolment into doctoral programmes, the incorporation of more coursework, a further standardization of the doctoral process, the introduction of structured quality assurance and accreditation and a further diversification of the programmes including the introduction of professional doctorates. The characteristics of the Dutch doctoral system as described in this chapter indicate that changes are already taking place. However, the pace of change will be gradual. Disciplinary cultures and long-standing doctoral practices are strong and will continue to lead to diverse practices.

How to fund doctoral training?

The scale and scope of doctoral training are predominantly bounded by finance: how much money is available and how is it allocated to the candidates and the institutions? The ambitions are high; government and universities would like to raise the number of Ph.D.s but the financial resources are limited. Without a substantial investment in extra Ph.D. positions, the Netherlands will remain a country with a relative modest number of Ph.D.s.

How to organize doctoral training

In the sciences, there is a tradition of bringing together doctoral candidates. It is in these organizational forms that a proper quality assurance mechanism can be implemented, that proper (research) facilities can be offered and that a stimulating interaction between researchers is possible. These issues must be addressed in any organizational format for doctoral training. The idea of research schools builds upon this. It is an interesting example of a relatively top-down policy innovation in doctoral education. The creation of critical mass, the structuring of doctoral education and the introduction of arrangements for quality assurance are considered to be important assets of the research schools. Universities realize that doctoral education can be an important dimension in their institutional profile, hence the development of institutionally-based graduate schools. The question of the design of graduate schools is moving back again from the (national) policy-maker to decentralized levels.

References

AWT (Adviewraad voor het Wetenschaps- en Technologiebeleid) (2005) *Briefadvies Onderzoeksloopbanen*. Den Haag: AWT.

Bergen Communiqué (2005) *The European Higher Education Area – Achieving the Goals*. Bergen: European Union.

Berlin Communiqué (2002) *Realising the European Higher Education Area*. Berlin: European Union.

Hesseling, P. (1986) *Frontiers of Learning: the PhD Octopus*. Dordrecht: Floris Publications.

KNAW (Koninklijke Academie voor Wetenschappen) (2005) *Protocol Erkenning Onderzoekscholen*. Amsterdam: KNAW.

OCW (Ministerie van Onderwijs, Cultuur en Wetenschap) (2005) *Onderzoekstalent op waarde geschat*. Den Haag: Ministerie van Onderwijs, Cultuur en Wetenschap.

Oost, H. and Sonneveld, H. (2005) *Rendement en duur van promoties in de Nederlandse onderzoekscholen. Beleidsgerichte studies Hoger onderwijs en Wetenschappelijk onderzoek 110*. Den Haag: Ministerie van Onderwijs, Cultuur en Wetenschap.

PNN (Promotienetwerk Nederland) (2006) *Tussen wens en werkelijkheid: carrièreperspectieven van jonge onderzoekers*. Leiden: PNN.

Sonneveld, H. and Oost, H. (2006) *Het promotiesucces van de Nederlandse onderzoekscholen. Afsluiting van een drieluik. Beleidsgerichte studies Hoger onderwijs en Wetenschappelijk onderzoek*. Den Haag: Ministerie van Onderwijs, Cultuur en Wetenschap.

Vereniging van Universiteiten (VSNU) (2002) *Kengetallen Universitair Onderzoek 2002*. Utrecht: VSNU.

Vereniging van Universiteiten (VSNU) (2004a) *Kengetallen Wetenschappelijk Personeel 2004*. Utrecht: VSNU.

Vereniging van Universiteiten (VSNU) (2004b) *Hora Est*. Utrecht: VSNU.

Wachelder, J.C.M. (1992) *Universiteit tussen Vorming en Opleiding: de modernisering van de Nederlandse universiteiten in de negentiende eeuw*. Hilversum: Verloren.

7

Doctoral education in Poland

Piotr W. Juchacz and Marek Kwiek

Introduction

Poland has a long tradition in doctoral education, dating back to the fifteenth century when such degrees were awarded at Jagiellonian University in Cracow. At present doctoral education takes place in both public and private universities, with over 33,000 students studying. There is a continuing academic tradition, emanating originally from Germany, of having two scientific degrees: the doctorate and the 'habilitation'. The future of this tradition however is subject to debate in the context of pressures for European harmonization – specifically the Bologna process. Indeed, Poland like so many other countries in Europe and beyond faces significant transformation in the coming years as pressures to redefine the doctorate and its purposes and outcomes are addressed.

The questionnaire

Table 7.1 The questionnaire

Question	Number	Comment
1 Total number of doctoral students studying	33,040	30,265 – public universities 2,775 – private universities. The data in the table are from 2004
2 Number of institutions offering doctoral programmes	No data	
3 Number of different doctoral awards (e.g. including professional doctorates)	2	Regular Ph.D. degree and Ph.D. in the arts

(Continued overleaf)

Table 7.1 (Continued)

Question	Number	Comment
4 Number of years over which doctorates have been offered in the country	Over 500	Since the fifteenth century (Jagiellonian University, Cracow)
5 Proportion of full-time to part-time students?	72% full-time, 28% part-time	23,027 full-time students to 8,949 part-time students
6 Average time to completion (in years)	68.5% of students complete their studies within 2 years; 25% within 4 years; 4.6% within 6 years; 1.9% longer than 6 years	The statistical data show only the number of years passing since the date of the opening of the doctorate procedure. Usually doctoral students open doctorate procedure on the second or third year of study
7 Success rates		No data available; the probable drop-out rate is relatively small, no more than 10% in the public sector
8 Typical age range of doctoral candidates	24–30	The vast majority of doctoral students begin doctoral studies immediately after graduation at (usually) age 24 and studies last (on average) 4–5 years
9 Proportion of male/female students	48.27% female	15,947 female students out of 33,040 in 2004
10 Proportion of doctoral students studying who are nationals of other countries	1.5%	488 foreigners in total (289 in public universities and 199 in private institutions)

Data source

Main Statistical Office (2005). See references.

The place of doctoral study in the national/international context

The place of the doctorate within the legislative framework

The procedures concerning doctoral studies and conferring doctoral degrees in Poland are regulated by two laws. The precise information concerning doctoral studies is presented in Part IV (Studies and students), Chapter 3 (Doctoral programmes) of the *Law on Higher Education* (2005) and in Chapter VI of *The Law on Scientific Degrees and the Scientific Title and on Degrees and the Title in the Area of Art* (2003). The precise rules concerning conferring doctoral degrees are presented in the latter law.

The doctorate and the habilitation

Two scientific degrees can be earned in Poland: the doctorate and the habilitation (the latter coming from the German academic tradition widely spread in Central Europe). In the Polish structure of higher education, the habilitation opens the way from being a junior faculty member to becoming a senior faculty member; however, full seniority of rank is only achieved with the award of the scientific title of professor. The habilitation, however, opens the way for an academic to become a university professor (a university function, without a scientific title). Background information on numbers, sex and distribution among disciplines of doctorates is given and discussed below. In the Polish context, it may also be useful to combine these data with the data concerning the habilitation.

Over the past four years, there have been significant discussions about the future of the habilitation in the training of faculty and in the academic career in general. Although opinions have varied, the status quo with regard to the existence of the two scientific degrees has been maintained and may be promoted for future legislative projects, despite Bologna-related European pressures to have only one degree in the academic career, the Ph.D. The strongest support for the abolition of the habilitation seems to be coming from trade union circles, and the strongest opposition from senior faculty who fear an (apparently unavoidable) lowering of academic standards (at least for as long as the standards for doctoral dissertations are not simultaneously raised).

Numbers of doctoral degrees awarded

The numbers of doctoral degrees (and habilitations) awarded in Poland in 2004, in higher education institutions, institutes of the Polish Academy of

Sciences, and in research and development institutes amounted to 5314 and 830, respectively. It should be noted that perhaps 80,000 people in Poland are believed to hold Ph.D. degrees, with an increase of 4000–5500 every year in the 2000s. Of these, slightly more than 41,000 were working in public higher education institutions in 1999 and the situation has not changed dramatically. Although people holding Ph.D. degrees are distributed among higher education institutions and research institutions and can be found in industry and administration, the principal places in which doctorates are concentrated are public higher education institutions.

Stipends

In the Polish higher education system, doctoral students rank between students and junior academic faculty. They have some of the privileges of faculty members; however, their social security coverage is the same as that of students and they do not receive regular salaries. Contributions to their pension schemes are not paid. Less than half of all doctoral students receive state-funded doctoral stipends, on a competitive basis, but with exemption from taxation. At the same time, doctoral students have poor chances of being employed after graduation in the public academic sector, for the number of positions available is very low in the vast majority of disciplines. The total amount of academics in Poland has only slightly risen in the last ten years, despite huge increases in the number of both students and doctoral students.

Funding issues

The funding of institutions

According to *The Law on Higher Education,* a public higher education institution receives state subsidies for: (i) tasks related to the teaching of full-time doctoral students and (ii) tasks related to non-reimbursable financial support for doctoral students. Also, a non-public (or private) higher education institution may be granted a subsidy for the tasks related to non-reimbursable financial support for doctoral students and may also be granted a subsidy to cover a part of fees paid by full-time doctoral students.

The funding of students

According to the *Law,* 'doctoral students may be awarded financial support in the form of: (i) a maintenance grant, (ii) an aid payment, (iii) a scholarship for learning achievements, (iv) a meals grant, (v) an accommodation grant, (vi) a special grant for disabled persons'. Additionally only full-time doctoral students may be awarded doctoral scholarships, which are funded by state budget subsidy.

There were 12,224 doctoral scholarships and 1134 doctor's scholarships (for assistants without Ph.D. degrees already employed in higher education institutions) in 2004. Of them, 112 and 47, respectively, were awarded in private higher education institutions.

It is worth mentioning that it is in the last few years that noticeable gradual growth of subsidies for doctoral students offered by local authorities and foundations has been observed.

Kinds of institution

Institutions within the national framework

Doctoral programmes are offered by academic institutions, research and development institutes and units of the Polish Academy of Sciences. According to *The Law on Higher Education,* 'organizational units of a higher education which are authorized to confer either the academic degree of habilitated doctor or the academic degree of PhD in at least two different disciplines of a given area of science may provide doctoral programmes in the corresponding disciplines'. Only those academic units (institutions, faculties, departments) which employ in a full-time mode at least eight academics with the scientific title of professor or that of habilitated doctor in a given discipline have the right to confer doctoral degrees.

In Poland, doctoral degrees are primarily awarded in top public academic institutions – with universities in the lead – followed by technical universities and academies of medicine. The quantitative trend is that of a large increase in both the numbers of doctoral students and of degrees awarded. The numbers of doctoral students increased 12 times between 1990 and 2004: from 2700 in 1990 to 10,500 in 1995, and to 33,000 in 2004. Also the numbers of doctorates awarded increased almost four times in the same period: from 1500 in 1991 to 2300 in 1995, and from 4400 in 2000 to 5700 in 2004.

At the same time, the number of undergraduate and graduate students in both the public and private sectors of higher education increased almost five times (from 403,800 to 1,926,000 in 2004, the trend being clearly stopped in 2004 and 2005 in comparison with radical growth in previous years). The number of doctoral students at the Polish Academy of Sciences is relatively small compared to the number in educational institutions – it is only 4.92 per cent (1625 doctorate students in 2004), as is the number of doctoral students in research institutes – 2.14 per cent (708 doctorate students in 2004). Consequently, the number of doctorates awarded at the Polish Academy of Sciences is relatively small as well, compared to the number of doctorates awarded in educational institutions – 2.8 per cent (162 doctorates awarded), as is the number of doctoral students in research institutes – 4.3 percent (246 doctorates awarded).

The organization of awarding institutions

Doctoral programmes are organized by departments or faculties of eligible academic institutions. In general, there are no graduate schools to run doctoral programmes: doctoral studies are offered as a continuation of post-graduate studies, for top graduates based on very strict selection procedures. Within the Bologna process, and based on the new law of 2005, doctoral students are third-cycle students at the university (the previous cycles being BA and MA, with the real distinction introduced only in recent years).

Forms of doctoral study

There are two kinds of doctoral degree – a scientific degree and a degree in a given domain of arts. No professional doctorates are possible within current legislation. So the only difference is between doctoral degrees conferred in academies of fine arts and in all other (eligible) academic institutions.

Students and their programmes of study

Requirements of doctoral students

The Law on Higher Education states that: 'Access to doctoral programmes shall be open to a person who holds the MA degree or an equivalent degree and fulfills the admission conditions laid down by a given higher education institution'. Usually there is the requirement of meeting the minimum level of average marks during the period of study (usually 4.00 – in the mandatory Polish scale from 2.0 failed to the maximum of 5.0, very good). Because of the number of candidates which is usually higher than that of places available (both with or without scholarships), there are usually oral introductory/ entrance exams, where the institutional admission committee consisting of professors of a given institute evaluate candidates partly on the basis of their previous accomplishments (studies and MA theses) and partly on the basis of the evaluation of their doctorate proposals.

Periods of study

Officially there are four years of doctoral studies in Poland (the scholarship can be taken during four years only). Universities treat differently students who have obtained scholarship abroad (a doctoral scholarship is suspended during the leave of absence abroad). Some universities include that time in the general four-year period, others do not. Quite often the rector agrees to extend the studying period to a so-called 'fifth year' with all doctoral student privileges maintained (especially without the necessity of paying the costs for the doctorate defence procedure, which has to be paid by all external candidates), but without scholarships.

Modes of study

There are officially two kinds of doctoral studies: full-time programmes and part-time programmes. As the *Law* clearly states, 'more than a half of the curriculum of a full-time doctoral programme shall require the presence of participants therein in the organizational unit providing the programme and shall comprise courses and research work requiring direct participation of academic staff or research tutors and doctoral students. Part-time doctoral programmes shall be organised in such a way as to ensure that doctoral programmes may be followed by persons in an employment relationship'. In public higher education institutions no tuition fees are charged for full-time doctoral studies, but can be charged for part-time doctoral programmes (especially in such lucrative areas of study such as economics).

Scholarships/internships

There are two kinds of student on a full-time doctoral programme: with scholarship (who cannot hold additionally any permanent job, both full-time and part-time) and without scholarship (this group consist of two kinds of student: firstly, students who have a post and do not want scholarships, and secondly students who have not received scholarships because the number of them is too small compared with the number of those students accepted in entrance exams; usually some of them get scholarship one or two years later, after the official opening of the doctorate procedure). The *Law* clarifies that 'doctoral students shall also be required to undertake internships involving the teaching of the courses or participation in the teaching courses. The maximum teaching load for participants in doctoral programmes may not exceed 90 teaching hours per year' (with the standard workload at universities being 210 for junior and 180 for senior staff). In practice, the law cited above is executed only towards full-time students who have scholarships, and only they are obliged to conduct 90 teaching hours. Also, fee-paying part-time students do not provide teaching in their institutions.

Career destinations

Current research on doctoral students in some areas (especially part-time fee-paying studies), indicates that only 20 per cent of them are interested in pursuing academic careers. The remaining 80 per cent may want to bring advanced credentials to the labour market or, more often, do not have any idea as to what they want to do in professional life, hoping to have additional time in which to choose (a widespread feeling of 'negative selection' exists for doctoral studies in certain disciplines; in other, more marketable disciplines, paid doctoral studies exist, in which the expected level of achievement of doctoral students is very low and no exceptional abilities are required). Very few doctoral students are interested in academic teaching. It is different in the area of humanities, where most doctoral students would like to continue their research in academic institutions.

An academic career in Poland today does not offer exciting job prospects in terms of remuneration and available research funding (the academic salary for full professor gross in 2005 was approximately €1800, the average salary for junior staff was about €600 gross). The labour market for new Ph.D.s in some disciplines is much larger abroad (especially in the USA) than in Poland – a situation that leads to the brain drain. Even though the number of doctoral students increased 12 times between 1990 and 2004, the number of academic staff members over that period did not increase substantially, compared with the growth in the number of students and doctoral students in the same period of time, with adverse consequences for chances for starting academic careers. Nevertheless the faculty number grew from 66,973 in the academic year 1995/6 to 85,760 in academic year 2003/4, almost 30 per cent within a decade. As a result, the chances of new doctorate-holders obtaining employment in higher education institutions or academies of sciences are limited. While a decade ago, Ph.D.s were produced mainly for academe, their holders now, in most cases, must seek employment outside the academic market.

Gender issues in doctoral education

There are no gender issues in relation to doctoral programmes. Presently almost half of the doctoral students are women (48.3 per cent). Almost the same proportion can be found among students who have completed a doctorate (47 per cent of females). But it should be stressed that on the next level of the academic career – habilitation – the proportion of females to males is only 30 per cent to 70 per cent. The higher the academic level, the lower the proportion of women (as in most European countries).

Social issues in doctoral education

Polish society is homogeneous, and in this sense there are no race issues in relation to doctoral programmes. There are only 1.5 per cent of foreign students (488 persons) among all doctoral students, but statistics information concerning the race of doctoral recipients is not collected. In 2004, 43 per cent of foreign students were of Polish origin. Among other nations represented, young people from neighbouring countries like Ukraine, Belarus or the Baltics dominate. There is also a small group of students from Central and South-East Asia.

It is worth mentioning that faculties of theology at public universities are always Roman Catholic theological faculties under the essential supervision of the archbishop for the area where the university is located.

Supervision

There is always one official scientific supervisor of a doctoral candidate who is proposed and elected during the opening of the doctorate procedure. The acceptance of the function of a professor conferring a degree, as well as that of reviewer of a doctorate thesis, is according to the *Law* a duty of the academic teacher. They are fully responsible for the academic development and progress of a doctorate candidate. But additionally, candidates every year have to present written information (including positive opinion of the supervisor) concerning the progress of their work to the director of the doctorate studies in the relevant department or faculty. Students with scholarships who have to teach are also supervised by the deputy director when teaching in the department.

Examination

The procedure is strictly described by the *Law* and consists of five steps.

Usually during the second or third year of doctoral studies, the candidate officially opens their doctorate procedure in front of the scientific council of the faculty or sometimes of the department (only scientifically very strong departments get the right to conduct doctorate procedures; they usually take place in the front of the faculty council). The law strictly says that 'eligible to take part in the voting shall be members of the board of the organisational unit concerned holding the academic title of professor or the academic degree of the doctor habilitated'. The candidate proposes the exact theme of a doctorate, presents its main thesis in a speech of approximately ten minutes and then is obliged to answer questions posed by the professors of the council. After discussion, the council votes on the opening of the doctorate; if positive, the council follows three steps: firstly, it designates a professor conferring a degree who has to be a person holding the academic title of professor or the academic degree of doctor habilitated in a given or related area of science or art; secondly, the council usually designates from its members a doctorate commission (six or seven professors) and thirdly it decides on the names of three examiners for the three obligatory doctoral exams (in the doctorate subject, in a related subject chosen by the candidate from the established list, and in a foreign language).

When the doctoral thesis is ready and accepted by the doctoral supervisor and all three doctoral exams have been passed, a doctorate commission accepts it and proposes to the scientific council the closing of the doctorate and the designation of two reviewers. The scientific council votes the closing of the doctorate and – if positive – designates two specialists in the field as reviewers: according to the law, 'at least two reviewers shall be appointed for the procedure leading to the conferment of the academic degree of doctor ... including not more than one who is employed in the same higher education institution or another research institution where the candidate for the degree of doctor is employed, or who is the member of the board of the organisational unit conducting the procedure' (they have three months to write the review).

When the doctorate commission receives two positive reviews and accepts them, it recommends to the scientific council the acceptance of the thesis and fixes the date of public defence.

The defence of the thesis takes place in the front of the members of the doctorate commission who for that occasion are accompanied by the director of a faculty (or department), the supervisor and both reviewers. The defence is open to the public, but in the final stage only the members of the commission have the right to vote. The defence starts with a 20–30 minute speech from the candidate who presents the main points of their thesis. Then both reviewers present their reviews and pose questions to the candidate. In the third step the candidate responds to the remarks or criticisms in the reviews and answers the reviewers' questions. In the next step members of the commission put questions along with members of the public. Finally the commission votes on acceptance of the public defence of the thesis and if affirmative recommends to the scientific council the conferring of a doctoral degree.

During a closed session of the scientific council, the recommendation is voted on and if affirmative the council confers a doctoral degree. The conferment takes effect immediately.

Other issues

It is important to remember that it is only the second academic degree, the habilitation degree, which opens the way to become a senior academic and gives the right to become a university professor (except for the arts). Academics with Ph.D. degrees in Poland are at the lower end of their academic careers – while a decade ago MA graduates were offered jobs at the best Polish universities, today the requirement is to be a Ph.D.-holder. The average time needed to get a habilitation degree is eight to ten years. All corporate privileges at the university begin with the latter degree: voting rights, the rights to supervise MA and Ph.D. theses and to be a reviewer of them, to head sub-units of departments etc.

Critical comments

Ph.D. studies in Poland are about to undergo a huge transformation in the coming years. While for decades they have been focused on producing young academics for the academic sector, with the fantastic increase in numbers they can no longer be treated as such. While the national system was able to accommodate 1500 doctoral recipients 15 years ago or over 2000 doctoral recipients 10 years ago, it seems impossible in the private sector to accommodate almost 6000 of them every year in the future. The solution might be academic jobs in private higher education institutions, or remodelling of doctoral studies so that they will be more useful to the non-academic labour market. Additionally, if the habilitation degree is to be discarded in the next five to ten years (which, within the processes of the Europeanization of Polish higher education may be the case), the role of Ph.D. studies and Ph.D. degrees will need to be dramatically changed, and their academic standards increased. As elsewhere in Europe, the academic profession in Poland no longer provides exciting career prospects, although it is still both highly valued and viewed as desirable and promising by society at large.

Bibliography

Kwiek, M. (2003a) Academe in transition: transformations in the Polish academic profession, *Higher Education*, 45(4): 455–76.

Kwiek, M. (2003b) The state, the market, and higher education, in M. Kwiek (ed.) *Challenges for the New Century. The University, Globalization, Central Europe*. Frankfurt: Peter Lang.

Kwiek, M. (2004a) The emergent European educational, policies under scrutiny. The Bologna process from a Central European perspective, *European Educational Research Journal*, 3(4): 759–80.

Kwiek, M. (2004b) The academic workplace in Poland, in J. Enders and E. de Weert (eds) *The International Attractiveness of the Academic Workplace in Europe*. Frankfurt: GEW.

Kwiek, M. (2004c) Doctoral studies in Europe: the case of Poland, in J. Sadlak (ed.) *Doctoral Studies and Qualifications in Europe and the United States: Status and Perspectives*. Bucharest: UNESCO-CEPES.

Main Statistical Office (2005) *Higher Education Institutions and Their Finances, 2004* (and previous years). Warsaw: GUS.

8

Doctoral education in the UK

Howard Green and Stuart Powell

Introduction

This chapter reviews the situation with regard to doctoral education in the UK. Some of the idiosyncrasies of the UK system and its complexities are described. There is also some analysis of supposed purposes (e.g. of government policies) weighed against the outcomes of actions. Pressures on the delivery of doctoral programmes and the various drivers for change are discussed.

The questionnaire

Table 8.1 The questionnaire

Question	Number	Comment
1 Total number of doctoral students studying	111,990	This number has been rising steadily over the last ten years
2 Number of institutions offering doctoral programmes	120 plus	There has been some change in institutional designation in the last 2 years. Some institutions have recently taken university status – but without as yet the ability to award research degrees. Some are accredited for research degrees by other universities. The University of London is a confederal organization with over 28 colleges and institutes

3	Number of different doctoral awards (e.g. including professional doctorates)	30 plus	Need to differentiate between different titles given to the same award (Ph.D., D.Litt, D.Phil) and an ever increasing number of named professional doctorates, taught doctorates, practice-based doctorates and the 'New Route Ph.D.'
4	Number of years over which doctorates have been offered in the country	700	Doctorates have been awarded in the UK since the thirteenth century – though titles and purposes have clearly changed much over this period
5	Proportion of full-time to part-time students	51:49	There are a large number of part-time students many of whom are in essence finishing their work part-time. As a consequence, the data probably inflates the number of students who are genuinely part-time
6	Average time to completion (in years)	Research Council students: 80%+ complete within 4 years, but they are only 30%+ of the cohort. For the rest the figure is much lower	The average is a meaningless figure in this context as there is significant variability (see HEFCE 2005)
7	Success rates	–	This data is not available
8	Typical age range of doctoral candidates	Full-time, 62% 24 and under (UK); part-time 89% over 24.72% 30 plus (UK)	While there is an increasing number of more mature students it is still the preserve of the young. A significant proportion of older part-time students are former full-timers
9	Proportion of male/female students	54:46	
10	Proportion of doctoral students studying who are nationals of other countries	45,440 of whom 13,800 are from the EU	Overseas students are now of fundamental importance to postgraduate research particularly in science and technology. EU students are becoming increasingly important

Referring to data sources

Much of the data discussed in this chapter can be found on the websites of the government-funded bodies, the HEFCE, HESA and QAA respectively: www.hefce.ac.uk/; www.hesa.ac.uk/; www.qaa.ac.uk/.

The place of doctoral study in the national/ international context

Structures within the UK

The UK comprises four countries each with a greater or lesser degree of self-government, with consequent divergences in the way in which higher education has developed, in particular with regard to funding. Where appropriate, we have noted them for comparative purposes; however, we do acknowledge that they make generalization about doctoral education in the UK problematic.

Drivers of change

The importance of research and the Ph.D. to the sustainability of the UK economy is seen as being of great significance to governments that fund both universities and students to undertake doctoral study. Discussion of the role of doctoral study and its value to the economy and society is not new – the government of the late 1960s set up committees to review the issues (e.g. Committee on Manpower Resources for Science and Technology 1968).

In the early 1990s the desire to make research, and the doctorate in particular, more relevant to the needs of the national economy intensified. Several national stakeholders began to question the nature and purpose of the Ph.D. Pressures for change were driven by three key concerns: (i) an apparent loss of international standing of the UK Ph.D., (ii) lack of personal and professional skills and (iii) disappointing completion rates.

The 1993 government White Paper *Realising our Potential* formalized the debate about research and research training, arguing that 'it is concerned, however, that the traditional PhD does not always match up to the needs of a career outside research in academia or an industrial research laboratory' (DTI 1993: 57). It went on to argue that there is a role for preparatory matters in research training when it suggested that 'for most students who have undertaken a first degree, the Master's qualification will provide an opportunity to acquire extra knowledge and skills . . . in preparation for a period of research training leading to a PhD or for employment' (p. 61).

In 1994 the Office of Science and Technology (OST) argued that those trained to postgraduate level should have skills better matched to the needs of potential employers, including those outside the academic. This should include elements of non-science specific training including at the very least communication skills and human, material and financial resource management skills (OST 1994).

The key driver for change in the mid/late 1990s came from the Harris Review of postgraduate education, both postgraduate taught (PGT) and postgraduate research (PGR). The impetus for this review came from concerns about quality, about growing numbers and, perhaps fundamentally, about the cost of provision, cross-subsidy and value for money. The analysis and conclusions on PGR began a chain reaction that is reflected in the majority of changes that we are currently observing. Key elements included: (i) the development of a code of practice; (ii) the selective funding of universities delivering research degrees; (iii) far greater attention to the supervisory process; and (iv) the inclusion of research training.

Training and industry linked initiatives

Employability is a word used increasingly across higher education in the UK and this is certainly applicable to the doctoral sector. Although demands for more employable research students date back more than two decades, the 1993 White Paper highlighted its significance. It observed that many successful Ph.D. candidates did not have the appropriate skills to work in industry (specifically in relation to the science base) and needed to have enhanced generic skills.

Value for money

Value for money represents a significant driver for change in the UK as successive governments increasingly recognize the costs of training doctoral students (most recently, see JM Consulting 2005). Through the respective funding councils, government continues to press for more effective doctoral training, better completion rates and higher quality students engaging in doctoral work. Several White Papers, from the seminal *Realising our Potential* to the more recent *Investing in Innovation* (OST 2002), have emphasized this requirement.

International forces

International forces are a key driver of change as a significant number of doctoral students, particularly in the sciences, are from overseas. The demands of overseas sponsors have been increasingly important in shaping the awards themselves and we have seen the development of the so-called 'New Route Ph.D.' as a direct response to international demands. This award, which is normally of four-year duration, includes more taught elements than does the 'traditional' Ph.D.

It is noteworthy that the demands from the European Union (EU) are perceived by many in the UK higher education sector as less significant. While the UK is a signatory to the Bologna Accord its practices pay little more than lip service to its demands. In part, this is because the only significant element that is not directly compliant with the Accord is the masters (the UK having a one-year postgraduate masters as opposed to the European two years). As far as the doctorate is concerned, the UK sees its three-year model, with apparently high completion rates, as one of excellence.

Workforce planning

It is perhaps noteworthy that absent from the drivers of change is any significant concern for the labour market and workforce planning. While there has been a slow realization than only a minority of doctorates will obtain academic appointment, there has been little discussion, other than by the British Academy, about the importance of academic placement (see e.g. the British Academy's Response to the Arts and Humanities Research Council's consultation on 'Doctoral research in the arts and humanities', accessible at www.britac.ac.uk/reports/ahrc2005/ahrcdocres.html). In the context of academic employers, little is said of the demand for doctorates and indeed there remains an open market with universities themselves dictating the level of provision.

Funding issues

Funding to institutions

The current arrangements for the funding of UK universities for research students are bound up in the structure known as the 'dual support system' of research funding which itself has been the subject of recent review. The dual support system provides universities that reach a particular level according to the Research Assessment Exercise (RAE), a funding stream reflecting the quality of the research referred to as 'QR'. The precise level of funding is determined by: (i) the quality rating; (ii) the number of staff rated in each department; and (iii) the academic subject under consideration. The complex issues that arise from this exercise and its effects are discussed more fully in Powell and Green (in press).

The other funding stream of the dual funding model comes from those agencies that fund specific projects. These include the research councils, the research charities, government departments and commercial organizations and companies.

The costs to UK universities for the delivery of doctoral programmes are funded through a similar dual support structure. The funding councils provide one element and students, frequently through a sponsor, provide the other through their payment of fees. Following the Roberts Review (Roberts 2003) an additional element (approximately £850 per full-time equivalent – FTE – per annum) has been added by government to support the delivery of research training for research council funded students only.

Indicative tuition fees and bench fee levels are set by the government and are subdivided into three broad categories: home and EU, overseas and Channel Islands. With some variability between disciplines there is broad parity of fees charged and little evidence that universities currently exploit the market by either significant variability between subjects or between universities with different market positions for research. In the case of the sponsors of full-time student fees the role of the research councils in supporting research students has declined over the period 1995/6–2001/2 from 46.5 per cent to 33.3 per cent of doctoral student fees. On the other hand the self-financing of fees, while only 15.4 per cent in 2001/2 has increased by 85.8 per cent during the period. Private industry, an insignificant funder at 4.6 per cent of the total, has become increasingly insignificant with a reduction of 19.6 per cent during the same period.

Self-financing is particularly important for part-time doctoral students who make approximately 46 per cent of the total. While not making such a significant contribution to the total number, both university and government department funding increased significantly, 37 per cent and 66 per cent respectively over the period 1995/6–2001/2. Notwithstanding the positive statements about the access agenda and the need to encourage more part-time research students, the research councils make only a minimal contribution to this group.

In December 2004 the English Funding Council announced that it was to change the payment to institutions and that a single payment, a supervision fee, would be paid to institutions for research students in departments rated 4 or above in the RAE 2001 (plus a small number of other departments receiving 'capability funding', see HEFCE 2004). One implication of this new approach is to withdraw funding from over 5000 university departments across the sector in the UK (see Powell and Green in press for a fuller discussion).

Funding to students: the stipend

Stipend is the term used here for the maintenance grant paid to doctoral students for the period of their research. In the UK the word is used interchangeably with bursary and scholarship. The stipend will cover all the domestic costs including accommodation, subsistence and transport.

The level of the stipend has come under scrutiny in the UK in recent years because of difficulties in attracting good quality candidates to research programmes and the possible difficulties in completion as students are obliged to take part-time employment to complement the stipend. The research councils noted an increase in unfilled studentships, both masters and doctoral, from approximately 4 per cent in 1997 to 11 per cent in 1999. Roberts (2003) observed that the level of the stipend fell by 4.5 per cent in real terms between 1971/2 and 1991/2; while during the same period starting salaries for graduates with an upper second first degree rose by more than 42 per cent. Despite the recent increases, from £6,800 in 2001 to £12,300 in 2006/7, stipends represent little advantage over the national minimum wage.

Kinds of institution

Who can deliver doctoral awards?

The issue of which institutions can deliver research degree programmes may be viewed from two perspectives: (i) university constitution and status; and (ii) the new approaches to funding. All UK universities are licensed to have Ph.D. programmes within their award portfolio as of right. Institutions that are not universities – such as the university colleges or specialist institutions – are able to run doctoral programmes in association with a university that acts as the awarding body. Recently there have been changes in the requirements to achieve university status and in practice most of the university colleges will eventually gain university status and subsequently be eligible to award doctorates.

The second key element in the equation relates more to the capacity to deliver, in relation to the Quality Assurance Agency (QAA) *Code of Practice* and in the funding, rather than in the constitutional right to so do. Implicit in the use of the QAA *Code of Practice* is a view that it will cause a reduction in the number of institutions that have the capability to deliver doctoral programmes. There is a clear message coming from the funding agencies that only in departments that are rated 4 and above in the RAE (put simply, the scale went from 0 to 5 – with 5 being the top) will in future be funded for doctoral programmes. Some institutions have stated that they will continue to offer doctoral programmes – even at a loss – for reasons of mission, status and profile enhancement; others may not.

Organization

By 1995 a significant number of universities had established graduate schools: 33 universities and one college of higher education had done so with a further 23 universities having definite plans to establish such systems (UKCGE 1995). By 2004 the graduate school had become the dominant model for the organization of graduate education (Woodward *et al.* 2004).

Beneath these headline figures there is a range of models of graduate school. The model adopted by any particular institution depends, in part at least, on the size of the university and the population of doctoral students. In cases where there are large numbers of doctoral students, graduate schools tend to be at faculty or departmental level. In universities with relatively few doctoral students the graduate school will tend to be at university level. The resources, facilities and responsibilities of graduate schools vary widely. So far in the UK there has been little development of discipline-based graduate schools at either institutional or regional level although these are being discussed in Scotland.

Forms of doctoral study

Doctoral awards

The doctoral award in the UK is very varied. This diversity and our under-standing of diverse structures and their purposes represent one of the major current concerns. Students can work towards doctoral awards with different nomenclatures – involving different levels of entry qualification, modes and kinds of study. The broad categories can be summarized as follows: Ph.D.; Ph.D. by published work; professional doctorate; practice-based doctorate; and higher doctorate (these categories are described in more detail in Green and Powell 2005).

Within these categories variance is also considerable both between and within institutions, all of which have their own regulations, requirements and understandings of the awards. There are also different understandings in the UK with regard to the purposes of doctoral education. We summarize three here; clearly these are not mutually exclusive.

- *The doctorate and the academic profession.* The notion of the doctorate as an apprenticeship for academia is predicated on two assumptions. First, that academics need a doctorate in order to practise their academic pro-fession and second that the doctorate provides the appropriate level of experiential learning to equip individuals for academic life.
- *The doctorate as an apprenticeship for industry.* Significant numbers of suc-cessful doctoral candidates follow careers in industry in a range of capaci-ties. The demands may relate specifically to research. Although the UK's performance in research and development is not at the top of the inter-national league, UK industry still takes large numbers of doctorates into research posts. The pharmaceutical and petrochemical industries are good examples.
- *The doctorate and the professions.* Data are not available within the UK on the number of employees in the professions (outside of academia) with doctor-ates and hence it is not possible to identify clearly the importance of the doctorate to specific professions. For many, the postgraduate diploma or masters is the passport to the profession rather than the doctorate (see Green and Powell 2005); the one exception here is the Doctor of Clinical

Psychology (DClinPsy) which is, in the UK, an 'entry level qualification' to clinical psychology or perhaps more accurately a licence to practise that profession.

Students and their programmes of study

Numbers, age structure, disciplines

There has been recent growth in the number of doctoral students in the UK; Table 8.2 illustrates this trend by giving the number of doctorates awarded over the last ten years.

The distribution of the awards is highly skewed across universities as is clearly seen in Table 8.3. Five universities, the Universities of Cambridge, Oxford, Birmingham, Manchester and University College London, all located in England, accounted for 25 per cent of the total awards in 2000.

Table 8.2 Total number of doctorates awarded by UK higher education institutions, 1996/7–2004/5

Year	Total	Annual Growth (%)
1996	10,800	
1997	11,860	9.8
1998	12,660	6.7
1999	13,140	3.8
2000	13,670	4.0
2001	14,115	3.2
2002	14,210	0.6
2003	14,875	4.4
2004	15,780	5.7

Source: HESA (2006: Table 12)

Table 8.3 The distribution of doctorates awarded by institution (2000)

Quartile	Number of universities
Upper	5
Second	9
Third	18
Lower	97

Source: Millichope (2001)

Table 8.4 Age structure: first year UK students 2004/5

Age	Type of student	
	Full-time	Part-time
Under 21	40	0
21–24	6,030	450
25–29	2,150	805
30 plus	2,220	3,610
Total	**10,440**	**4,865**

Source: HESA (available on the HESA website www.hesa.ac.uk, Tables 1d and 1h)

Table 8.4 gives a breakdown of the student population by age and across the modes of full-time and part-time study. It can be seen here that the preponderance of full-time students fall within the 21–24 age bracket while for part-time students the clear majority are within the 30 plus category. However full-time study is not the sole preserve of the under 25s and the table highlights the significant minority of students over the age of 30 studying full-time.

Overseas students

The demand for doctoral research programmes has risen considerably over the past ten years although there is some evidence that this has now levelled off, illustrating the attractive nature of the UK Ph.D. Much of the growth in overseas student demand has been funded by private sources; 40 per cent of the 39,000 postgraduate research students were funded in part or in full from UK sources including institutional scholarships and fee waivers (British Council 2004) (see Figure 1.1).

There are several reasons for these increases. From the pre-Harris days of the early 1990s there has been a significant change in the way in which the doctorate is delivered and quality assured. The QAA's *Code of Practice for Postgraduate Research Awards*, and the associated institutional audit of process is arguably a major factor in reassuring international students and sponsors of the quality of the doctorate. The language of delivery is also significant, particularly in science where English is now the common international language. Clearly the UK is not the only English language-speaking country offering doctorates.

Expected time to completion is a further significant factor in attracting overseas students to the UK. Recent evidence suggests that overseas students (along with their UK peers) complete in significantly shorter periods than in many other countries.

Destination of successful doctoral candidates

We noted earlier that there are various potential destinations for the successful doctoral candidate. The first destination figures in Table 8.5 illustrate the wide range of employment destinations – and the limited importance of academic employment.

Pressures to complete

In 2004 HEFCE completed a study into doctoral submission and completion rates across the sector (HEFCE 2005). The study incorporated all degrees that are examined predominantly through research, thus including the professional doctorates. This work presented a picture that was far from the optimistic one coming from the research councils. It emphasized the importance of funding, age, mode of study, discipline and institution in the explanation of time to completion. The study revealed that after seven years of study 71 per cent of full-time students had completed; only 34 per cent of part-time students had completed.

Student status

Currently, a research student in the UK may have the status of a student or a member of staff. In the former case, they will be funded on a grant or bursary and be subject to institutional regulation. As a member of staff, research assistant, graduate teaching assistant (GTA) or lecturer, the terms

Table 8.5 First destination of research council funded Ph.D. graduates

	1994	*1996*	*1998*	*2000*
Total number of leavers	3,166	3,201	3,735	3,262
Of which destination unknown	1,057	621	938	766
Known destinations	2,109	2,580	2,797	2,496
Of which	%	%	%	%
Permanent academic appointment	5	5	5	5
Fixed-term academic appointment	29	21	26	25
Further training (excluding teaching)	5	4	4	4
School teaching or teacher training	3	2	2	2
Private sector, industry or commerce	22	33	29	24
Government or other public sector	5	5	6	5
Other employment	4	2	4	4
Not employed	19	18	15	18
Overseas	10	9	10	13

Source: OST Set Statistics Table 8.5: 13, www.dti.gov.uk

of engagement and the associated regulations are completely different. Consequently in a science research laboratory we might find eight doctoral candidates, each with different conditions: the student on a well-funded research council stipend, the student who is self-funding, the student who is institutionally poorly funded, a part-time student with no funding, a research assistant on a short term contract, a research fellow on a permanent contract, a member of the lecturing staff undertaking a Ph.D. part-time and an overseas student funded generously by their sponsor government.

Supervision

In the UK 'who can supervise' is not regulated at national level as it is in some other countries. Universities with research degree awarding powers impose their own rules with regard to the criteria that a member of staff needs to fulfil in order to become part of a supervisory team and indeed the areas within which research degree study may be offered. However, at national level the QAA *Code of Practice* (QAA 2004) does set out broad principles upon which universities are subsequently audited: for example, supervision is undertaken by teams, supervisors will receive some training and the supervision itself will be recognized within the member of staff's overall workload. So, individual institutions may set up their own systems for selecting, training and monitoring the performance of research degree supervisors but these will fall within the context of the *Code* and the institutions are required to justify their rules and regulations accordingly.

Similarly the research councils have recognized the importance of the supervisory process to successful award completion – for example, this is formalized within the 2001 Economic and Social Research Council (ESRC) training guidelines.

Examination

Examining

The approach to examination of the doctorate is a further element of the process that has received attention recently, in part because of empirical research that has confirmed that examining is a less than structured affair (e.g. Underwood 1999; Tinkler and Jackson 2004).

While normally a viva is an integral element of examination there is evidence about a lack of clarity as to its purpose from both an institutional perspective (Powell and McCauley 2002) and in terms of the perceptions of the various participants (Tinkler and Jackson 2004). For example, the viva may be interpreted as an examination in the broadest sense of the term (and here questioning may extend beyond the work presented in the thesis itself to encompass issues of the candidate's knowledge of related subject matter) or as merely a matter of verification of authenticity.

Search for criteria

The UK *National Qualifications Framework* (QAA 2001) describes doctoral level work as that which makes a significant contribution to knowledge and which is original. Institutions interpret this description in the way in which they set out criteria. Some use 'contribution to knowledge and to the application of that knowledge'; some include the notion of 'publishability'. This last indicator is usually expressed in a somewhat imprecise way, however, in some disciplines the pressure to publish is more explicit; for example, the British Psychological Society (BPS/UCOSDA 1995) suggest that a doctoral submission should be equivalent to at least two articles in refereed journals.

Any other issues

The quality regime

Of particular interest is the way in which universities respond to the demands of the QAA *Code of Practice*. As Green and Powell (2004) noted, the increased complexity of the *Code* may create problems for those universities that have relatively small numbers of research students – probably over 50 per cent of the total number of universities – causing them to reconsider the financial viability of delivering doctorates at all. The revised *Code*, launched in September 2004, is a longer and more thorough document than the original 1996 *Code*; it was prepared with the help of representatives from the sector and responds to the views of the Better Regulation Review Group (BRRG). The guidance sections of the first edition of the *Code* are replaced by explanatory text. The QAA emphasizes that the *Code* provides a reference to widely agreed approaches to good practice in the relevant areas.

Institutional audit

The institutional audit is a second element of the QAA's work that will influence the doctoral process in institutions. The process of institutional audit was introduced in 2002/3 and developed out of the continuation audit process. In theory and as far as doctoral work is concerned, both processes examine how institutions are responding to the *Code of Practice*. A 'special audit' of all institutions was undertaken in 2005 to provide a national picture of institutional response to the new *Code*. The overall conclusion of this was very positive.

Critical comment

We recognize four issues that are of particular current significance within the UK doctoral system:

- the diversity of awards leading to lack of clarity of their status and purpose;
- the need to develop an organizational delivery structure which encourages efficient yet accessible provision;
- a need for government and the funding councils to recognize the real costs of delivery of doctoral programmes and fund them appropriately;
- the challenges posed by the globalization of the doctoral market.

References

British Council (2004) *Vision 2020: Forecasting International Student Mobility*. London: British Council.

BPS/UCOSDA (British Psychological Society and Universities and Colleges' Staff Development Unit) (1995) *Guidelines for Assessment of the PhD in Psychology and Related Disciplines*. Sheffield: UCOSDA.

Committee on Manpower Resources for Science and Technology (1968) *Interim report of the Working Group on Manpower Parameters for Scientific Growth*, Cmnd 3102. London: HMSO.

DTI (Department of Trade & Industry) (1993) *Realising our Potential: A Strategy for Science, Engineering and Technology*, Cmnd 2250. London: HMSO.

Green, D.H. and Powell, S.D. (2004) The high price of good quality, *The Independent Education*, 13 October.

Green, D.H. and Powell, S.D. (2005) *Doctoral Study in Contemporary Higher Education*. Buckingham: Open University Press.

HEFCE (Higher Education Funding Council of England) (2004) *Funding for Research Degree Programmes*, www.hefce.ac.uk/research/postgrad/rdpfund.htm (accessed 20 January 2005).

HEFCE (Higher Education Funding Council for England) (2005) *PhD Research Degrees: Entry and Completion*, HEFCE2005/2, www.hefce.ac.uk (accessed 12 January 2005).

HESA (Higher Education Statistics Agency) (2006) *Students in Higher Education Institutions 2004/05*. Cheltenham: HESA.

JM Consulting (2005) *Costs of Training and Supervising Postgraduate Research Students. A Report to HEFCE by JM Consulting Ltd.* www.hefce.ac.uk/pubs/rdreports/2005/ (accessed 4 February 2005).

Millichope, R. (2001) Doctorates awarded from United Kingdom higher education institutions, *Statistics Focus*, 3(2).

OST (Office of Science and Technology) (1994) *Consultative Document: A New Structure for Postgraduate Research Trainings, Supported by Research Councils*. London: Cabinet Office.

OST (Office of Science and Technology) (2002) *Investing in Innovation: A Strategy for Science, Engineering and Technology*. London: OST.

Powell, S.D. and Green, H. (in press) The national funding of doctoral training –

warnings from the English experience, *Journal of Higher Education Policy and Management.*

Powell, S.D. and McCauley, C. (2002) Research degree examining – common principles and divergent practices, *Quality Assurance in Education (Special Edition 'Standards and the Doctoral Award'),* 10(2): 104–16.

QAA (Quality Assurance Agency) (2001) *National Qualifications Framework.* www.qaa.ac.uk/crntwork/nqf/ewni2001/contents.htm (accessed 27 August 2004).

QAA (Quality Assurance Agency) (2004) *Code of Practice for the Assurance of Academic Quality and Standards in Higher Education: Section 1: Postgraduate Research Programmes,* 2nd edn). Gloucester: QAA.

Roberts, G. (2003) *Review of the Research Assessment Exercise. Report for the Funding Bodies,* HEFCE Issues for consultation May 2003, www.ra-review.ac.uk/reports/roberts/ roberts_summary.doc (accessed 20 January 2005).

Tinkler, P. and Jackson, C. (2004) *The Doctoral Examination Process: A Handbook for Students, Examiners and Supervisors.* Buckingham: Open University Press.

UKCGE (UK Council for Graduate Education) (1995) *Graduate Schools Survey.* Warwick: UKCGE, www.ukcge.ac.uk/report_downloads.html (accessed 20 January 2005).

Underwood, S. (1999) *What is a PhD? Towards a Discussion Paper.* Lancaster: Higher Education Development Centre.

Woodward, D., Denicolo, P., Hayward, S. and Long, E. (2004) *Review of Graduate Schools Survey.* Lichfield: UKCGE, www.ukcge.ac.uk/filesup/Graduateschools.pdf (accessed 20 January 2005).

Part 3
Australia, Canada and the USA

In Part 3 we include countries from the English-speaking world that predominate in terms of producing doctorates. These are major international competitors for the other countries in this book. All have strong reputations and consistent track records over recent years in terms of developing aspects of doctoral study. All attract research students from elsewhere and all are technologically advanced.

It is also the case that each has developed its own distinctive system for doctoral study and each has dealt with global issues in its own, sometimes idiosyncratic, way.

9

Doctoral education in Australia

Barbara Evans

Introduction

Doctoral education in Australia has grown from an education system that emulated, and in its early years depended heavily on, UK traditions (Evans *et al.* in press). This has had several consequences in regard to the structure, breadth and duration of current Australian doctoral programmes.

The first four years of secondary study in Australia are broad and academic, usually requiring coverage of all disciplines. This is followed by two final years of study that can be much more specialized, especially in the sciences. Only five subjects are normally undertaken in the final year, one of which must be English.

Undergraduate degrees then build on this discipline base and can involve degree requirements of 75 per cent or more in a four-year programme to be 'in the discipline' (e.g. physics and maths). This is less so in the humanities, but may still be over 50 per cent (Hall *et al.* 2006). The fourth year is often a distinct 'honours year' undertaken after completion of the undergraduate degree and involving a significant research project and some advanced coursework.

The other important factor that impacts on Australian doctoral research programmes is government funding. Australia is highly uniform in the funding provided to higher degree research students *across the cohort* – the great majority of domestic students pay no fees and receive a living stipend if they are enrolled full-time. As a consequence of both the discipline-focused undergraduate education and four-year funding for doctoral tuition, doctoral education programmes are shorter and more discipline-focused in Australia than the USA and about the same length as in the UK.

There is less (if any) formal discipline-based coursework and no preliminary examination within the Ph.D.; most students are expected to have completed this work during their previous discipline-based study. However there is a serious confirmation of candidature process, which involves written work, an oral presentation and formal interview by a committee, after about 12 months of candidature. There is also an increasing requirement for development of generic capabilities and professional and research skills within Australian Ph.D. programmes; but these are not for 'credit'.

The questionnaire

Table 9.1 The questionnaire

Question	Number	Comment
1 Total number of doctoral students studying	37,511	Of these 35,875 were research doctoral candidates. Does not include students enrolled in a masters programme who may (or may not) later convert to doctoral candidature. Conversions numbers are reducing with increasing direct entry to the Ph.D.
2 Number of institutions offering doctoral programmes	39	All Universities are entitled to offer doctoral programmes
3 Number of different doctoral awards (e.g. including professional doctorates)?	Many doctoral award programmes including Ph.D., EdD, MD, SJD and DPsych. By far the greatest majority are Ph.D.s	Refers to taught and research doctorates, where students are enrolled in a doctoral programme for a number of years. Does not include those such as DSc, DLitt, DEng., 'higher doctorates' awarded on the basis of a 'lifetime's work'
4 Number of years over which doctorates have been offered in the country	First Ph.D.s awarded in 1948	
5 Proportion of full-time to part-time students	60.9:39.1%	Higher proportions of part-time students in education, law and arts; lower in the sciences
6 Average time to completion (in years)	5.5 elapsed years (for all commencers)	This includes full-time and part-time students and any leave taken. Effective full-time duration more like 4–4.5 years
7 Success rates	Completion rate for 1992 entering cohort in 1999 (8 years) was 53%	This DEST study estimated that final completion rate would be approximately 65%. Success rates vary across disciplines (higher in sciences than humanities); origin of student (higher for internationals than locals); enrolment type (higher for full-time students); and age (higher for younger students)

8 Typical age range of doctoral candidates	From early 20s upwards – average age 37	Tends to fall into two groups – early twenties and full-time, and later 30s+ and part-time. Older students more likely to be in humanities, particularly education; younger students predominate in the sciences
9 Proportion of male/ female students	1.4:48.6%	
10 Proportion of doctoral students studying who are nationals of other countries	In 2005, approx 1 in 6 (16.7%) were internationals	In 2005 approximately 1 in 5 (20%) of completions were internationals

Data sources

The figures in Table 9.1 are based on DEST data (2004) for 2003, except for Questions 6 and 7, which are based on older DEST data (1992 entering doctoral cohort).

See websites in the chapter for ongoing data.

The place of doctoral study in the national/ international context

The role of the doctorate in relation to national research policy

Universities are recognized as significant producers of new knowledge through research and research training. Higher degree by research (HDR) students are recognized as major participants in this knowledge production. The realization of the potential of knowledge production is seen to be critical to the progress of Australia's innovation system (Gallagher 2000). The government is a major contributor to the costs of research training (see below).

Concerns about long completion times and low completion rates for higher degrees by research, raised in the government 1999 White Paper *Knowledge and Innovation* (Kemp 1999) were supported by a subsequent paper analysing national completion rates, describing factors relevant to successful completion and considering 'wastage' associated with non-completions (Martin *et al.* 1999).

In 2000, the Commonwealth government embarked upon research and research training (R&RT) policy reform, including incentives to institutions to improve their RT outcomes and increased funding to improve Australia's capacity for economic return from research and development (R&D) in biotechnology and related fields (Gallagher 2000). Universities were encouraged to participate in all stages of the innovation cycle. Universities are required to prepare R&RT management plans – structured quantitative and qualitative reports on their objectives, policies, approaches, circumstances and outcomes.

National quality audit

A broad national quality audit of higher education institutions is conducted through the Australian Universities Quality Agency (AUQA). Established early in 2000, AUQA is responsible for auditing the quality of Australian universities, including assessment of R&RT performance and outcomes. Its audit reports are publicly available on the AUQA website (see end of chapter).

Funding issues

The funding of institutions

Australian universities receive funds from Commonwealth and state governments, student contributions, fees and other sources such as bequests, royalties and consultancies (see Table 9.2). The largest component is Commonwealth government grants, which increased from $4566m in 1996 to $5307m in 2004 (an increase of 16 per cent). However this represents a decline from 57 per cent of overall university funding in 1996 to only 41 per cent in 2004. The difference has been made up from university fees and student charges.

Table 9.2 University Revenue by main source, 1996, 2004

University revenue	1998		2004	
	$m	%	$m	%
Commonwealthgovernment grants	4,191	51%	5,307	41%
State government	93	1%	315	2%
HECS	1,662	17%	1,983	15%
Fees and charges	1,547	16%	3,137	24%
Other sources*	1,240	15%	2,282	18%
Total university revenue ($m)	**8456**		**13,024**	

Source: DEST Selected Higher Education Finance Statistics

*Includes 'donations and bequests', 'royalties, trademarks & licences' and consultancy & contract research from 2000

The introduction of the Research Training Scheme (RTS) in 2001 altered significantly the way that universities received funds for research training. The major change was a shift from student load to completions as a major part of the allocation formula. In 2000 there were about 24,100 HDR places in the system, of which 21,500 were fee exempt. With the introduction of the RTS, an estimated 21,644 RTS-funded places were provided for.

The objectives of the RTS were to:

- enhance the quality of research training provision in Australia;
- improve the responsiveness of institutions to the needs of their students;
- encourage institutions to develop their own research training profiles;
- ensure the relevance of the degree programmes to labour market requirements;
- improve the efficiency and effectiveness of research training.

In 2005, the Australian government provided over A$550 million to universities to support research training through the RTS. These funds are distributed to universities based on their research performance compared with all other universities. The components of the formula are 50 per cent HDR completions, 40 per cent research income and 10 per cent publications. These are weighted for 'high-cost (sciences)' or 'low-cost (humanities)' disciplines at 2.35 to 1.00, and at 2:1 for doctorates:masters programmes. This scheme effectively provides 'fee free' places for domestic research students for up to two years for masters and four years for doctoral programmes. In 2004, approximately 82 per cent of RTS enrolments overall were in doctoral programmes. However, the proportion of masters:doctoral enrolments varies widely between different institutions, some of which choose to allocate their RTS places only to doctoral candidates.

In 2006, Australia entered a new phase of quality assurance and funding with the proposed introduction of a new instrument – the Research Quality Framework (RQF). The RTS will probably continue but it is likely to incorporate RQF outcomes in a modified allocation formula. There is an intention to develop measures of the quality of RT and the National Council of Deans and Directors of Graduate Studies (DDOGS) are expected to be key players in this. However this is likely to be part of the second round as appropriate quality measures are yet to be determined.

The funding of candidates

Most domestic HDR students do not pay tuition fees (or accrue further tuition debt) – 88 per cent full-time equivalent (FTE) student load held an RTS place in 2003 (DEST 2004 data). RTS-funded places provide free tuition for research doctoral enrolment for four years full-time or eight years part-time. Some universities choose to enroll more HDR students than they have RTS places and they can charge fees to these 'over quota' students, and also to overtime students (students who have exceeded their RTS entitlement), but in practice this is rarely if ever done.

Most full-time research doctoral students also receive a scholarship of (currently) approximately AUS$19,000 a year for up to three and a half years to cover living expenses. These scholarships are funded from a number of sources including the Commonwealth government (1550 scholarships), universities, research funding bodies such as the Australian Research Council and National Health and Medical Research Council, or through other research projects, organizations and foundations. Part-time students are not normally eligible for living stipend scholarships and they usually fund their living expenses from their employment income.

Universities normally charge tuition fees for international students. However, the Commonwealth government provides 330 tuition scholarships per year to international doctoral students for three to four years. These students would normally receive an additional scholarship for living expenses from the university at which they are enrolled. The Commonwealth government also provides scholarships to international students from particular developing countries, for both tuition and living expenses, through its foreign aid mechanisms.

Kinds of institution

Institutions offering doctoral awards

There are 39 universities in Australia and, as universities, all are entitled to award doctoral degrees. However, there is considerable diversity in their age, size and research profile and some of the newer and smaller universities have limited research capacity and experience to provide good quality doctoral research programmes.

Organization of awarding institutions

Discipline-based research is conducted in academic departments. Graduate schools provide additional academic activities and generic skills programmes, leadership programmes and career planning. They also usually have overall authority for enrolment, candidature management, examination, supervision, internal policy development and quality assurance.

Graduate schools

DDOGS was established in 1994. Whether or not they have a formal graduate school, most universities participate in this network, which meets biannually to share experience, develop policy, prepare submissions to the government and generally cooperate for improvement of research education across the country. It has proved to be an extraordinarily collegial body and is nationally recognized and consulted for its special expertise in research training matters. While graduate schools in Australia do not usually have a large role in the administration of postgraduate coursework programmes, their programmes and activities are normally available to all postgraduate students.

As an example of its work, DDOGS has recently considered quality, quality assurance and best practice in Australian doctoral education, and developed national best practice guidelines regarding the structure, content and examination of doctoral programmes (e.g. *Framework for Best Practice in Doctoral Education in Australia*, see www.ddogs.edu.au/cgi-bin/papers.pl).

Postgraduate associations

Within most Australian universities, postgraduate student associations play a highly effective and valued role in providing programmes, interdisciplinary opportunities, advocacy and support for doctoral students.

Nationally, the Council of Australian Postgraduate Associations (CAPA, founded in 1979) is the peak body representing Australia's more than 250,000 postgraduate students. In 2005, CAPA had 33 member postgraduate associations, as well as the National Indigenous Postgraduate Association Aboriginal Corporation (NIPAAC, see below).

CAPA seeks to coordinate postgraduate representation, advance the interests of postgraduate students and defend postgraduate student rights nationally. Importantly it represents the interests and concerns of postgraduate students to the Commonwealth government and higher education peak bodies such as the Australian Vice-Chancellors' Committee, the Australian Research Council and DDOGS. (for more information about its activities see www.capa.edu.au).

Forms of doctoral study

Different forms of doctoral study and different doctoral qualifications

The Australian Qualifications Framework (AQF) is a unified system of national educational qualifications across all sectors – schools, vocational education and training and the higher education sector. It states that 'the Doctoral degree recognises a substantial original contribution to knowledge in the form of new knowledge or significant and original adaptation, application and interpretation of existing knowledge'. Doctoral programme outcomes may take the form of a comprehensive critical review of literature, empirical research, creative work or other systematic approach embedded in a field or discipline, and/or they may be based on advanced and sustained critical reflection and analysis of professional theory and practice.

DDOGS *Best Practice Framework* states that a graduate of a doctoral degree programme should have demonstrated the capacity to:

• design and implement at a high level of originality and quality, either an original research project(s) of significance to a discipline or cross-disciplinary field, or a project(s) addressing an important problem or question concerning policy and/or practice in a profession or industry; and

• present, using one or more media, a substantial and intellectually coherent product or product(s) such as a thesis, dissertation and artefacts, or exegesis and portfolio of creative works and/or performance, for submission to external examination against international standards.

Each university should also formally identify the desired academic, professional and personal attributes of the graduates of its doctoral programmes and check that each of its doctoral programmes provides candidates with the opportunity to develop these attributes.

Broad categories of doctoral degrees

Because of eligibility for RTS funding, the fundamental distinction in Australia is between doctorates by research and doctorates by coursework. Research doctorates are defined by the Commonwealth government as being at least 66 per cent research. These are sometimes also referred to as 'taught' doctorates, meaning that students are *enrolled* under supervision in a doctoral programme for a number of years, to distinguish them from higher doctorates. Professional doctorates may be either research or coursework and they normally require professional experience before entry and/or during candidature. The research project often has a professional orientation.

By far the greatest majority of doctoral enrolments in Australia are in the Ph.D., which may contain some hurdle coursework. Other supervised research doctorates include the Doctor of Education (EdD), Doctor of Medicine (MD), Doctor of Juridical Science (SJD) and Doctor of Psychology (DPsych).

Coursework professional doctorates are less than 66 per cent research and usually include a component of professional practice. There are very few coursework doctorate students – only about 2.5 per cent of all doctoral FTE student enrolments in 2004.

The Ph.D.

Over recent decades the Ph.D. in Australia has become increasingly flexible, accommodating new areas of human endeavour such as the creative and performing arts as appropriate 'disciplines' for research. Ph.D. rules have been extended to accommodate these new specialities, and the ways in which research can be carried out and theses presented. The Ph.D. has also accommodated an increased demand from governments and the community for relevance and applied value of the work undertaken.

Increasingly as elsewhere, Ph.D. graduates have varying employment outcomes and the Ph.D. is no longer seen simply as an apprenticeship for entering academia or research. Ph.D.s in professional fields have increased strongly since the late 1980s. Interestingly it is becoming apparent that the Ph.D. in many professional fields is proving more attractive than professional doctorates.

Students and their programmes of study

Entry qualifications required of candidates

Entry requirements for doctoral study are normally a masters degree or a four-year bachelors honours degree, with honours first class (H1) or honours upper second class (H2A) grades (equivalent to a grade point average of about 3.3 to 3.5) *and* a demonstrated capacity to undertake significant research in the proposed doctoral field. Entry to professional doctorates may also require significant professional practice either prior to and/or as part of the programme.

Periods and modes of study

Most doctoral degrees are stated to be of at least three years full-time (FT) duration and RTS places provide funds for up to four years. Doctoral study can also be undertaken in part-time (PT) modes, which is usually considered to be half-time, thus eight years.

Students may transfer between FT and PT enrolment. Transfer from FT to PT often occurs towards the end of candidature to allow more time to complete the work, or to write up. Part-time enrolment is higher in humanities and arts disciplines, especially education, with many later career professionals returning to higher study.

Programme structure and content

DDOGS *Best Practice Guidelines* (2006) state that doctoral programmes should 'comprise a combination of research with doctoral coursework and professional practice and enquiry as appropriate, such as:

- a supervised research and scholarship programme of at least three years' FTE study;
- a coursework, research and scholarship programme of at least three years' FTE study, with at least two years' FTE research and scholarship; or
- a professional practice and enquiry, and coursework programme, together with at least two years' FTE research and scholarship, totalling at least three years' FTE.'

The Council's position is that research is the fundamental substance of a doctorate and that a best practice doctorate should not be earned solely or substantially on the basis of coursework. The research and scholarship component(s) of a best practice doctoral programme should be at least equivalent to two years' FTE doctoral study. Coursework within a doctorate should be related to research education, whether this be for making a significant contribution to knowledge for the discipline or a profession/professional practice.

Usual elements of Australian Ph.D. programmes include the major research project, research skills preparation, preparing relevant ethics and grant applications, attending and presenting seminars, defined writing requirements at each stage of candidature, developing generic skills, oral presentations and overseas research visits. Publication during candidature is encouraged, particularly in the sciences.

There is considerable variation in the nature and amount of 'coursework' required in different Ph.D. programmes. However, most programmes include some components that could be broadly described as coursework. Government regulation precludes more than 33.3 per cent coursework in a research doctorate.

Most Australian universities have a rigorous hurdle usually termed 'confirmation of candidature' at about 12 months. This normally includes evidence of the acquisition of necessary technical and methodological skills, completion of any required coursework subjects, completion of an adequate amount of research, submission of a significant piece of writing, a public presentation on the project and an interview by a 'confirmation committee'.

For FT students, 'allowable' outside work commitments are generally limited to no more than six to eight hours per week. Developing teaching experience is encouraged, but it is expected to be included within the allowable six to eight hours. Students who are not on a scholarship may not have such limitations placed upon them; however, normal progress for a full-time student is expected and monitored.

Issues of gender, race or religion in relation to doctoral study

Because doctoral research education is essentially 'fee free' to eligible domestic students, issues of gender, race and religion are less apparent than in some other countries. RTS places are awarded to students competitively, largely on academic merit, and there are many living stipend scholarships available for FT students. The balance between male and female doctoral enrolments is very close with 51 per cent male and 49 per cent female enrolments.

Nevertheless, the proportion of indigenous Australian doctoral students is worryingly low, much less (0.7 per cent in 2004) than the proportion of Aboriginal and Torres Strait Islander peoples in the Australian population (about 2 per cent) (DEST data). While enrolments are increasing slowly, in relative terms they have not kept pace with the overall growth in the indigenous Australian population despite a number of national and institutional initiatives to support participation. A high proportion of indigenous students are enrolled in the education and health fields, which are areas of major concern and emphasis within and for indigenous communities (Evans *et al.* in press).

NIPAAC has focused on supporting and promoting Indigenous postgraduate education since 1989 (see NIPAAC website). For example, it provides cultural diversity awareness information packs for the student community.

Employment destinations

Across all fields of study, 89 per cent of research masters and Ph.D. graduates in 2004 available for full-time work were in full-time employment; 65 per cent of these were still working for their final year employer. The main occupations are shown in Table 9.3 (GCA data 2004). A trend for higher proportions of available female graduates to still be seeking full-time employment has existed for more than a decade (see Figure 9.1).

Supervision

The nationally accepted DDOGS guidelines state that 'a principal supervisor should be appointed to coordinate the research of each candidate. This person should be assisted by a colleague (such as an associate supervisor) or colleagues (such as an advisory team, supervisory panel) who may have different roles in the supervision process'. In practice recently there has been increased encouragement of panel supervision.

The principal supervisor should have expertise in the field of study, hold a doctoral qualification or equivalent, be research active in a relevant

Table 9.3 Main occupations of masters research and Ph.D. students who graduated in 2003 and are in full-time employment

Main Occupations if in Full-time Employment (%)			
	M	F	All
Teaching Professional	26.4	29.6	28.0
Science Professional	23.0	24.6	23.8
Other Professional	11.4	16.8	14.1
Manager/Administrator	11.8	11.5	11.7
Health Professional	6.8	5.3	6.0
Business Professional	6.5	3.8	5.2
Eng. Professional	7.0	1.4	4.2
Med./Sci. Tech. Officer	2.7	2.0	2.4
All Others	4.4	5.1	4.7
All	**100**	**100**	**100**
Total Number	1,103	1,065	2,168

Note: of all 2003 graduates, 89% were in this category.

Source: Postgraduate Destinations (2004)

discipline or disciplines, have sufficient time and resources to provide a quality learning experience for the candidate, and have training and/or experience in the supervisory process.

The Department of Education, Science and Training (DEST) requires each university to have a code of practice outlining the rights and responsibilities

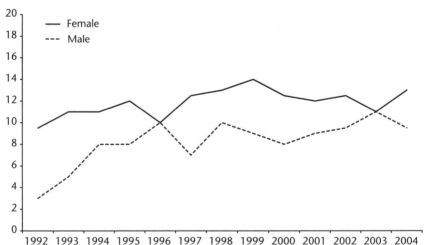

Figure 9.1 Percentage of masters research and Ph.D. graduates available for full-time employment, still seeking full-time work (by gender) 1992–2004

Source: Postgraduate Destinations (2004) *The Report of the Graduate Destination Survey,* www.graduatecareers.com.au

of doctoral students and the university, and annual signoff in universities' R&RT management plans on (a) the number of supervisions (holding a higher degree qualification), (b) the number of supervisors who undertook formal supervisors training and (c) the number of staff who supervised at least one HDR student to completion.

Examination

Successful completion of an Australian Ph.D. is based on the assessment of the research thesis by two or more independent and expert examiners, at least two of which must be external to the candidate's university. Use of international examiners is encouraged. The RTS mandates the use of external examiners in that it states that: 'the assessment process must involve at least one qualified examiner external to the institution'. The examination process is transparent and provides an external quality assurance of Ph.D. standards and outcomes.

While the Ph.D. degree is awarded entirely on the basis of the external examination of the research thesis, professional doctorates are usually awarded on performance across a combination of coursework, professional and research requirements. DDOGS doctoral guidelines state that the research and scholarship component should comprise at least two-thirds of the work.

An oral defence is rarely required of candidates in Australia. However, a public presentation of their work before academic colleagues from within and often beyond their department is normally expected or required. This presentation usually occurs prior to final submission, thus providing an opportunity for collegial commentary and critique, and for verification of the student's 'ownership' of the work.

Typically, the department or faculty in which the student is enrolled nominates examiners to the university. Supervisors are not allowed to be examiners but they have an important role to play in the examination process. They provide advice and context information to the examining committee through the chair of examiners, who is usually an independent senior member of the department.

Each examiner submits an independent detailed written report on the thesis and makes recommendations to the university regarding the award of the degree. The chair of examiners reviews the examiners' reports before the responsible university committee determines on the outcome. Examiners' recommendations are normally followed, except in rare circumstances where there are irregularities in procedure or significant disagreement. Usually candidates are required to make some amendments to bring the thesis to the highest possible standard before the university confers the degree.

It is expected that the recent development and endorsement of the DDOGS guidelines *Framework for Best Practice in Doctoral Examination in*

Australia (2005) will lead to greater consistency and quality of examination practice nationally.

Any other issues

Developing global perspectives for students is becoming increasingly important in the training of Ph.D. students in Australia and the international mobility of Australian Ph.D. students during candidature is increasing. There has always been a widespread encouragement for international experience within the doctoral experience, probably because of Australia's comparative geographic isolation. Joint doctoral programmes, such as the French *co-tutelle*, have required development of procedures for international co-supervision and assuring quality of distance supervision. There is a need for new relationships between players and more nimble responses by universities.

Critical comment

There are a number of aspects of doctoral education in Australia that have been identified as being in need of improvement. In various combinations, academics, students, researchers, government and industry representatives are working to find more efficient and effective methods to:

- improve completion rates;
- measure the quality of research training and its outcomes;
- improve knowledge transfer between universities and the wider community;
- better prepare students for entering work;
- develop international collaborations in doctoral education programmes;
- benchmark our practices and outcomes internationally;
- ensure equity and access for the brightest students;
- to do this in a time of declining government funding to universities.

References

Evans, T., Evans, B. and Marsh, H. (in press) Australia, in M. Nerad and M. Heggelund (eds) *Forces and Forms of Change in Doctoral Education Internationally*. Washington: University of Washington Press.

Gallagher, M. (2000) New directions in Australian research and research training policy – some questions for researchers. Paper presented to the Annual Conference of The Australian Network for Higher Education Policy Research, Canberra, 2000.

Hall, F., Evans, B. and Nerad, M. (2006) Feasibility of international comparisons of PhD program times-to-degree (TTD) and completion rates. Proceedings of the Quality in Postgraduate Research National Conference, Adelaide.

Kemp, D.A. (1999) *Knowledge and Innovation: A Policy Statement on Research and Research Training.* Canberra: Department of Education, Training and Youth Affairs.

Martin, Y.M., Maclachlan, M. and Karmel, T. (1999) *Postgraduate Completion Rates.* Canberra: Department of Education, Training and Youth Affairs, Higher Education Division.

Postgraduate Destinations (2004) *The Report of the Graduate Destination Survey,* www.graduatecareers.com.au.

Relevant websites

Australian Council of Deans and Directors of Graduate Studies (DDOGS): www.ddogs.edu.au

Australian Qualifications Framework (AQF): www.aqf.edu.au

Australian Universities Quality Agency (AUQA): www.dest.gov.au/sectors/higher_education/policy_issues_reviews/key_issues/assuring_quality_in_higher_education/the_australian_universities_quality_agency_auqa.htm

Australian Vice-Chancellors Committee (AVCC): www.avcc.edu.au

Council of Australian Postgraduate Associations (CAPA): www.capa.edu.au

Department of Education, Science and Training (DEST): www.dest.gov.au/sectors/higher_education

for Improving Research Supervision and Training (fIRST): www.first.edu.au

Graduate Careers Australia (GCA): www.graduatecareers.com.au

National Indigenous Postgraduate Association Aboriginal Corporation (NIPAAC): www.nipaac.edu.au

10

Doctoral education in Canada: a valued national product facing the challenges of institutional differentiation

Louis Maheu

Introduction

Universities within the Canadian educational landscape are only a few hundred years old, with pioneer institutions appearing in the first half of the nineteenth century. As elsewhere in the world, these first institutions were devoted mostly to the professional training of physicians, lawyers and barristers as well as clergymen of various denominations, with limited activities in diverse fields of the arts and sciences. New universities did subsequently appear during both the nineteenth and twentieth centuries, bringing the overall number of universities in Canada to more than 90 institutions.

Canada has an ambitious national strategy that involves reaching the top five countries in the world for research and development and innovation performance; the Canadian Ph.D. enterprise is seen as central to this ambition. At the beginning of the twenty-first century, Canadians aged 25 to 64 rank first among the Organization for Economic Cooperation and Development (OECD) countries for post-secondary education (Allen and Vaillancourt 2004: 5). However this is tilted much more toward non-university, post-secondary education as opposed to university training, where the USA leads the way. In university provision, Canada is having difficulties in distinguishing itself from countries like Australia, Japan and the United Kingdom (Riddell 2003: 91). In recent years, the Canadian Ph.D. annual production has generally made, in absolute numbers, the tail end of the 15 leading doctorate-producing countries (Syverson and Bagley undated: 3; NSF 2004). Leadership, vision and inspired institutional agency are seen as prerequisites for a strong programme, paving the way to better control of structural opportunities underpinning the needed expansion of the Canadian Ph.D.

The questionnaire

Table 10.1 The questionnaire

1 Total number of doctoral students studying	32,006	2003[1]
2 Number of institutions offering doctoral programmes	48	2003[2]
3 Number of different doctoral awards (e.g. including professional doctorates)	About 6	Ph.D. plus professional doctorates mainly in psychology, education, music, theology, law
4 Number of years over which doctorates have been offered in the country	109	46[3]
5 Proportion of full-time to part-time students	92.9%	Full-time (2003)[4]
6 Average time to completion (in years)	5 years, 8 months	Graduates, 1993 cohort, 10 years later[5]
	5 years, 10 months	Graduates (2003–4)[6]
7 Success rates	60.2%	Graduates, 1993 cohort, 10 years later[5]
8 Typical age range of doctoral candidates	24–33	Inferred from the median bracket age of the 2003–4 graduates (30–39) and their mean time to completion (approximately 6 years)[6]
9 Proportion of male/female students	54.2% male 45.8% female	2003[7]
10 Proportion of doctoral students studying who are nationals of other countries	21.1% international students	2003[8]

Data sources are as follows:
1 Lebel (2005)
2 Lebel (2005)
3 Gingras (1991)
4 Lebel (2005)
5 G10 Data Exchange (2003)
6 Gluszynski and Peters (2005)
7 Lebel (2005)
8 Lebel (2005)

Data sources

The sources of the information in Table 10.1 are listed at the base of the table.

The place of doctoral study in the national/ international context

Origins

As in many industrial societies, Canadian graduate studies really started growing after the Second World War. The 1920s started modestly with a few hundred yearly enrolments. Then, from about 3000 graduate students in 1945, total enrolments reached near 5000 at the beginning of the 1950s, before ending the decade with 6518 full-time students (Urquhart and Buckley 1983: 340–57). In Canada as elsewhere, the 1960s represented an important jump ahead with total graduate enrolments reaching more than 40,000 in 1970, of which 33,000 were full-time and nearly 10,000 were at the Ph.D. level. The figures for 1980 were more than 60,000 total enrolments, 35,000 full-time and 13,000 at Ph.D. level (Urquhart and Buckley 1983: 340–57; Lebel 2005: 3–4). However, the number of doctorates granted has increased very slowly. Globally, there were a little more than 20 such degrees granted yearly in the first part of the 1920s and nearly a hundred in 1945. At the end of the 1950s there were still only 300 yearly degrees granted. Again, the 1960s made a real difference: Ph.D.s granted multiplied by five, reaching a peak of 1625 degrees in 1970. In the mid-1970s, a yearly figure of 2000 was attained (Urquhart and Buckley 1983: 504–12; Leacy 1999).

The national political backdrop of Canadian graduate education

As a modern government committed to a knowledge-based economy, the Canadian federal government has engaged the country with rigorous science, technology and research policies. This trend became even more evident throughout the 1990s, as well as at the turn of the new century. More and more decisively a terrain of federal jurisdiction, science and research policies confronted provincial jurisdictions when they entailed links, or for that matter overlaps, with education, or more precisely still, with higher education policies and management.

Canada does not have a national Department of Education. Education at all levels, including post-secondary institutions such as community colleges and universities, and consequently the financing of education, is the responsibility of provincial governments.

Funding

Federal funding

Provincial governments assume financial responsibility for education not only with their own resources, but also with federal transfer funds. Whether targeted as a specific item or not, tied or untied to conditions and whether at an appropriate level or not, these transfer funds have an unsurprisingly hectic history (Cameron 2004, 2005). They were cut severely in the mid-1990s when the government wanted to control its chronic deficits and mounting debt. Universities were then required to adapt, since most provinces did not substitute more resources to compensate for these cuts.

Diversity of funding

Finding a diversity of funding sources became a real challenge, with a large differentiation in each university's capacity to achieve this goal. Overall, by the beginning of the twenty-first century, in comparison with the beginning of the 1970s, provincial income sources for universities had decreased by 23 per cent to reach 46 per cent of total sources (Snowdon 2004: 170–6). Student fees, as well as gifts and donations, significantly increased from 6 to 7 per cent respectively to represent, at the end of the period, 22 and 10 per cent of total university income sources respectively. Federal participation also rose to 13 per cent of total sources during this period, mainly for sponsored research.

Research granting agencies

The Canadian research agenda has its own characteristics. Very early on, the government took charge of it and since then it has maintained a large degree of, not always undisputed, control over it (Cameron 2004). Investing directly in research activities, including university-based research, the federal government created, and also funds, three research-granting agencies. They currently run various research grant programmes and student fellowships for the natural and engineering sciences, the health sciences and the social sciences and humanities. New federal initiatives for research and development, with university-based research holding a central position on the radar screen, were gradually implemented during the second part of the 1990s. They include:

- the strengthening of a previously launched policy of centres and networks of excellence scattered about the country;
- the introduction of foundations, notably the Canada Foundation for Innovation and the Canada Millennium Scholarship Foundation;

- the transformation and re-enforcement of granting agencies;
- the distribution of 2000 Canada research chairs for outstanding faculty members among Canadian universities on the basis of their institutional research of previous years (Cameron 2004; Prichard 2000).

In 2004, two policy papers clarified the federal government's latest innovation strategy in respect of research and development as well as academic research and training programmes for research. Their respective titles were evocative: *Achieving Excellence: Investing in People, Knowledge and Opportunities* (Industry Canada 2004a) and *Knowledge Matters: Skills and Learning for Canadians* (Industry Canada 2004b). With the main objective of ranking among the top five countries for research and development by 2010, the federal government set very demanding goals. Among its highest priorities were to double its support for research and development and support university-based research accordingly by giving more financial resources to granting agencies and gradually implementing a permanent programme to directly support the indirect costs of university research.

Measures were announced to enlarge graduate student funding provided by granting agencies and a totally new programme was launched in 2003: the 'Canada Graduate Scholarship Program' under which 2000 fellowships each for both masters and doctoral students are offered yearly. With these came very challenging targets for university graduate training programmes. Every year up to 2010, enrolments to both masters and doctoral programmes within Canadian universities should increase by 5 per cent (Industry Canada 2004b). Hence, Canada's innovation strategy gives a stimulating push to Canadian research-intensive universities and their training programmes for research, by definition mainly the Ph.D. (Clark 1995).

Kinds of institution

General trends in numbers of Ph.D. students across Canadian institutions

With 32,006 in 2003, Canadian Ph.D. enrolments increased by 9.1 per cent in comparison with the previous academic year. From 1995 to 1999 inclusively, these enrolments were generally stable or decreasing; they started growing again in 2000, the increase being steeper in the last two years (Lebel 2005: 3). Degrees conferred in 2003 reached 3861, a 3.5 per cent increase on the previous year. After being stable or declining between 1999 and 2001, the number of Ph.D. degrees granted yearly started growing again (Lebel 2005: 73). Globally, in the last ten years or so, Ph.D. training unfortunately remained stable.

Concentration in some institutions

These figures do not show the strong Ph.D. concentration within some institutions, and consequently the differentiation of training missions between universities. Only six of the 48 Canadian universities registered at least a few Ph.D. students in 2003, and exactly 6 per cent of all Canadian universities make up more than 50 per cent of total enrolments. Eleven institutions, which represent 12 per cent of all Canadian universities, account for more than 66 per cent of all Ph.D. enrolments.

The same concentration exists in respect of degrees conferred. Here too, six universities, the same six discussed above, granted more than 50 per cent of all degrees conferred in 2003, and ten universities granted more than 66 per cent of all Ph.D.s. This concentration pattern is not new: more or less the same six institutions have, since the beginning of the 1990s, accounted for a large proportion of doctoral students and of the degrees conferred. All six are research-intensive universities, and among them are found all the universities belonging to the G-10 group. Since the 1990s, this informal network has acted as a pressure group to influence policy and decision-making, and capacity-building in favour of the development of research-intensive universities in the country.

Graduate schools

In his seminal work on modern universities, Clark (1995: 155–8, 225–6) suggested that a differentiated tier for graduate studies within modern universities is a structural condition for strategic development at that level. To reach outstanding graduate studies and fruitful linkages of research to training, encompassing teaching and study, these universities relied heavily upon the graduate school (Clark 1995; Ben-David 1977: 81–3, 1984). As established by the existence of a graduate school, all of the Canadian universities which make up more than 50 per cent of Ph.D. enrolments and degrees conferred have a differentiated tier for graduate studies. In addition, 75 per cent of Ph.D. enrolments are to universities with a graduate school, except two institutions (one of which did have a school in the past). Their functions may significantly vary, but the point is that the very existence of graduate schools, some of which have existed for a fairly long period of time, does indicate mission differentiation within research-intensive universities.

Forms of doctoral study

At doctoral level, the Ph.D. curriculum and training is overtly within the mainstream of all teaching, supervision and study activities within Canadian universities. However, some institutions offer other curricula and doctoral degrees to smaller, specific student populations. Professional doctoral training and degrees are offered mainly in education (Ed D: Doctorate in Education), law (LLD/JSD, Juris Scientiae Doctorate), music (Doctorate in Music), psychology (Clinical Psychology Doctorate) and theology (Doctorate in Theology). Not all universities offer these degrees, nor is each of these degrees offered within a single institution, although a single institution may offer distinct doctoral programmes in the same fields. Some of these programmes include a dissertation of some kind (thus a certain research piece is produced by admitted students), while others use high-level performance activity as a substitute, for example the composing of original pieces of music or high quality artistic interpretations.

Students and their programmes of study

Masters awards

All universities apply selection requirements to prospective students, including, for some institutions, formal tests and examinations. Admission to all types of doctoral programme most often requires a masters degree and high level marks. Although the masters degree is currently the focal point of intense transformation and change due to mass higher education pressure on graduate training (Geiger 1992; Clark 1995), the Canadian graduate studies culture nonetheless values the masters degree. Admission to the Ph.D. after completion of the masters remains much more the norm within Canadian universities than in other North American universities.

International students

International students also value masters-level training within Canadian graduate studies. In the last ten years, international masters student enrolment has increased yearly. These numbers have been regularly and significantly higher than those at the doctoral level. At the Ph.D. level, there were even decreases in international student enrolments from the end of the 1990s up to the beginning of the twenty-first century. However, there have been sharp increases in the last two years, as a result, in good part, of tighter American immigration policies after the 2001 events of 9/11. International students now represent 21.1 per cent of all doctoral students (Lebel 2005: 39).

Gender issues

Feminization of Canadian graduate studies is an obvious trend of the last decades. Women are now in the majority at the masters level, with

52 per cent of all enrolments, the outcome of important and very steady yearly increases. At the doctoral level, in the last ten years or so, the increases in the enrolment of women have been both regular and impressive. From 39 per cent of the total doctoral student population in 1994, the figure rose to almost 46 per cent in 2003 (Lebel 2005: 15). Have Canadian graduate studies and the Ph.D. become a haven for women? Globally, Canadian universities have not introduced numerous innovations in graduate studies management to support women in their access to these degrees. For example, it seems only a small number of them offer maternity leave fellowships for women students (Eisenkraft 2004: 8–9).

Social issues

Aboriginal students confront important inequalities in respect to access to university training. As Williams reports (2004: 516), the 2001 census shows 7.8 per cent of aboriginals aged 25 to 34 had completed a university degree, in contrast to 27.6 per cent of the general population belonging to the same age group. Without hesitation, we may suggest that the educational participation gap is far more severe between these two groups for graduate studies.

Full-time and part-time registration

Doctoral training requires, as most institutional policies would specify, full-time registration. To access a fellowship, the same status is almost always required by granting agencies, as well as by institutional graduate student funding policies. Moreover, institutions tend to systematically report those engaged in dissertation writing as full-time students regardless of how they actually occupy their working hours. According to official national statistics, 92.9 per cent of doctoral students study full-time (Lebel 2005: 63). However, inside knowledge of graduate student study patterns, and the detailed track records of graduate schools, show large disparities in registration status along disciplinary lines. Humanities and social sciences doctoral students choose, more than others, to engage in part-time training during the course of their studies. Lower full-time status is a characteristic of education, management and administration, arts and human sciences and social science students, while mathematics, computer science, engineering, physical and life sciences students tend to enrol more full-time (Lebel 2005: 67). 'Time to completion' data show long durations of doctoral study, mainly in the humanities and social sciences. These fields are of course known for more part-time studies and stop-outs during training; trends that contribute to longer durations of study.

Funding sources for individual students

Typically, Ph.D. students make use of four different funding sources, the two most important being doctoral fellowship programmes and teaching and research assistantships. Then come personal and familial savings and incomes, followed by all other funding sources. These funding patterns reflect how Ph.D. graduates of the year 2003–4 financed their studies. For more than half of them (52 per cent), doctoral fellowships were the main funding source, and for another 20 per cent it was teaching and research assistantships. Universities have a major responsibility here: their in-house fellowships and teaching, as well as research assistantships, represent the most important student funding sources (Gluszynski and Peters 2005: 11–13, 30). Surprisingly enough, almost half of doctoral students (46 per cent) report no debt for their undergraduate and graduate studies combined; for their graduate studies, the proportion of students without debt is even higher (56 per cent). Debt ranges vary, but a figure of less than $20,000 (Canadian dollars) seems to be typical for the majority of those facing debt for undergraduate and/or graduate studies (Gluszynski and Peters 2005: 11–13, 30).

At a more systemic level, increased tuition fees have been, in almost all provinces, a partial response to reduced federal transfer funds for post-secondary education, particularly in the last decade, and to generalized reduced investments in education by provincial governments. Fees increased by a factor of three between 1971–2 and 2001–2 (Snowdon 2004: 172–6) and increases were steep in the 1990s up to 2004 (Fortin 2004: 370–2; Williams 2004: 519). Not surprisingly, students' average indebtedness for a four-year undergraduate programme almost doubled, reaching more than $21,000 in 2001, as did government expenditures for student assistance in the mid-1990s, tilted much more though toward loans than grants (Junor and Usher 2004; Williams 2004: 519–20).

Supervision

A questionnaire recently submitted to deans of graduate studies of leading Canadian universities for doctoral training shows that a committee, which includes the supervisor, is the dominant model of doctoral study and thesis supervision. In institutions where the norm is different, committee supervision still exists for a certain number of programmes.

Examination

Examination procedures have large variations across Canadian universities. As a key feature of the Ph.D., and normally the entry door to writing the dissertation, if not to access the 'advanced candidacy' status, comprehensive examinations most often have an oral component consisting of a defence before committee. They may also include a written part, resembling more a written paper than a formal questionnaire. Almost all doctoral training ends with a final oral examination that constitutes the dissertation defence before a committee. Membership of dissertation committees may vary a lot between institutions, but the compulsory participation of one reviewer, external to the university, is almost universal.

Other issues

Outputs of doctoral education

A close and in-depth analysis of doctoral student training depends upon availability and quality of data. Good quality data sets are very scarce. Recently, two data sources became available, each providing data sets that represent an interesting starting point. Statistics Canada proposes an initial analysis of its recently implemented yearly Survey of Earned Doctorates, modelled upon its American counterpart at the beginning of the twentieth century. The analysis covers Ph.D. graduates of a single year only, from 1 July 2003 to 30 June 2004. This sample shows a mean time to completion (see also below) of five years and ten months for all students, the duration of study being longer (six years and eight months) for students from the human and social sciences. At 36 years as a mean, graduates get their degree rather old. More than half of them (56 per cent) are within the bracket of 30–39 years of age, and 20 per cent are younger (less than 29) (Gluszynski and Peters 2005: 8–9). As an approximate median age range, we may then make the hypothesis that current doctoral students are now between 24 and 33 years of age.

Time to completion

Another data source, the G10 Data Exchange (2003), adds more complex information to doctoral student track records within some Canadian universities. Data collected in recent years include a few cohort studies on academic progression of doctoral students entering their programme at the beginning of the 1990s, their academic status within ten research-intensive Canadian universities being observed more or less ten years later. Of the 1993 doctoral student cohort, 60.2 per cent had completed their degree in the winter of 2002 with a mean time to completion of five years and eight months. Large variations along disciplinary lines show the most successful and rapid students are enrolled in life, physical and applied sciences, followed by social science students. The humanities has the lowest graduation percentage and the longest time to completion. Surprisingly, students wait a long time to withdraw from their doctoral studies without a degree. Half of them do so in two years and eight months; here again physical and applied students are faster (two years) and humanities students may remain for a longer period of time: more than three years (G10 Data Exchange 2003).

Career destinations

Statistics Canada's Survey of Earned Doctorates provides data on the career plans of Ph.D. graduates. Three out of four of the 2003–4 graduates have clearly identified career plans. More than half (56 per cent) of them intend to work in research and development and teaching activities related to service industries: education mainly, but also professional, scientific and technological, as well as health and welfare services. The others plan to pursue their training in one way or another: more than a third (34 per cent) will undertake formal postdoctoral training with appropriate fellowships. Globally, the latter is more attractive for life sciences graduates, of which 64 per cent foresee adding such an experience to their training trajectory. A large majority of graduates (80 per cent) intend to work or pursue their training in Canada, and three out of four foreign students have the same plan, as do more than 60 per cent of international students having completed their degree in Canada. Amongst those leaving the country, almost half intend to return after a certain period of time and roughly 40 per cent have not yet made up their mind on this issue (Gluszynski and Peters 2005: 14–16, 18–20).

Critical comment – challenges ahead

The social contract model

It has been suggested that a 'social contract' between universities and governments has been the structural factor underpinning the development of Canadian higher education in the last decades. Sceptics are right when they question the social contract model's capacity to adequately explain how complex structural dimensions and tension-driven stakeholder relations impact on university development (Cameron 2005: 287–9). Sustainable trust, the necessary glue shared by partners to a social contract, cannot easily be the outcome of relations fuelled by divergent and opposing interests, as well as unequal institutional capacity to master constantly evolving opportunity structures. A more sophisticated analysis should establish that Canadian universities function like an institution-led system, having to maintain relationships with a number of state departments at diverse levels of the political system, and develop market-type relations to various resources and assets (Clark 2004: 179–84). To promote graduate studies and doctoral education at the requested level, a number of Canadian universities must become much more entrepreneurial. Globally their organizational structure must bring managerial leadership and collegial entrepreneurship to a higher efficiency level so that institutional means of volition-building produce more sustainable transformation (Clark 2004: 93–5).

More degree completion and quality assurance as reputation markers

On the short-term agenda are two other challenges for the Canadian Ph.D. enterprise, which both entail new complex structuring connections between universities, governments and markets. To attract high-quality and outstanding scholars, substantive research funds and infrastructures, extended partnerships with highly profiled counterparts and diversified funding sources, an institution has to perform well in terms of reputation and prestige. A second-level quality assurance for Canadian Ph.D.s, encompassing a nationwide and international benchmarking of doctoral education indicators, constitutes a challenge for any institution wanting to better its position in the reputation and prestige market. For the time being, leadership or vision is lacking to provide the Canadian Ph.D. enterprise, beyond in-house or in some instances provincial assessments, with a second-level national and international exercise of quality assurance for Ph.D. training and degrees offered. A leading doctorate-producing country requires such a tool to internationally promote its doctoral education (OECD 1999).

The second challenge, closely linked to the former above, points to urgent policies specially designed to master the excessively high level of dropouts apparent within the Canadian Ph.D. enterprise. A general figure of close to 40 per cent of dropouts raises significant questions, even more so when we know that this figure is higher in specific disciplinary fields. New structuring connections between universities and governments, combined with market-type relations to assets must produce a better output for the overall Canadian Ph.D. enterprise. This is an end result that requires without doubt more leadership and vision from universities and their academic units. In efficiently mastering the structural conditions to success within graduate and doctoral education, universities clearly constitute themselves as an institutional agency helping diverse stakeholders to converge for a goal valued by individual students, members of faculty and university partners.

References

Allen, M. and Vaillancourt, C. (2004) *Class of 2000: Profile of Postsecondary Graduates and Student Debt.* Ottawa: Statistics Canada.

Ben-David, J. (1977) *Centers of Learning: Britain, France, Germany, United States.* New York: McGraw-Hill.

Ben-David, J. (1984) *The Scientist's Role in Society : A Comparative Study.* Englewood Cliffs, NJ: Prentice-Hall.

Cameron, D.M. (2004) Collaborative federalism and postsecondary education: be careful what you wish for, in C.M. Beach *et al.* (eds) *Higher Education in Canada.* Montreal: McGill-Queen's University Press.

Cameron, D.M. (2005) Post-secondary education and research: wither Canadian federalism? in F. Iacobucci and C. Tuohy (eds) *Taking Public Universities Seriously.* Toronto: Toronto University Press.

Clark, B.C. (1995) *Places of Inquiry, Research and Advanced Education in Modern Universities.* Berkeley, CA: University of California Press.

Clark, B.C. (2004) *Sustaining Change in Universities: Continuities in Case Studies and Concepts.* Maidenhead: Open University Press.

Eisenkraft, H. (2004) In a family way, *University Affairs,* June/July.

G10 Data Exchange (2003) *The 1993 Cohort Study Final Report: Project of Graduate Students Academic Progression.* Montreal: G10 Data Exchange Initiative.

Geiger, R.L. (1992) Introduction, Section II: the institutional fabric of the higher education system, in B.R. Clark and G. Neave (eds) *The Encyclopedia of Higher Education,* Vol. 2, *Analytical Perspectives.* Oxford: Pergamon Press.

Gingras, Y. (1991) *Les origines de la recherche scientifique au Canada; le cas des physiciens.* Montréal: Boréal.

Gluszynski, T. and Peters, V. (2005) *Survey of Earned Doctorates: A Profile of Doctoral Degree Recipients.* Ottawa: Statistics Canada.

Industry Canada (2004a) *Achieving Excellence: Investing in People, Knowledge and Opportunities.* Ottawa: Industry Canada.

Industry Canada (2004b) *Knowledge Matters: Skills and Learning for Canadians.*

Junor, S. and Usher, A. (2004) *The Price of Knowledge: Access and Student Finance in Canada.* Montreal: Canada Millennium Scholarship Foundation.

Leacy, F.H. (ed.) (1999) *Historical Statistics of Canada, Section W, Education,* 2nd edn. Ottawa: Statistics Canada.

Lebel, J. (2005) *35th Statistical Report, 1994–2003.* Ottawa: Canadian Association for Graduate Studies/CAGS.

NSF (National Science Foundation) (2004) *Science and Engineering Indicators, 2004.* Arlington, VA: National Science Foundation.

OECD (Organization for Economic Cooperation and Development) (1999) *Quality and Internationalization in Higher Education.* Paris: OECD.

Prichard, J.R. (2000) Federal support for higher education and research in Canada: the new paradigm. Killam Annual Lecture.

Riddell, W.C. (2003) *The Role of Government in Post-Secondary Education in Ontario,* background paper for the Panel on the Role of Government in Ontario. Vancouver: Department of Economics, University of British Columbia.

Snowdon, K. (2004) 'Muddy' data: university financing in Canada, in C.M. Beach *et al.* (eds) *Higher Education in Canada.* Montreal: McGill-Queen's University Press.

Syverson, P.D. and Bagley, L.R. (undated) *Fact Sheet on Graduate Education Worldwide.* Washington: Council of Graduate Schools.

Urquhart, M.C. and Buckley, K.A.H. (eds) (1983) *Historical Statistics of Canada.* Toronto: Macmillan.

Williams, M.S. (2004) Access to public universities: adressing systemic inequalities, in F. Iacobucci and C. Tuohy (eds) *Taking Public Universities Seriously.* Toronto: University of Toronto Press.

11

Doctoral education in the USA

Maresi Nerad

Introduction

Since the mid-1990s the USA has annually awarded about 40,000 doctorates (42,155 were awarded in 2004). This is currently the largest number of Ph.D.s produced by a single country (medical doctorates and doctorates of jurisprudence are not included in this figure).

In comparison, in 2001 the 25 European Union (EU) states produced 73,000 doctorates in total. That same year the six major Asian countries combined (China, India, Japan, Kyrgyzstan, South Korea and Taiwan) produced 47,489 doctorates – only slightly more than the USA did alone.

In 2004, the greatest number of US doctorates were awarded in the life sciences (8819) followed by the social sciences (6795), education (6635), physical sciences (6049), mathematics and engineering (5776), humanities (5476) and business and other so-called professional fields (2614), such as public health, social work, architecture etc.

The questionnaire

Table 11.1 The questionnaire (figures are from 2003 and 2004)

Question	Number	Comment
1 Total number of doctoral students studying	837,640 masters and doctoral students combined (graduate students) were enrolled in doctoral granting institutions	In the USA it is difficult to disaggregate doctoral enrolment from master's level enrolment, because students may change degree goals during their studies. Even within the same programme, students may be admitted to either a masters/ Ph.D. track or immediately to the Ph.D. degree track

(Continued overleaf)

Table 11.1 (Continued)

Question	Number	Comment
2 Number of institutions offering doctoral programmes	419	
3 Number of different doctoral awards	24	US doctoral degrees can be grouped into two types. The majority of doctoral degrees are Ph.D.s (the doctor of philosophy). The remainder includes 23 professional research doctorates such as the DFA (doctor of fine arts) or the EdD (doctor of education). The doctor of jurisprudence (JD) and the medical doctorate (MD) are not considered professional research doctorates
4 Number of years over which doctorates have been offered in the US	Since the late nineteenth century	In 1861 the first US doctoral degree was granted at Yale University
5 Proportion of full-time to part-time students	More students are enrolled on a full-time basis than part-time	At the major research universities, two-thirds of doctoral students are full-time and a third are part-time. At other doctoral granting institutions, slightly more graduate students are part-time than full-time students. In general, more masters students than doctoral students study part-time than full-time
6 Average time to completion	Median time to degree: 8 years	The time is measured from entrance to graduate school until doctoral degree completion – thus masters degrees and time spent on hiatus or withdrawn are included. Completion times vary widely by fields of study, being about 5–7 years on average in the natural sciences and engineering, and 6–10 years in the social sciences and humanities

7 Success rates	Around 60%	Completion rates vary widely by fields of study: engineering and the natural sciences have the highest completion rates; humanities and the arts have the lowest
8 Typical age range of doctoral candidates	Median age at completion of degree: 33.3 years; average range is 31.7–43.1 years	Age at completion of degree varies by field of study. Engineers and scientists are generally the youngest; education doctorates are often the oldest
9 Proportion of male/ female students	61% of graduate students (enrolled masters and doctoral students) are women; 39% are men. 45% of Ph.D. recipients were women; 55% were men	Women received 45% of all doctorates in 2004
10 Proportion of doctoral students who are nationals of other countries	14%	

Data sources

The data overview comes from various sources. Enrolment data are collected annually by the CGS/GRE Survey of Graduate Enrolment.[1] Data about degrees offered and the number of doctoral granting institutions come from the annual Survey of Earned Doctorates, sponsored by six US governmental associations.[2]

The place of doctoral study in the national context

Scientific research and doctoral studies are closely intertwined in the USA. Since the beginning of US doctoral education – the founding of Johns Hopkins University in 1876 is often regarded as the establishment of doctoral education – scientific research and graduate education became linked organizationally in the graduate school. While there is research and development undertaken in private industry, basic research is largely undertaken within the major universities supplemented by large federal and philanthropic sponsorships of the research. The doctorate-granting universities are the only place where scholars who undertake scientific research are educated and trained.

Over 400 institutions currently award doctoral degrees, and the number is steadily increasing. In 2004 there were 419 such universities that produced on average 1001 doctorates. However, a relatively small number of these universities award a relatively large number of doctorates. About 50 per cent of all US doctoral degrees are awarded by 49 universities. This indicates that doctoral education is primarily concentrated in a few institutions – the major research universities – of which the majority are members of the American Association of Universities.

Issues of funding

The USA has both public and private universities. Public universities fall under the sovereignty of the 50 US states. Private institutions are funded by endowments, philanthropy, investments and property holdings, and student fees. A student who is studying for a doctorate at a private institution, once accepted, however, is funded very similarly to a student in a public university. Funding for doctoral education in both public and private institutions comes from various sources: instruction and student advising is funded by the state; research is largely funded by entities within the US federal government (see Note 2) through research grants and contracts to individual professors and campuses as well as by private foundations and contracts with corporations.

Doctoral students are funded through fellowships from the US government, private foundations and individual university sources, or through research and teaching assistantships. Teaching assistantships are typically 50 per cent (part-time) appointments provided by the state for study at public institutions. Research assistantships are generally funded by professors' individual research grants or through traineeships funded from governmental grants. Nearly all natural science, engineering and many social science students work 50 per cent (part-time) as research assistants, and their assistantships are often related to their dissertation research. In addition, most universities grant financial support by waiving fees and tuition. There are also federal and private student loan programmes.

Kinds of institution

As indicated earlier, an increasing number of US universities award doctoral degrees. Each new doctoral degree programme needs to be approved by the university's state higher education board.

By using the most widely accepted higher education classifications created by the Carnegie Foundation for the Advancement of Teaching, doctoral-granting universities can be classified into two main types of institution: research-extensive and research-intensive.

- research-extensive universities award 50 or more doctoral degrees per year across at least 15 disciplines;
- research-intensive universities offer few doctoral programmes and award fewer doctoral degrees, at least 10 doctoral degrees per year across three or more disciplines, or at least 20 doctoral degrees per year overall.

As a way to coordinate their various graduate programmes, US universities early on established the concept of a 'graduate school', a central administrative unit that oversees all masters degree study, doctoral education and post-doctoral training on a campus. As a result, US universities are called 'vertical universities', consisting of a first tier – the undergraduate college – that is largely committed to general education; and a second tier – graduate education – that provides specialized education and training where doctoral students join their professors in the laboratories and seminars. A graduate dean oversees this second tier to ensure that those policies and procedures that govern the quality of the graduate education (including, for example, admission of students and dissertation requirements) are adhered to. In order to be effective, the graduate dean belongs to the inner circle of the university president.

The roles and functions of the graduate school are manifold. It monitors student progress, grants degrees, collects dissertations and approves new degree programmes. It increasingly raises money from philanthropic sources for doctoral student fellowships and establishes procedures for financial support. It is an advocate for the intellectual development of students, and supports faculty and academic staff in their roles as advisers. In its monitoring function, the graduate school focuses on access and equity, student retention and progress, time-to-degree, career development and doctoral educational outcomes.

Forms of doctoral study

There are two basic types of doctoral degrees awarded in the USA: the doctor of philosophy, the Ph.D., which is the research doctorate, and the professional research doctorate. Currently there exist 23 professional research doctorates, such as the Doctor of Engineering (DEng), the Doctor of Fine Arts (DFA) and the Doctor of Education (EdD). The Doctor of Jurisprudence (JD) and the Medical Doctorate (MD) are not considered professional research doctorates. The majority of doctoral degrees are Ph.D.s as this is the major research doctorate and the general requirement for becoming a professor. Professional doctorates most often lead to employment in the field outside the university. There are usually fewer research methodology courses (such as advanced statistics courses) required, internships are often included in the study course and the dissertation is more applied in nature.

Students and their programmes of study

Admission to doctoral study is extremely competitive, as with the admission also comes a commitment by the programme to financially support the student. Admission criteria are generally based on the student's undergraduate grade point average; their scores on a three-part national graduate entrance examination consisting of a verbal, analytical and quantitative component; three letters of recommendation from undergraduate professors; and a 'Statement of Purpose' essay.

While there are many variations, a doctoral study programme generally involves (1) coursework, (2) a series of exams, often called the general exam or qualifying exam, (3) a dissertation proposal, (4) an original piece of research (the dissertation) and (5) the public defence of the dissertation research.

Depending on the field of study, the coursework, for example, may last three years and consist mainly of seminars. The general exam serves to demonstrate the knowledge of the field acquired during these coursework years, and may often be demonstrated in a publishable piece of work.

At present the average time-to-degree in the natural sciences and engineering ranges between five and seven years. The range is generally longer, six to ten years, for social sciences and the humanities. This time is calculated from the time of entrance in graduate school until exit with a doctoral degree. This time most often includes time spent in masters study *en route* to the doctoral degree. The differential timing is partly due to the better funding available for natural science and engineering students, and partly due to a more structured process in a laboratory environment.

Most Ph.D. students are full-time, although they generally also work 20 hours per week either as research or as teaching assistants throughout their doctoral study period. Science and engineering students usually work as paid research assistants, doing research on work related to their dissertation. Social science and humanities students work far more often as teaching assistants, and rarely have the opportunity to be paid to work on their dissertation.

Part-time students can be found mainly among professional doctoral degree students such as in education, social work or public health fields.

The number of women receiving US doctorates has steadily increased since the Second World War. During the last ten years the proportion of doctorates awarded to women exceeded 40 per cent. In 2004, nearly half of all doctoral degrees awarded (45.4 per cent) were awarded to women.

Currently, 20 per cent of all US citizens who earn doctorates belong to racial/ethnic minority groups.

Supervision

Each doctoral student has one chosen main adviser as well as a dissertation committee of five professors. Two of these committee professors are required to come from outside the doctoral programme. In general, US doctoral students have a fairly close relationship to their main dissertation adviser. In recent years much attention has been paid to the faculty/student relationship and mentoring has become the preferred model. A mentor, in contrast to an adviser, nurtures, protects, guides and socializes the student into a professional of their field. A faculty mentor plays an active role in the student's job search after degree completion. In short, faculty often take on a role beyond simply advising on programme requirements and dissertation guidance.

Examination

As described earlier, a typical doctoral student passes a number of examinations both oral and written in nature. At most universities the doctoral student has a five-professor examination committee that includes one graduate school representative. This representative's duty is to ensure that the examination proceeds in a fair manner and that graduate school policies are followed. The written dissertation is required to be approved by at least three committee members and is most often 'defended' publicly.

Statistical information

Doctoral education statistics are fairly rich due to the long established data collection surveys by the National Science Foundation. A summary report of the national Survey of Earned Doctorates is published annually by the National Opinion Research Center of the University of Chicago. This survey is administered at the time a doctoral student submits their dissertation to the graduate school. This survey is funded by six federal agencies (see Note 2). In recent years, the National Endowment for the Humanities funding from the US government has been drastically reduced, thus their contribution to funding humanities doctorates appears to be in jeopardy.

Critical comments

As universities have come under scrutiny and are asked to demonstrate accountability for their resources, doctoral education has been criticized on several fronts: its long time-to-degree in some fields, its assumed dropout rate and its lack of data on doctoral completion and doctoral placement information. Spearheaded by the Council of Graduate Schools, the professional association of graduate deans, an effort to collect comprehensive doctoral completion data is currently under way.

However, there is still little national effort to collect Ph.D. placement data and retrospective doctoral programme evaluations in a more systematic way. The Center for Innovation and Research in Graduate Education (CIRGE) at the University of Washington has become a national centre dedicated to collecting Ph.D. career path information, as well as aggregating doctoral programme quality assessments from doctoral recipients. CIRGE has completed three national career path studies to date: the *PhDs – Ten Years Later* study (biochemistry, computer science, electrical engineering, English, mathematics and political science), *Art History PhDs – A Decade Later* and *Social Science PhDs – 5 Years Out* (anthropology, communication studies, geography, history, political science and sociology). The surveys included about 65 US universities and had a response rate between 50 and 70 per cent. They were funded mainly by private foundations such as the Andrew Mellon Foundation, the Getty Foundation, the Ford Foundation and the National Science Foundation.[3]

Conclusions

As US doctoral education continues to grow and evolve, it will become more imperative to track, study and understand the programmes' effectiveness – including the educational outcomes of the Ph.D. US doctoral education will continue to need to respond to external market forces, including meeting demands for interdisciplinary-trained scholars who can solve large societal problems, and do so while working in teams and across national boundaries. It will also need to reconcile internal forces that impede change, such as disciplinary and departmental budgeting and faculty promotions, as it strives to be innovative and relevant to societal needs and contribute to knowledge creation. Given the trend of reduced governmental funding for higher education, US doctoral programmes need to become even more creative in financially supporting their doctoral students.

Notes

1 Administered annually by the Council of Graduate Schools, the professional association of Graduate Deans.
2 The National Science Foundation (NSF), the two National Institutes of Health (NIH), the Department of Energy (DOE), United States Department of Agriculture (USDA) and National Aeronautic and Space Administration (NASA).
3 See CIRGE website, www.cirge.washington.edu.

Part 4

Countries with Emerging Potential

Part 4 includes countries that may be seen to have emerging potential both as suppliers of postgraduate students and as providers of postgraduate programmes. In some cases this potential is enormous and if brought to fruition may change significantly the map of postgraduate provision globally over the years to come.

These countries developed their systems often in respect of those of other neighbours with establish postgraduate provision. Yet none have mimicked other systems exclusively. Each has developed its own sets of procedures – often following social contexts that challenge some of the accepted norms within other groups of countries.

12

Doctoral education in Brazil

Renato Janine Ribeiro

Introduction

This chapter reviews the situation with regard to doctoral education in Brazil. The way in which doctoral programmes are related to the needs of a vast and diverse country are noted and particular issues such as the rigorous quality control mechanisms in place in the country are carefully described. Brazil is a country with nearly 40,000 doctoral students and a further 66,000 studying for masters degrees. In specific academic areas it has some of the most highly regarded provision of doctoral education in the southern hemisphere.

The questionnaire

Table 12.1 The questionnaire (data refer to 2004)

Question	Number	Comment
1 Total number of doctoral students studying	38,948	66,306 students are preparing their masters degrees
2 Number of institutions offering doctoral programmes?	87	87 institutions of higher education offer 976 programmes
3 Number of different doctoral awards (e.g. including professional doctorates)	1	Professional doctorates are not offered though professional masters are
4 Number of years over which doctorates have been offered in the country	41	Doctorates have been awarded on a regular basis since at least the 1930s, but since 1965 Brazil has had a graduate studies policy

(Continued overleaf)

Table 12.1 (Continued)

Question	Number	Comment
5 Proportion of full-time to part-time students	70%	Data refer to the current proportion of bursaries against non-bursaries
6 Average time to completion (in years)	4.08	
7 Success rates	75%	Data refer only to bursaries, which comprise about 50% of doctoral students
8 Typical age range of doctoral candidates	28	When they enter doctoral programmes (considering CNPq data about their bursaries)
9 Proportion of male/female students	48% male, 52% female	
10 Proportion of doctoral students studying who are nationals of other countries	1.5%	

Data sources

Capes (most data are available at http://ged.capes.gov.br/AgDw/silverstream/pages/frPesquisaColeta.html) and CNPq (http://fomentonacional.cnpq.br/dmfomento/home/index.jsp).

The place of doctoral study in the national/international context

Relationship with national research policy

Doctoral studies play an important role in Brazilian research policy. Research policy has as its main institutions Capes (Coordination for the Improvement of Higher Level Personnel), an agency that belongs to the Ministry of Education and deals with doctoral and master degree programmes, and CNPq (National Council for Scientific and Technological Development), part of the Ministry of Science and Technology, which supports research. We also have state agencies, known as FAPs (Research Support Foundations), the most important one being Fapesp, the São Paulo state funding agency.

Indicative current budgets are as follows.

- Capes budget is R$671,450,000 (or approx. US$301,098,000 at the 13 February 2006 rate of US$1.00 = R$2.23).
- CNPq's R$807,000,000 (or approx. US$361,888,000);
- Fapesp's R$510,206,000 (or approx. US$228,800,000).

Evaluation and accreditation

Since the 1970s, graduate studies programmes have been a major concern of Brazilian governments, both military (until 1985) and democratic (since that year). Graduate studies are the only field in education where Brazil has a performance that is internationally recognized as very good. This is due to a strong evaluation policy of accreditation that includes a new evaluation every three years and the closure of programmes that do not meet standards of quality that are continuously raised, in accordance with international standards (5 per cent were closed in 2001, 2 per cent in 2004). It should be noted that there is no independent evaluation of research groups as such: they are evaluated according to their performance in the training of new masters and doctors. This means, on the one hand, that evaluation will give a strong role to scientific production and, on the other, that research groups are strongly stimulated to renew themselves by receiving new (doctoral) students. This quasi-obligation for research groups to act also as graduate programmes has generated rich results, improving the quality of scientists and their research.

Funding issues

Most doctoral candidates are funded by the two federal agencies, Capes (49 per cent of all doctoral students) and CNPq (33 per cent). State-owned funding agencies or FAPs fund 13 per cent of the students.

Institutions are also funded by the agencies, but mostly by Capes, CNPq and Fapesp. Institutional funding usually takes the shape of extra money that is given to institutions according, mainly, to the number of candidates they have. However, it also takes into account their rank in the Capes evaluation, the presence or not of distinguished researchers (who are evaluated by CNPq and receive grants from this agency) and the relevance of their field of studies. For example, for funding matters, engineering is deemed a priority while law is not (it should be noted here that most doctoral students in law will not ask for grants, since they already work and earn money as lawyers).

Kinds of institution

Doctoral awards are offered by three major kinds of institutions of higher education (IHEs): federal, state-owned and private. Federal IHEs offer most programmes – 535 as of 31 December 2004 – followed by state-owned (352) and private (51).

However, if we rank institutions according to the number of awards, we will see that, in 2004, 4075 (or 46 per cent) of new doctorates came from state IHEs, 3924 (or 44 per cent) from federal ones and 856 (a little less than 10 per cent) from private ones. Of the new doctorates produced by state IHEs, 2119 came from USP (University of São Paulo), 1121 from Unicamp (University of Campinas) and 607 from UNESP (State University of São Paulo), meaning that 3847 (or 43.4 per cent) of the new titles were awarded by universities owned by the State of São Paulo; the other state-owned universities were responsible for no more than 228 awards (of those, 132 came from the two universities that belong to the State of Rio de Janeiro and 72 were produced by two owned by the State of Paraná). Most of the other Brazilian 24 states sponsor universities, but these are usually 'young' (i.e. relatively newly established) and do not have doctoral programmes.

The Federal Universities of Rio de Janeiro (782 doctors), Rio Grande do Sul (383), Minas Gerais (350) and Santa Catarina (203) took the lead among federal IHEs. The Catholic Universities of São Paulo (329 new doctorates) and Rio de Janeiro (194) were the strongest in the private sector. Among private IHEs awarding doctoral degrees, those that seek profit have a negligible number of doctoral programmes.

Relationship between graduate and undergraduate programmes

Institutions that award doctoral programmes are organized in different ways, but usually we try not to sever graduate and undergraduate programmes, so that most members of doctoral programmes teach also at undergraduate level. To teach at a doctoral programme a necessary condition (but not the only one) is to hold a doctorate and be engaged in scientific research. Brazil has some 254,000 faculty members at more than 2000 IHEs, but only about 54,000 are doctors. In the approximately 200 IHEs with graduate studies programmes (including both masters and doctoral degrees) we have 32,364 doctors. This means that more than 20,000 doctors teach only at the undergraduate level, while most of the 32,364 doctors engaged in graduate studies programmes also teach at the undergraduate level.

Brazilian IHEs are usually organized in departments (for undergraduate teaching) and programmes (for graduate studies), even though many doctors may teach in both. Capes has been instrumental in establishing an autonomous culture for graduate studies, which includes a budget (coming from Capes and indirectly from other agencies and even, in a small measure, from state-owned or private corporations) controlled by the programme coordinator, the importance of evaluation (which is quite recent at the undergraduate studies level and until now has not closed any IHE or undergraduate programme) and, last but not least, a strong sense among the academic community that they are responsible for the quality of graduate studies.

Forms of doctoral study

Presently we have only one doctoral qualification, the equivalent of a Ph.D. Professional masters were introduced in the mid-1990s, but all doctorates are academic. However, at least a third of those holding a doctorate do not work in the academic world. This feature may be understood as meaning that many doctors, most of all in professional fields such as law and dentistry, get their degrees in order to foster their personal careers; however, since some fields of academe strongly oppose professional masters degrees, the creation of professional doctorates is not on our agenda.

Students and their programmes of study

Evaluation of programmes

Programmes are largely autonomous concerning the criteria they adopt in order to select candidates, but they will later be evaluated according to the quality of the doctors they produce. Selection usually follows some procedures:

- doctoral programmes usually require the candidate to present a research project that will be evaluated by a panel;
- candidates that are selected will have a personal supervisor; during the thesis work, that will usually last four years, they may change their supervisor (or, conversely, their supervisor may send them to a colleague) but this is not usual;
- most students will be funded during their period of study.

Teaching and modes of study

Teaching is offered usually in two semesters per year: March–June and July–December. However, this applies only to teaching; research is not interrupted during the other months of the year. Doctoral students usually have few classes – no more than one or two semesters in total – and from the second to the fourth year of study they will do their research.

Study can be undertaken in part-time mode, but this is not usual. Bursaries (41 per cent of all doctoral students) need to study full-time. Among the non-bursaries, most are already faculty members who often get paid leave of absence in order to study and then write their theses. This means that funding, both direct and indirect, is widespread. This also implies that a great majority will study full-time and that they will finish their thesis work in approximately four years. Those who have a non-academic job that keeps them from studying full-time will take a longer time to conclude their work, but this is not the rule.

Employment destinations

We have been very concerned by the employment that successful doctoral candidates go to when they receive their award. The last comprehensive study on this point dates from the mid-1990s: at that time two-thirds of the doctors went to universities and a third to other sectors (primarily corporations but also public service). It is noteworthy that, among the holders of masters degrees, these proportions were inverted: only a third went to academe, while two-thirds went to other employment, in both the private and public sectors.

Social issues

Concerning gender issues, they are not identifiable in relation to doctoral study. Women constitute more than half of Brazilian doctoral students. Some programmes deal with gender studies, related both to women and to homosexuality. Ethnic issues are not identifiable either, and we lack precise data about the number of Afro-descendent students in our doctoral programmes. In 2005, the Federal University of Bahia (the region of Brazil where African heritage is more present) began the first Brazilian doctoral programme dealing with Afro-Brazilian issues. President Luis Inacio Lula da Silva's government has taken several steps toward affirmative action, but until now it is understood as a policy for undergraduate, not graduate, studies. Issues of religion are not very important in Brazilian society and so they have little weight in our doctoral world. However, as we have already shown, the most important private IHEs that award doctoral degrees are confessional, Catholic or Protestant, but they must follow the same rules that are effective for lay institutions.

Supervision

Candidates must be supervised, continuously, by one supervisor. We stimulate 'sandwich' periods abroad, which means that in the third year of thesis work hundreds of students go to the USA, France, Germany, the UK or other countries for one or two semesters, where they will have another supervisor. If possible, this co-supervisor will be invited for the final examination of the thesis. However, since costs can be high, some examinations are being held with the foreign member of the panel addressing the candidate by video-conference. Also, in Brazil we encourage co-supervision of theses, either with a co-supervisor of the same programme or with someone who teaches in another institution.

Examination

Examination procedure is composed of two important steps. One or two semesters before candidates conclude their thesis they undergo a qualifying exam before a panel of three doctors, one of them being their supervisor. When they conclude their work, a final examination takes place before a jury of five doctors, one of them being their supervisor and at least two coming from another IHE. The presence of external examiners is mandatory.

Other issues

'Quasi self-government' of graduate studies

There are some major points that should be stressed concerning doctoral studies in Brazil. International experience attests to the crucial role of external evaluation by peers in the field of advanced education. This has been done in Brazil since the Federal Union began to regulate graduate studies in the 1960s and especially the 1970s (the Capes evaluation was initiated in 1976). Very interesting is what we could call a *quasi self-government* of graduate studies. It is true that the Board of Capes is appointed by the President of the Republic and can be dismissed with no formalities – as, for that matter, is the Board of CNPq (but not the Board of Fapesp) – but the job would be very difficult for a president and directors with no support in the academic community. The 2000 or so Brazilian graduate studies pro-grammes (among them, 1000 of doctoral programmes, almost all of which also award masters degrees) are evaluated in one of 45 fields of knowledge (e.g. philosophy, ecology or physics). Every field has a representative, who is appointed – after all programmes are heard and have nominated people for the function – for a three-year term. They elect among themselves 16 of the 24 members of Capes' CTC, which is the Portuguese acronym for *Conselho Técnico Científico*, or Technical and Scientific Council. Capes has another council – its Superior Council – which is in charge of some important decisions, but the crucial decisions are made by the CTC.

The most important deliberations of the CTC concern two matters: first, it can approve new programmes. Every year some 450–70 new programmes are proposed; every one of them is evaluated by the field to which it belongs. The representative forms a committee that approves (or not) the proposed programme. The committee's opinion is then sent to the CTC, which can endorse it or change it. The CTC usually follows the opinion of the representative, but sometimes – let us say in less than 5 per cent of cases – it changes it. Some 150 to 200 new programmes are approved every year, a third or more of them at doctoral level.

Triennial evaluation

The second matter is triennial evaluation. Committees are also constituted in every field of knowledge, but, instead of dealing with specific proposals, they evaluate the system as a whole. A field can have from just a few programmes (less than a dozen, e.g. anthropology) to more than a hundred (e.g. agrarian sciences). The evaluation considers the following.

- The scientific production of the faculty members, who should be doctors with recent publications in journals and/or books respected by their fellow researchers.
- A good balance between the faculty members, meaning all (and not only a few) should be engaged in both research and the training of candidates.
- The quality of the papers, dissertations and theses submitted by the candidates.

Grades are awarded to the programmes, ranging from 1 to 7. Grades 1 and 2 mean the programme will not be allowed to continue in the graduate studies system. Grades 3, 4, and 5 mean respectively 'fair', 'good' and 'very good'. Grades 6 and 7 mean the programme has a truly international level, measured by standards of publication in the best journals of the field or other criteria recognized by the peers of its field of knowledge. In the last triennial evaluation (2004), 36 programmes – 2 per cent of the 1816 then evaluated – received grades 1 and 2 and were closed.

Integration of masters and doctoral studies

We should not forget that the Brazilian system integrates (academic) doctorate, academic masters and professional masters degrees, whereas many countries separate these titles. More and more the masters degree comes to be thought of as something inferior to a doctorate, but in Brazil we consider that it is a good thing to link masters degree courses to doctoral programmes. Doctorates can help the junior courses. And, given the enormous distances in Brazil and the difficulties most IHEs face in order to create doctoral programmes, especially in the Amazonian Basin and in the centre-west states of the country, masters degree courses can be very useful, since they congregate doctors and keep them doing their research. More than a third of Brazilian doctors do not teach at the graduate level. This is a major concern of those engaged in scientific policy. Doctors that do not belong to a programme will most likely stop doing their research. They can be good teachers (though clearly this is not a certainty), but their research will not help the institution, the students or the country. This problem can be addressed in several ways. We can stimulate new programmes in the less developed states of the country: this is the goal of *Acelera, Amazônia* (Speed up, Amazon), which will spend some US$2,000,000 per year in the next few years. We can also create DINTER's ('Inter-institutional Doctorates'), meaning that some of the best doctoral programmes will send their faculty members to other states' IHEs, where they will train new doctors – instead of making these candidates from the Amazonian region go to the south-west and south. We can also encourage the use of the web, of videoconferencing and other forms of networks that will help bridge geographical and social distances in a large country. Solidarity – meaning a grade 6 or 7 programme will help a grade 3 programme in one of the less developed states – will be mandatory from 2007 in order to get or keep grades 6 or 7.

Age of candidates and completion rates

We should note something about the typical age of candidates when they begin their thesis work. If we take as our source CNPq data about their bursaries, we see that their age average is 30. Since CNPq and Capes scholarships are given for a four-year period, this means the average age to begin a doctorate is 28 and to finish is 32. This also implies that most candidates have attained a masters degree before beginning their thesis. It is very likely that we can lower this age, if we encourage undergraduate students to begin some kind of research even before getting their degree. When we do that (and we do), they finish both their dissertation and thesis one or more years before those who did not begin scientific research until the completion of their undergraduate grade, even though they take some four years to complete their doctoral studies. But we should also keep in mind that many doctoral students, mostly in the human sciences and the humanities, begin their doctoral work later than in other fields and their completion times are longer than, say, in biological sciences.

Critical comment

Variability of cost across disciplines

One of our major challenges concerns the fact that it is much easier to create programmes when there is no need of laboratories. Costs are very low if you want to have a law or business programme, but it is not certain that they will help the social or economic development of the country. We need engineering and technological programmes. We also need programmes, as in public health, that can help us bridge social gaps that are now deemed to be unacceptable. This means we should try and change the directions that we have been developing in the Brazilian educational system: if we look at the PNPG 2005–10, Table 12, available at www.capes.gov.br/capes/portal/conteudo/10/PNPG.htm, we can see that applied social sciences – which include business, law and economics – have grown from 5 per cent to 7.9 per cent of the number of doctoral programmes in the seven and a half years from 1996 to mid-2004, meaning a growth of almost 60 per cent, while engineering has increased from 9.8 to 10.3 per cent, which means a growth of only 5 per cent.

The professional masters degrees

PNPG, the Portuguese acronym for the National Plan of Graduate Studies 2005–10, defines the main goals Brazil will have to face in the field of doctoral (and masters degree) programmes in the next few years. For several years our scientific policy has emphasized the need to transfer scientific knowledge to the productive sector and to foster the competitiveness and productivity of our enterprises. One of the tools conceived to do that is the professional masters degree. However, in 2004, we produced only 1081 new professional masters, against a total of 25,651 academic masters. It is very likely that several or maybe many among these latter 25,651 are – in fact – professional rather than academic masters, but the programmes themselves do not yet acknowledge this. The present Board of Capes has broadened the meaning of the professional masters award and emphasizes the idea that this tool should not only help increase economic production, but also contribute to the reduction of social inequalities, which means sectors such as health, education, sports and culture should also be prioritized. A workshop held at São Paulo by Capes in March–April, 2005 was an important initiative to reduce misunderstanding and increase cooperation concerning professional masters programmes.

Geographic inequalities

A third priority is the reduction of geographic inequalities in the country. Broadly speaking, we have several regions in Brazil: São Paulo, with the neighbouring States of Minas Gerais and Rio de Janeiro and also the city of Brasilia, have the best standards of scientific production and the best scores in the evaluation. The three states to the south follow. Then we have the north-east states, and at the end of the line the Amazonian Basin and the centre-west states. Of course there are excellent programmes in all regions – Recife, for instance, in the north-east, houses one of the best doctorates in physics of the southern hemisphere – but as a whole those in the north-east/north/centre-west face more difficulties than do those in the south and south-west circuit. In the Amazonian region distances mean costs can greatly increase. In spite of this, there is a moral obligation towards the citizens of these regions to integrate them into the graduate studies system. This is also in the national interest: everybody knows how rich the Amazonian Basin is in terms of biodiversity, and this is deemed to be a major issue in forthcoming years. Last but not least, is it not strange that the region where most of the Brazilian native people live houses no doctorate in ethnology at all? Capes is presently stimulating the programmes in anthropology to constitute a doctorate either in Amazonas or Pará State.

Cost benefits

PNPG implies costs. Brazil has been increasing her doctorate programmes at a pace of 10 to sometimes 15 per cent per year, considering either the number of doctors that get their degree every year or the number of existing programmes. This has been done to a large extent due to the Capes evaluation system: it means that those teachers who did not do their best were strongly stimulated to perform better and better, to publish, to present their work at the best congresses, to submit their papers to the best journals, to supervise more students (or less, if someone was supervising more than, say, six students at a given time). We can say this has been a policy based on voluntarism, meaning the political will to increase the quality of our scientific production. This was largely successful during the two Fernando Henrique Cardoso presidential terms (1995–2002). However, it is possible that this policy is no more able to get good results without new money. To be more specific, the Cardoso years were very hard for federal universities, which – in spite of being the best evaluated both in graduate programmes (by Capes) and in undergraduate courses (by the newly devised tool known as *Exame Nacional de Cursos*, or National Courses Examination) – lost many of their faculty members without having them replaced. If we want to go from the 8855 new doctors we had in 2004 (against 5335 in 2000) to some 15,000 new doctors in 2010 – keeping exactly the same pace of growth we had in the last five years – we will have to pour new money into laboratories, libraries, teachers and candidate funding. We know exactly how much money we will need, if we sum all sources that can be available: R$1,663,500,000 (or US$746,000,000), not per year but in the five years until 2010. It is not an easy task but we are sure that this sum will not be misspent: evaluation will ensure that money put into graduate studies will be well employed.

Further reading

Ribeiro, R.J. (2002) *A Universidade e a Vida Atual: Fellini não via filmes* (*University and Present-Day Life: Fellini did not see Films*). Rio de Janeiro: Elsevier/Campus.

www.capes.gov.br Capes's site has plenty of information about Brazilian graduate policy, and links for the programmes and IHEs that award doctoral and masters degrees.

www.cnpq.br CNPq's site gathers data about scientific research in Brazil. Lattes platform is noteworthy, since more than 500,000 résumés are available, including those of all Brazilians engaged in research.

13

Doctoral education in China

Lee Zhuang

Introduction

China is a country with immense potential in all aspects of higher education. In terms of doctoral study it has a relatively short history, spanning as it does a mere 25 years. Yet in that time there has been a significant growth in the number of doctoral candidates, with the 20 years from 1983 to 2003 seeing an increase from approximately 18 to 188,000. As with so many other countries cited in this book, this rapid growth has brought with it problems; and questions are now being raised about quality of candidates, transparency of processes and over-stretched capacity. China has experienced what is termed a 'Great Leap Forward' in terms of Ph.D. study and this chapter sketches out its origins, the drivers underpinning change and some of the consequences.

The questionnaire

Table 13.1 The questionnaire

Question	Number	Comment
1 Total number of doctoral students studying	165,600[i]	At time of writing, this figure was the latest aggregate figure for 2004 released by the Chinese Ministry of Education (MoE) in an official report on the country's education in that year
2 Number of institutions offering doctoral programmes	Not available	There are no official statistics showing how many and which Chinese academic institutions offer doctoral programmes (Ph.D.s). According to figures released by the MoE, in 2004 769[ii] institutions offered masters and Ph.D. programmes. These included 454 regular higher education

(Continued overleaf)

Table 13.1 (Continued)

Question	Number	Comment
		institutes and 315 research institutes (RIs). There is a different set of statistics which indicated that by the end of 2004 there were over 1,900 bases where Ph.D. programmes were offered but in 2005 alone there were over 2,700 fresh applications from institutions to offer Ph.D. programmes[iii]
3 Number of different doctoral awards (e.g. including professional doctorates)	1	Currently there is no authoritative source of information giving a full account of the different doctoral awards. Going through a range of Ph.D. recruitment information from a variety of Chinese universities, it seems that all Ph.D. programmes offered by state HEIs and RIs fall into the conventional category of being predominantly research based but there is a small number of private or joint venture institutions (e.g. DBA Centre of China based in Beijing)[iv] that offer Doctor of Business Administration
4 Number of years over which doctorates have been offered in the country	25	In February 1980, China's National People's Congress approved a landmark piece of legislation on the country's higher degree framework to include bachelor, masters and doctor of philosophy. This piece of legislation took effect on 1 Jan 1981 with the first cohort of 18 students awarded a Ph.D. on 27 May 1983 (Lu 2004)
5 Proportion of full-time to part-time students	28.9:1[v]	Strictly speaking, this ratio is full-time to non-full-time. The ratio was worked out using the numbers obtained from the official statistics of 2003 provided by the Chinese MoE
6 Average time to completion (in years)	3–4 full-time[vi]	No official statistics exist to show the average length of time it takes for a Ph.D. candidate to complete the programme but there is evidence to suggest that an increasing number of them cannot complete on time (Xu 2005)
7 Success rates	0 failure rate	No official statistics were available at the time of writing but the real figures are likely to be low due to the traditional Chinese practice of 'strict at entry and relax at exit' ('*yan jin kuan chu*')

8 Typical age range of doctoral candidates	No statistics available	The upper age limit of 40 was extended to 45 in 2004. In practice, this usually does not matter as most Chinese students prefer to complete all levels of education one after another without a break
9 Proportion of male/ female students	3.46:1	This was worked out using the numbers obtained from the official statistics of 2003 provided by the Chinese MoE
10 Proportion of doctoral students studying who are nationals of other countries	No statistics available	There were no official statistics on this but an educated guess would suggest that the number is very small due to language barriers, as most state approved Ph.D. supervisors are not able to supervise in languages other than Chinese

Notes

i   At the time of writing, the latest official statistics on doctoral provision in China with some breakdown information rather than just aggregate numbers were only available up to 2003 while aggregate figures were available for 2004.

ii April 2005. *Statistical Report on China National Development of Education in 2004*, Ministry of Education of the People's Republic of China. Full data set can be obtained from www.moe.gov.

iii As Note ii.

iv Editorial, 2005. 'The key to overcoming the current crisis in Ph.D. education', *Education Observation*, full text in Chinese can be found at http://learning.sohu.com.

v   The DBA Centre of China is a joint venture institution between American City University and the Chinese Association of Experienced Professors. More details can be found (in Chinese only) at www.cbma.org.

vi These figures were taken from the Annual Statistical Report on Education for 2003 published by the Chinese Ministry of Education. The table on full-time postgraduate students in 2003 published by the Chinese MoE can be found at www.moe.gov.cn. The table on part-time postgraduate students in 2003 can be found at the same site.

vii Chinese MoE, 1991. *Higher Education Law of the People's Republic of China* (effective from 1 January 1991). Full text in Chinese can be found at www.moe.gov.cn.

Data source

In compiling the table, where possible the latest official statistics were sourced from the Ministry of Education (MoE) of the People's Republic of China, a government ministry responsible for all aspects of state education at all levels ranging from primary education to higher education including doctoral provision. Statistics released by the MoE are thus considered the most complete and authoritative but not always accurate and timely due to the size of the country and the scale of its higher education provision. As the history of doctoral education in China is relatively short, its infrastructure is still developing. This is one of the reasons why only a few statistics are available and they are not always comparable to those seen in the other countries with a longer history of doctoral provision.

The place of doctoral study in the national context

'Higher' and 'adult' education institutes

Chinese higher education institutes (HEIs) are conventionally divided into regular HEIs and adult education institutes (AEIs). The former offer a wide range of award-bearing programmes in terms of subject disciplines and levels of study while the latter tend to have a relatively narrow range of subject disciplines, which are either non-award bearing or at sub-degree levels (e.g. the two- or three-year full-time diploma).

An HEI typically offers higher diploma programmes (two or three years), degrees and, subject to approval of the Chinese MoE, masters and Ph.D. programmes. Their students tend to come straight from high schools, having been successful in the annual National College Entrance examinations. An AEI, on the other hand, tends to provide vocational programmes to those who are already in employment. 'Up-skilling' and knowledge renewal are emphasized more than gaining qualifications, although topping up to the next level qualification is often possible either at the same institution or at a different one. The source of students is thus seen as a dividing factor between an HEI and an AEI. An increasing number of regular HEIs in China have been approved by the Chinese government to offer Ph.D. programmes but none of the AEIs have been, or will be, approved to do so at least for the foreseeable future.

Government approval to offer Ph.D. programmes

In China, Ph.D. programmes are offered by selected regular HEIs and research institutes (RIs) subject to strict government approval procedures. The Chinese MoE views Ph.D. education as the highest form of academic enquiry and tends to associate this with the country's science and technology as well as economic development priorities. As such, in each round of approval strict criteria and quotas are imposed on institutions wishing to apply to host doctoral programmes. For instance, a government White Paper on approving degree-awarding applications in 2005 (the tenth round of approval) stipulated that applications were restricted to regular HEIs and approval would be granted to no more than 15 institutions.[1] To qualify for this round of application, an HEI must have been approved by the government to offer masters programmes prior to 1996.

Ph.D. provision in Chinese was non-existent until February 1980 when the National People's Congress approved a landmark piece of legislation on the country's higher degree framework to include bachelor, masters and doctor of philosophy. This piece of legislation took effect on 1 Jan 1981 with the first cohort of 18 students awarded a Ph.D. on 27 May 1983 (Lu 2004).

Since then, Ph.D. provision has been growing at an unprecedented speed. The year 2003 alone saw a fresh enrolment of 48,700 and 18,000 Ph.D.s were awarded (Lu 2004).

An institution that gains approval to offer Ph.D. programmes tends to be regarded as having high-level research competence and thus attract more external research funding both from the government and other private sources. It is therefore highly desirable for institutions to gain government approval to host Ph.D. programmes in as many subject disciplines as possible and at the earliest opportunity. This explains the recent surge in applications from institutions seeking approval to offer Ph.D. programmes. As mentioned in Question 2 of the questionnaire, in 2005 alone there were over 2700 new applications submitted to the MoE.

Funding issues

Funding of full-time students

All full-time Ph.D. students in China are recruited through the state planning system. By source of funding, they fall into three categories, namely: (1) state planned, (2) sponsored and (3) self-funded.

Students in the first category are funded by the government and are not tied to any employment destinations. Funding is provided to the host institution on an annual basis. It may include an element of bursary to cover the cost of living. Self-evidently, the funding for the second category comes from sponsoring organizations and students are contractually bound to work for them for an agreed period of time after completion. The funding tends to cover the fees but not maintenance. The host institution can often find some paid teaching or research work for the students to help them cover the cost of living. As for the third category, some sources suggest that in 2004, 40 per cent of full-time postgraduate students (including masters and Ph.D.s) were self-funded (Wang 2005) but it was not clear how big the proportion was for Ph.D.s.

Funding of part-time students

For non-full-time Ph.D. students, funding arrangements tend to be less well defined. Many students in this category are actually young academics working as full-time lecturers. If they pursue a Ph.D. within their own institution there will be no fee to pay to an external body. There may be a notional internal transfer of payment between different departments. If, however, their own institution is unable to supervise their proposed topic of research they may need to apply to a different institution, in which case the issue of funding will need to be addressed. In the first instance, the individuals may need to pay the fees themselves. Most academic institutions will reimburse a proportion of fees for their staff undertaking a Ph.D. programme at a different institution provided their staff agree to work for them for an agreed period of time after gaining the qualification. Currently, the annual fees charged for doing a Ph.D. vary from one institution to another but are usually in the range of 10,000 to 20,000 RMB (about £700–1400).

Kinds of institution

Ph.D. programmes and the 'programme base'

As mentioned above, there are two kinds of institution that offer Ph.D. programmes, regular HEIs and RIs. The former refers to state universities that offer a wide range of award programmes at both undergraduate and postgraduate levels. It must be noted that not all HEIs are approved to run Ph.D. programmes. RIs are academic research institutions that undertake government commissioned or commercial research. They do not offer taught programmes and only a small number of them are approved by the government to offer postgraduate programmes including Ph.D.s. In 2004 there were 769 institutions offering masters and Ph.D. programmes, of which 454 were regular HEIs and 315 RIs. Again, it was not clear just how many in each category host Ph.D. programmes.

No official statistics are available indicating how many academic institutions offer Ph.D. programmes. Instead, the concept of 'programme base' is used in official statistics. A Ph.D. programme base is a subject discipline located within a regular HEI or a RI that has been approved by the Chinese MoE to host a Ph.D. programme. An approved institution may have more than one Ph.D. programme base and different institutions may offer Ph.D. programmes in the same or similar subject areas. For this reason, the figure of 1900 Ph.D. programme bases that existed in 2004 indicates neither the total number of Ph.D. programmes nor the total number of institutions offering them in the country.

Graduate schools

Not all Chinese HEIs are approved to set up a graduate school. Where an institution has one, Ph.D. programmes tend to be located there. The concept of graduate school was first introduced to China in August 1984 with the approval of 22 HEIs among the first to establish a graduate school from within. In April 1996, the MoE approved a further 10 HEIs to open a graduate school. In June 2000, another 22 HEIs were approved to join them and two years later in May 2002, another two were approved. By then, altogether 56 HEIs had been approved to set up a graduate school. According to the Chinese MoE, these graduate schools are responsible for 76 per cent of Ph.D. and 55 per cent of masters students in the country.[2]

There are strict requirements for an HEI to set up a graduate school. These include teaching quality, research quality, ratio of postgraduate students to undergraduate students, ratio of Ph.D.s to masters, proportion of academic staff with a masters and Ph.D. qualification, excellent research infrastructure, etc. Applications are considered and approved by the State Education Committee.[3]

Forms of doctoral study

Currently, there is only one main form of doctoral study in China, which is full-time, supervised with the requirement that each student undertakes a minimum of 13 credits of compulsory taught subjects. In China, a credit equates to one contact hour per week over one semester (which is typically 14 to 16 weeks long).

The compulsory taught subjects typically include Marxism (or something similar), a foreign language – most likely to be English – one subject fundamental to the proposed topic of research and another one delivered by the supervisor. It is interesting to note that research methodology is not among the compulsory taught subjects.

Professional doctorate programmes have not yet been introduced but a small number of business schools have started offering Doctor of Business Administration with a much higher taught content.

In order to enrol onto a Ph.D. programme, a candidate needs to sit in a national entry examination for postgraduate study, which typically takes place in the spring. For doctoral study, the compulsory subject examined is English. If a student successfully attains the level required by the host institution, they will then be invited to take further examinations with that institution, followed by an interview and sometimes a second interview with the supervisor. The subjects to be examined are left to the institutions to decide and the results are considered in conjunction with the candidate's background and performance in the interview.

Students and their programmes of study

Prior qualifications, age and mode of study

A Ph.D. candidate is expected to have a masters degree and normally be under the age of 40. As most Chinese students like to complete all levels of education in one go, i.e. from high school to university undergraduate, masters and Ph.D., the age limit is normally not an issue.

In China, the notion of 'part-time' study is very new and the figures released by the MoE on non-full-time Ph.D. students (see Table 13.1, Note vi) actually indicate those who study while in employment. Whether these students study on a full-time basis or a part-time basis depends on the level of sponsorship they receive from their sponsoring organization. Some employers may allow their staff to take time off work to attend all the compulsory taught classes while others may leave it to their individual staff to juggle between work and study. It is generally expected that these students will put in a lot of their private time.

Duration of Ph.D. study

The typical duration of a Ph.D. programme is three years full-time but in some cases an extension is possible. The majority of students study on a full-time basis. One exception to this is young academics who are usually encouraged by their place of work to undertake Ph.D. studies. Technically they are not full-time students as they are in full-time employment. During their study their normal teaching load will be reduced, though not to zero level. They are still expected to complete the programme within the normal period of three years.

Destinations of Ph.D.-holders

There are no statistics showing employment destinations of Ph.D.-holders in China. Personal observations suggest that a large proportion of successful candidates work in academia although an increasing number of them are now occupying key positions in the banking, insurance and stock exchange industries.

Gender and ethnicity

Although statistics suggest that nearly three-quarters of Ph.D. students are male, this is more the result of personal choice rather than a gender issue *per se*. In China, since the Cultural Revolution ended in 1976 and with the introduction of the 'one-child' policy, sex discrimination in higher education is much less common.

China is a multi-ethnic country with the Han majority accounting for over 95 per cent of the total population. There are 55 nationally identified ethnic minorities, many of whom have their own languages, both spoken and written. Mainstream higher education caters primarily for speakers of the Han language (also known as Mandarin or putonghua), and as a result members of ethnic minorities may sometimes feel disadvantaged. Having said that, most universities take this into account when admitting students from the minority groups. However, due to the new and evolving nature of Ph.D. education in China, a consistent policy of supporting non-Mandarin speakers has not yet emerged.

Language of study

The issue of language also has implications for foreign nationals wishing to study for a Ph.D. in China. While in recent years most Chinese universities have welcomed overseas students onto their programmes, the number undertaking a Ph.D. is relatively small and largely confined to those who are from Chinese-speaking communities outside the country, such as Singapore and Malaysia. For non-speakers of the Chinese language the most notable barrier is the language, as very few Ph.D. supervisors are able to supervise in English. Having reviewed a number of recent Ph.D. recruitment flyers from a number of different universities in China directed at overseas applicants, it turns out that none of them specified the minimum entry requirement in terms of the Chinese language. This may be due to the fact that Chinese language testing for non-Chinese speakers is still developing and there is not yet a clearly established threshold an overseas applicant must reach in order to effectively pursue a Ph.D. programme in Chinese.

Religion

As China is largely an atheist country, religious belief is not normally an issue for consideration at the point of admission. Moreover, where there are large Muslim communities, such as Beijing and Xi'an, universities will operate some distinct facilities such as separate canteens to cater for Muslim students.

Supervision

Normally, when applying for a Ph.D. programme at a particular institution, a candidate often has a clear preference for a particular supervisor and tends to tailor their application to reflect the research interest of that supervisor. The candidate may have heard about the supervisor via friends or read their published work prior to submitting the application. Quite often, famous Ph.D. supervisors get over-subscribed and thus have to turn down applications.

If successfully admitted, a candidate will be supervised continuously by the same supervisor, known in the UK as the principal supervisor. If necessary, the supervisor will bring in additional colleagues, internal or external, to form a supervising team. The team arrangement can be ad hoc or formal. If the latter is the case, formal permission will need to be sought from the research degrees committee of the host institution.

In China, to qualify as a Ph.D. supervisor, one is normally expected to be: a) a full professor for at least five years, b) a leading researcher in the relevant field, c) have supervised at least one cohort of masters dissertations to completion (please note that it takes two to three years to complete a masters degree in China), and d) in possession of a Ph.D. qualification if born after the founding of the People's Republic of China.

There is a lot of social kudos associated with being a Ph.D. supervisor because it is seen as a recognition of one's academic capabilities in the highest form. For this reason, senior academics in HEIs approved by the MoE to host Ph.D. programmes are keen to become Ph.D. supervisors at the earliest opportunity. Applications are submitted to the research degrees committee within the relevant HEI and approval of new Ph.D. supervisors is granted on an annual basis. For those who have become approved supervisors, they will proudly display it on their business cards using the Chinese expression *bodao*.

Examination

There is no established common procedure for organizing a Ph.D. examination in China. The detailed practice varies from one institution to the next and between academic disciplines. What is described here is taken from different sources, which indicates a typical pattern.

Before reaching the examination stage, a candidate must demonstrate that they have:

- completed all the compulsory taught modules;
- undertaken all the relevant research deemed necessary to complete the programme;
- published at least three pieces of work based on the research in recognized academic journals;
- completed the thesis to the required standard.

Having satisfied the above conditions, the following typical procedure will then begin:

1 The candidate makes a formal request to the research degrees committee or an equivalent body within the institution for the viva – obviously with the agreement of the supervisor who has read the final draft of the thesis and is happy with it. This step usually entails the candidate completing an official request form.

2 Upon receipt of the formal request, the committee or an equivalent body within the hosting institution undertakes to appoint a viva secretary who could be internal or external to the institution and will liaise between the candidate and the examining team during the viva stage. Naturally, the viva secretary should be totally familiar with the relevant rules and regulations concerning the Ph.D. programmes within the institution.

3 The committee undertakes to appoint five or seven (some institutions require nine; even numbers are avoided to prevent a draw in the voting) appropriately qualified senior academics to form the examining team. Normally, at least 80 per cent of the examiners must be professors or in an

equivalent position in the relevant research field. At least three examiners must be Ph.D. supervisors themselves. Two to three of the examiners must be external to the host institution. The principal supervisor can be one of the examiners but cannot act as the chair.

4 The viva secretary arranges copies of the thesis with an examiner's report form to be sent to all the examiners approximately one month prior to the proposed date of viva. The examiners are given a date prior to the viva by which they will have to read and returned their written reports.

5 The viva secretary collates the written feedback from all the examiners and produces a summary report which, based on the actual feedback, may recommend to the committee that the viva should go ahead or the candidate be asked to undertake further work.

6 During the actual viva, the chair formally opens the viva, followed by the viva secretary briefly introducing the background of the candidate who then takes over to give a formal presentation of between 30 to 60 minutes duration. This then leads to the formal questioning. There is no formal guidance on how long this should last.

7 The panel of examiners then holds a private meeting to consider their evaluation of the thesis and the candidate's performance during the viva.

8 A resolution is reached by anonymous voting. Broadly speaking, the resolution either confirms that the candidate has achieved all the programme objectives and therefore recommends the award of a Ph.D. or rejects the thesis and recommends the candidate rework it within a specified period of time. Some institutions grade a Ph.D. thesis into distinction, merit, pass and fail while others don't.

9 After a resolution has been reached, the chair reconvenes the meeting with the attendance of the candidate and announces the outcome of the viva.

10 The viva secretary formally takes the minutes during the viva and completes all the relevant paperwork.

In the past, very few Ph.D. candidates have failed because they were given extra time to rework their thesis. There have been discussions in the academic community in China about whether tighter control should be exercised over the time it takes to complete a Ph.D. and whether if a candidate fails to meet the deadline they should be deemed to have failed the programme. Naturally, there is also a lot of resistance to this idea due to the severe loss of face this would cause to the candidates and their supervisors. To most students and supervisors alike, not being able to enrol onto a Ph.D. programme is far less humiliating than failing to complete it.

Other issues

The Chinese higher education system was completely disbanded during the Cultural Revolution which lasted for ten years between 1966 and 1976. The system of National College Entry Examinations was reintroduced in 1978. Ph.D. education was not formally introduced until 1981. For this reason the infrastructure to support this level of education is still developing and evolving and thus statistics comparable to those found in the UK and other more Ph.D.-advanced countries are hard to come by. This has resulted in Table 13.1 being somewhat sketchy.

Critical comment

Ph.D. education in China is relatively young but fast developing. As mentioned earlier in this chapter, within the past two decades, the annual number of Ph.D. graduates jumped from 18 in 1983 to 188,000 in 2003 (Lu 2004). According to some commentators, in terms of Ph.D. education, it took China only 20 years to achieve what took the USA over 100 years to accomplish.

Other observers are questioning the sustainability of this fast development. They describe it as China's 'Great Leap Forward' in Ph.D. education and have uncovered some worrying signs of a crisis (Xu 2005). These include slipping quality of applicants, lack of transparency in the recruitment process, over-stretched supervision capacity and lack of objectivity in the examining process. In addition, Xu found that, in keeping with the traditional Chinese approach to teaching and learning, most Ph.D. programmes are over-supervised and lack truly 'independent' research. The absence of emphasis on research methodologies is evidence of this, though some might argue that Ph.D. candidates should have already acquired the necessary research skills through their previous masters education. While this may be true in many institutions in the UK, it is rarely the case in China as research methodology is not normally taught as part of masters education.

Notes

1 Chinese MoE, 2005. 'Announcement on the 10th Round of Approval for Institutions Wishing to Apply for New Postgraduate Qualification Awarding Power', Ref. Degree [2005] Number 15. Full text in Chinese available at www.moe.edu.cn/edoas/website18/info12675.htm.
2 Chinese MoE, 2005. 'Background to Graduate Schools', Chinese Ministry of Education, 26 June 2005. Full text in Chinese available at www.moe.gov.cn/.
3 Chinese MoE, 2005. 'Interim Regulations on Requirements of Establishing a Graduate School', 14 July 2005. Full text in Chinese available at www.moe.gov.cn/.

References

Lu, N. (2004) The changes in the educational history of new China, PhD graduates from 18 to 18.8k, *New China Net*, 10 March. Full text in Chinese can be found at www.sina.com.cn.

Wang, D. (2005) Recognising the oversupply of PhD programmes, *People Net*, 10 October. Full text in Chinese available at http://edu.people.com.cn/GB/8216/47717/47723/3754919.html.

Xu, Z. (2005) Time to put a break on the Great Leap Forward in PhD Education, *China Education Pioneer Net*, 11 July. Full text available at www.ep-china.net. (In the past couple of years there have been press reports on the impact of the 'Great Leap Forward' in Ph.D. education in China and 'not being able to complete on time' has been cited as evidence of slipping quality of applicants.)

14

Doctoral education in India

Sudhanshu Bhushan

Introduction

India has one of the largest higher education systems in the world with over 10 million students enrolled in universities across the sub-continent. Of these 0.65 are engaged in doctoral study. This population is set to increase with agreement reached in 2005 to the effect that the number of doctoral students should increase fivefold over the next ten years. At present just under a third of all doctoral study is carried out in 'professional' domains. This chapter explores how the doctorate is developing in this large and growing academic environment.

The questionnaire

Table 14.1 The questionnaire

Question	Number	Comment
1　Total number of doctoral students studying	65,491 (0.66%)	Number in parentheses relates to percentage enrolment of students in research (doctorates) to total enrolment in higher education in 2003–4
2　Number of institutions offering doctoral programmes	315	Only universities/deemed universities/ institutions of national importance confer doctoral degrees and students are enrolled in university departments/university colleges and affiliated colleges. There were 16,885 university and affiliated colleges in 2003–4, but not all of them have doctoral programmes
3　Number of different doctoral awards (e.g. including professional doctorates)	15 (142)	1 Doctorate of Letters or Doctor of Literature (D.Litt. or Litt.D.); 2 Doctor of Philosophy (Ph.D. or D.Phil.); 3 Doctor of Oriental Learning (DOL); 4 Doctor of Laws (LL.D.);

5 Doctor of Laws (D.L.); 6 Doctor of Science (D.Sc. or Sc.D.); 7 Doctor of Medicine (M.D.); 8 Doctor of Hygiene (D.Hy.); 9 Doctor of Music (D.Mus.); 10 Doctor of Education (D.Ed.); 11 Doctor of Engineering (D.Eng.); 12 Doctor of Medicine (in cardiology) (D.M.); 13 Doctor of Ayurvedic Medicine (D.AyM); 14 Vidya Vachaspati; and 15 Master of Philosophy (M. Phil.), as per the notification of the University Grants Commission (UGC). The figure in parentheses indicates total degrees specified by the UGC for award of degrees by the universities. Doctoral degrees constitute 10% of the total degrees

4	Number of years over which doctorates have been offered in the country	Since 1857	1857 saw the establishment of three universities, which led to the beginning of doctoral programmes. In post-independence period, under the UGC Act 1956, the first notification related to doctoral degrees was made on 1 December, 1958
5	Proportion of full-time to part-time students	100%	A doctoral programme is full-time study, however a very small proportion of employed candidates pursue doctoral studies simultaneously, i.e. part-time
6	Average time to completion (in years)	3–5	Average time is not empirically verified. It is based on the period of fellowship offered by the government
7	Success rate	22%	Estimate is based on the ratio of total doctorates awarded (13,733) and the enrolment of students in research (62,213) in 2002–3
8	Typical age range of doctoral candidates	23–26	The majority come into doctoral programmes straight from a bachelor degree of three years and thereafter completing two years of a masters degree. A higher age range does exist due to employed teachers/professionals enrolling themselves at later stage of life
9	Proportion of male/ female students	61:39	Refers to 2003–4
10	Proportion of doctoral students studying who are nationals of other countries	Less than 1%	Based on the annual reports of some reputed institutions

Data sources

University Grants Commission (UGC) *Annual Report 2003–4*. This is a yearly publication that contains information on enrolment in higher education, number of institutions in higher education, total doctorates awarded in a year and number of fellowships awarded through National Education Testing (NET). Different doctoral awards are notified in The UGC Act 1956 (as modified up to 20 December 1985) and rules and regulations under the act (see www.ugc.ac.in). Data on the proportion of full-time to part-time students, average time to completion, proportion of doctoral students studying who are nationals of other countries and typical age range of doctoral candidates are given in the comments to Table 14.1.

The place of doctoral study in the national/international context

The place of doctoral study in national research policy in India has been guided by asymmetries in policies and practices. At the level of concept, the role of universities was to explore ideas and knowledge. Doctoral-level research was the instrument through which knowledge could be cultivated and disseminated through two domains – teaching and research. At the level of practice the share of the higher education sector in the total research and development (R&D) expenditure is a meagre 2.9 per cent. (Department of Science and Technology 2002). In the field of research the concentration of resources in bodies outside the universities, in research laboratories under the Council of Scientific and Industrial Research (CSIR), other research institutions and industries both in the public and private sectors is responsible for a rather low expenditure on R&D in the higher education sector. Low R&D expenditure not only affects doctoral level of research but is also responsible for the low level of basic research in the universities. At the same time, poor university/industry linkages have not encouraged industrial collaboration.

Nonetheless, the place of doctoral study cannot simply be evaluated in terms of R&D expenditure in higher education and its contribution in basic and applied research. In India the view is taken that successful doctoral candidates are the finest human resources; they have acquired the highest levels of knowledge in the relevant field. Success at doctoral level means the development of a continuing aptitude for independent scientific enquiry and therefore those with a doctorate should have great potential to serve as good teachers, scientists or leaders in all sectors of development.

This, however, poses a dilemma both from the national as well as the international perspective. The finest human resources that India has may be attracted towards industries and they may not advance their careers in the universities and research institutions. As a result, diffusion of doctoral-level knowledge may take place in different sectors of the economy but the sustenance of universities in terms of a pool of researchers may be threatened. At the same time, advanced countries also attract the best talent, creating a 'brain drain'. While the outward mobility of doctorates should not be prevented by means of any specific policy, universities should be able to attract talent so that inward mobility of aspirants for doctoral study compensates to a great extent the loss of talent due to any brain drain. From an international perspective, therefore, there is a need to raise the infrastructure and facilities for doctorates in the universities in order to retain existing talent and attract new talent.

Funding issues

Only universities, deemed universities and institutions of national importance, confer doctoral degrees. Therefore, aspirants for a doctorate register for the doctorate in university departments, university colleges and colleges affiliated to the universities. Any aspirant who is desirous of financial assistance for the period of doctoral study from the government will have to be successful in a competitive written test called the National Education Test (NET) (conducted twice a year) at national level, conducted by the UGC in the fields of humanities (including languages), social sciences, forensic science, environmental sciences, computer science and applications and electronic science, and by the Council for Scientific and Industrial Research (CSIR) in life sciences, physical sciences, chemical sciences, mathematical sciences and earth atmospheric, ocean and planetary sciences.

The results of NET in 2003 showed that out of 97,603 students who sat the test in humanities and social sciences only 764 students (0.78 per cent) qualified for a junior research fellowship (JRF). A considerably large number of JRFs (1883 in 2003) were provided through CSIR for science doctorates. Qualifying tests do not bestow a fellowship upon the candidate. They are entitled to the fellowship after registration in a doctoral programme in the universities. This indicates a hard reality that less than 1 per cent of aspirants undertaking the examination get the necessary funding support from the UGC. A similar situation exists in science. In engineering and technology competitive examination such as NET is not held. Some 50 JRFs are available for doctoral studies every year in engineering and technology through direct interviews. During 2003–4, UGC awarded 20 JRFs and seven research associateships to foreign students from developing countries.

Many join a doctoral programme without support from the UGC and the CSIR and seek short-term limited fellowships or contingency grants from CSIR or other research institutions. The majority do not get funding support.

A certain number of Senior Research Fellowships (SRFs) are awarded each year by CSIR (see www.csir.res.in) directly to professional graduates in engineering, medicine, veterinary studies and agriculture. The Indian Council of Social Science Research (ICSSR) (see www.icssr.org) awards doctoral fellowships directly under the centrally administered Doctoral Fellowships Scheme. Additionally, the Council allocates 50 fellowships annually to 18 of its research institutes spread all over India. The Council also has three other schemes to assist doctoral scholars – Doctoral Fellowships for Foreign Nationals, Short-term Doctoral Fellowships and a Contingency Grant for doctoral Scholars in social sciences, not in receipt of any assistance. For the promotion of historical research, the Council of Historical Research provides 355 JRFs for doctoral studies and 47 general/postdoctoral fellowships are awarded. The Council of Philosophical Research and the Council of Agricultural Research also award fellowships to doctoral aspirants in these respective subjects.

Those in the teaching profession can apply for the teacher's fellowship. Subject to the fulfilment of certain conditions, teachers get salary protection and contingency grants from the UGC after they are registered for a doctorate programme.

Kinds of institution

Students are enrolled in university departments, university colleges and affiliated colleges. Out of 65,491 students enrolled for doctoral research 58,321 were in university departments or university colleges and 7170 were in affiliated colleges in 2003–4. The concept of the research university is lacking in India. All postgraduate departments are research and teaching units. As a result there is a proliferation of doctorates in university departments but research universities concentrating on doctorates are smaller in number.

There are some research institutions funded by the Indian Council of Social Science Research and research laboratories funded by the Council of Scientific and Industrial Research, where doctoral studies are undertaken that are accredited by a university. There is an Inter-University Center for Astronomy and Astrophysics (IUCAA) at Pune, and 37 students have worked for a Ph.D. there. It has on an average ten post-doctorates per year. There is also an inter-university Consortium of Atomic Energy Facilities at Indore with branch centres at Kolkata and Mumbai where, under the collaborative research schemes, university teachers engage in doctoral programmes. During 2002–3 more than ten students completed a Ph.D. there. The Nuclear Science Center (NSC) is another inter-university centre providing a world-class facility for accelerator-based research. In 2003–4 about 55 students utilized the NSC facilities for their Ph.D. work.

Forms of doctoral study

Doctoral studies are offered in the arts, science and commerce in all universities imparting general education. Doctorates are also offered in some professions such as ayurvedic medicine, education, engineering, health sciences, law, medicine, medicine (in cardiology) and music. Some doctoral degrees such as *vidyavaridhi* (Ph.D.) and *vidyavachasapti* (D.Litt.) are given in Tibetan studies.

M.Phil. programmes were introduced in the late 1970s. In India the M.Phil. is a pre-doctorate qualification of one or two years after which a candidate may continue on a doctoral programme or may discontinue after getting the initial exposure to research. An M.Phil. programme is completed in two parts – Part 1 for coursework and Part 2 for the dissertation. Some argue that this is pre-Ph.D. training, meant to prepare a student with a postgraduate degree for research, others say that Part 1 is virtually an extension of the masters programme, while hardly any worthwhile research can be done in the six months (actually less than that) of Part 2 (see Shah 2005).

Students and their programmes of study

Required qualifications

For admission to an M.Phil. programme a candidate is required to hold a postgraduate qualification of two years after a first degree in higher education (i.e. a bachelors degree) of three years. The M.Phil. is of one or two years' duration. A candidate may directly be admitted to a doctoral programme after an M.Phil. in a relevant subject. In terms of policy the M.Phil. is seen in India as a preparatory stage to the doctoral degree in some universities. However, in many universities a candidate is directly registered on the doctoral programme after a postgraduate qualification of two years. There is no competitive examination to test the research aptitude of the researcher, except for the fellowship. As a result anybody holding a postgraduate qualification may be registered for Ph.D.

A candidate is required to submit a research proposal to the university department. The board of studies examines the research proposal and if it is found satisfactory in terms of research design and relevance of topic, allocates the supervisor. The research proposal is then finally approved by the university. In terms of necessary professional qualification the minimum qualification for Doctor of Medicine is four and a half years and one year of internship of Bachelor of Medicine & Bachelor of Surgery (M.B.B.S. or M.B. & B.S.).

Periods of study

The period of study for the doctorate is three years as per the UGC guideline. In some universities it is three years after an M.Phil., which amounts to four years of study for a doctorate. The minimum period of research at doctorate level is three years after provisional registration but may extend well beyond this.

Part-time and full-time modes

There is a flexi-model with respect to part- and full-time modes of doctorate. After an initial period of coursework which may require full-time study, a candidate is required to submit a proposal. After the proposal is accepted, it is optional whether a candidate pursues their doctoral studies part-time or full-time. Where there is no coursework, a candidate is free to pursue full- or part-time study as per the provisions in the respective universities. Those who are already employed in a profession prefer to pursue their doctorates part-time. They naturally take a substantial number of years to write the dissertation. Candidates who are awarded JRF/SRF are supposed to do full-time research work.

Kinds of employment

After doctoral study some researchers join teaching and research institutions such as universities, colleges, CSIR laboratories, R&D wings of defence and industrial establishments. Those who are already in a profession register for doctorates and acquire professional knowledge that qualifies them to be specialist human resources. Thus there are clearly two trends – one joining the teaching and research profession and further pursuing a research career, and the other acquiring specialist knowledge that makes them capable of taking objective decisions at a high level. However, employment is not guaranteed. Therefore a minor proportion of doctorate-holders may remain unemployed in search of a better job for a short period of time, called the 'waiting period of employment'.

Gender

The enrolment of women as a percentage of total enrolment has consistently been increasing at all stages of higher education – at the graduate level (first degree level of three years) from 10.8 per cent in 1950–1 to 40 per cent in 2002–3, and at the postgraduate level from 17.3 per cent to 42 per cent during the same period. At the level of research the percentage of women enrolled at doctoral level has consistently been increasing, from 14.1 per cent in 1950–1 to 39 per cent in 2002–3. Enrolment at the doctoral level was 6 per cent of the total enrolment at postgraduate level in 2002–3, which means the transition to the doctorate is quite low. Data on disciplinary choices by females at the doctorate level is not available. If female enrolment at graduate level by disciplines is any indication, women's preference for science, electronics and computer engineering may have grown at the research level over the past few years (see Chanana 2004).

Supervision

Supervision of doctoral study is a critical element of a doctoral programme. The quality of doctoral work is said to depend upon the quality of supervision. As soon as the proposal for research is approved, candidates are allotted a supervisor. Students may sometimes have the option to choose a supervisor depending upon their research interest and the supervisor's willingness to guide the student. There is also flexibility for a research student to choose an external supervisor with the consent and approval of the departmental research committee. The practice of team supervision is not widely prevalent in Indian universities. There are also no qualifications, except the one for a teacher, laid down for the supervisor.

During the period of supervision a Ph.D. scholar works in continuous interaction with the supervisor and shares the findings of the research in seminars. A six-monthly progress report prepared by the student is to be approved by the supervisor. Students are also encouraged to publish their research findings. Finally, after the dissertation is submitted the report of the supervisor, among other requirements, is the basis for evaluating the dissertation.

The quality of supervision depends on the knowledge and expertise of the supervisor. Sometimes the topic of the dissertation may fall outside the expertise of the supervisor and as a result the student may be deprived of expert comment.

Examination

In India it is accepted that evaluation of the doctoral dissertation is key to the quality of doctorates. After the formal evaluation by the supervisor, they suggest to the student some names for an external evaluator. Examiners from foreign universities may be suggested. Normally the dissertation is sent to the two examiners approved by the board of studies. The examiners submit an evaluation report in which they specifically note their recommendation – approval or revision – for the dissertation. If the dissertation is approved by both examiners, a viva examination is arranged in which the student defends the thesis. The viva is open to all and candidates may be questioned by any one of them.

Although in terms of procedure the process of evaluation is rigorous, there are several matters which need to be addressed. First of all, the system of selection of examiners should be changed. National panels of specialist examiners should be created. Second, the time between the submission of dissertation and the viva examination is often too long. Third, the number of candidates supervised should not be a criterion for promotion, as it gives rise to a kind of 'rat race' to produce doctorates.

Other issues

Structural constraints

Barring a few, universities in India suffer from infrastructural constraints, such as lack of journals, equipment, laboratories, libraries and IT facilities. Additionally, the teaching workload in departments in relation to available faculty is high. Even after spending four years at doctoral level there is no guarantee of a secure job. Most of the education and research institutions, being controlled by the government, are unable to offer the salary and conditions found in the corporate sector. As a result, there is no incentive for successful doctoral candidates to join the academy.

Quantity vs. quality

India has one of the largest networks of institutions of higher education. Ten million students are enrolled and doctorates make up 0.65 per cent of total enrolment. The university system consists of three years of first degree and two years of postgraduate study. Expansion at the graduate level has adversely affected postgraduate research by taking up too much teaching time. The recommendation of the Task Force for Basic Scientific Research in Universities notes is that the number of Ph.D.s should increase fivefold within a span of ten years, while maintaining proper standards (Governments of India 2005). Further expansion, however, demands that universities concentrate on developing standards at the postgraduate and doctorate levels and a separate system should be created for managing the graduate colleges in a university. This will reduce the load on universities.

University research linkages

Doctoral candidates register themselves only in university departments, where they work on various research projects. This means there is a one-way linkage between the university and research institutions and laboratories. The decline in the standards of research in universities is bound to affect the research institutions and laboratories as well. If it were possible to create a reverse linkage between research institutions, laboratories and universities, expertise available in the former could be used to upgrade the quality of doctorates in the latter. As a matter of general principle, mutual relationships and linkages would help to develop the quality of doctorates. In the Indian context this requires that UGC, ICSSR, CSIR, CHR, CPR and ICAR should develop two-way linkages between universities and all research institutions engaged in different disciplines and professions (Shah 2005).

Disciplinary choices

Doctorates by disciplinary choice indicate that 37 and 33 per cent of research students were awarded doctorates in arts and science respectively in 2002–3. The professionals constituted the rest with 30 per cent of doctorate (including commerce) degrees awarded in this area in 2002–3. If we look at the trend during 1997–8 and 2002–3, there has been 3 per cent increase in professional doctorates (see Figures 14.1 and 14.2 for representations of the proportions at the two time periods and Table 14.2 for the trend over the past six years).

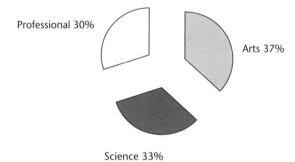

Professional 30% Arts 37%

Science 33%

Figure 14.1 Doctorates awarded in 2002–3.

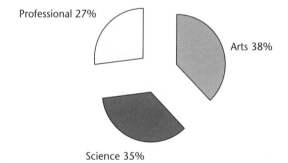

Professional 27% Arts 38%

Science 35%

Figure 14.2 Doctorates awarded in 1997–8.

Critical comment

Pre-doctoral study

As stated earlier, the M.Phil. is a pre-doctoral requirement. It cannot, however, be uniformly applied in all the universities. Besides, there is no standardization in terms of time, and the time period for an M.Phil. varies from one to two years of study. In the universities the minimum eligibility for the

Table 14.2 Number of doctorate degrees awarded by faculty

Faculty	Number of doctorate degrees awarded					
	2002–3[$]	*2001–2*	*2000–1*	*1999–2000*	*1998–9*[$]	*1997–8*
Arts	5,034	4,524	4,398	4,280	4,231	4,256
Science	4,497	3,955	3,727	3,885	3,832	3,896
Commerce/management	857	728	621	571	567[#]	517[#]
Education	554	420	399	364	363	310
Engineering/technology	779	734	778	723	682	696
Medicine	243	219	221	228	225	195
Agriculture	1,042	838	889	787	732	806
Veterinary science	153	110	110	146	136	101
Law	138	110	105	74	74	75
Others*	436	336	296	238	225	255
Total	13,733	11,974	11,534	11,296	11,067	11,107

Source: UGC Annual Report
* Others includes music/fine arts, library science, physical education, journalism, social work, etc.
$ Provisional
# Only commerce

appointment of a lecturer is M.Phil./Ph.D. As a result there is a tendency to discontinue after the M.Phil. and get a lecturership. The Ph.D. is then earned later to assist with promotion. As a result the M.Phil. as a pre-doctoral qualification is defeated. In fact, in my view, the M.Phil. has failed to serve the purpose for which it was created.

Financing doctorates

It is a matter of great concern that government funding for doctoral fellowships is declining, reflected in the falling number of qualifying students in the UGC-JRF test for fellowship. The number of qualifying students fell from 550 in June 1993 to 347 in December 1999 and further to 340 in December 2003 (see Bandyopadhyay 2003). The number of fellowships offered is too small to attract the best talent for doctoral research in the universities. In addition, higher salaries are offered to even the lowest executive in the corporate sector. Research is now attracting second- and third-grade talent. This is a matter of concern for policy-makers. The present dilemma can be solved by the following means: (1) by raising the number and value of fellowships;

(2) by linking the output of doctorates to industry and in turn getting funding support from industry; (3) by linking doctorates to projects supported by the government and civil societies; (4) shifting the preference of funding from research institutions to doctorates in the universities. In other words, the doctorates may be partly linked to the applied research and treated *as* potential income and not as a *means to* potential income in terms of better job prospects.

Monitoring and evaluation

Monitoring during the period of a doctoral programme suffers from a number of deficiencies. Normally the supervisor who has guided the maximum number of scholars is approached by the student for guidance. As a result they are overburdened and do not devote adequate time to the supervision. They may suggest repetitive studies so that the same methodology may be applied in a number of projects (see Mulimani 2003). In order to improve the quality of dissertations there should be some minimum conditions relating to the research credentials of the supervisor and the number of doctoral candidates that a supervisor can guide simultaneously.

There appears to be a mutual obligation of examiners to approve the thesis on a reciprocal basis without going into the merit of the thesis. There are also several instances in which the examiner is chosen without the required specialization in the topic. Due to the weak supervision and evaluation process there are instances of plagiarism. Even when such instances are found, little action is taken. Measures therefore should be in place to ensure that evaluation of dissertations is not simply a formality (see Dahiya 2003; Kapoor 2003).

Doctoral output

The topic of the dissertation is sometimes chosen depending on the ease with which the data can be generated rather than its relevance. As a result the dissertation may not have value in terms of new knowledge. It is also possible that the same topic be chosen for more than one dissertation, as there is no up-to-date repository of all dissertations. Doctoral output should therefore also be linked with the creation of patents.

References

Bandyopadhyay, M. (2003) *Quality Control of Doctoral Research: Role of Research Fellowship.* New Delhi: Association of Indian Universities (AIU).
Chanana, K. (2004) Gender and disciplinary choices: women in higher education in India, paper presented at the UNESCO Colloquium on Research and Higher

Education Policy, 'Knowledge, Access and Governance: Strategies for Change', Paris, 1–3 December.

Dahiya, L.N. (2003) *Quality of Doctoral Research in India: Some Monitoring and Control Issues*. New Delhi: Association of Indian Universities (AIU).

Department of Science and Technology (2002) *Research and Development Statistics 2000–01*. New Delhi: Government of India, Ministry of Science and Technology.

Governments of India (2005) *Task Force for Basic Scientific Research in Universities*, www.ugc.ac.in.

Kapoor, J.N. (2003) *Raising the standard of the Ph.D. Programmes: Some Suggestions*. New Dehli: Association of Indian Universities (AIU).

Mulimani, V.H. (2003) *Standards for the Ph.D. Degree*. New Delhi: Association of Indian Universities (AIU).

Shah, A.M. (2005) Higher education and research: roots of mediocrity, *Economic and Political Weekly*, 28 May – 4 June, www.epw.org.in.

15

Doctoral education in Japan

Shinichi Yamamoto

Introduction

Doctoral study began in Japan in the late nineteenth century when the first modern university, the 'Imperial University', was established in Tokyo in 1887. The intention was to introduce the most advanced knowledge from overseas and to train a future elite intellectual group within the workforce. From these early beginnings Japan now has approximately 75,000 students studying at doctoral level. Doctoral education is centrally controlled in as much as doctoral degree programmes in Japan are allowed only if the granting university is authorized by the relevant government minister. In common with many other countries Japan faces difficulties in terms of the future of its provision of doctoral education with the supply of doctoral students expected to exceed demand by 2010.

The questionnaire

Table 15.1 The questionnaire

Question	Number	Comment
1 Total number of doctoral students studying	74,907	In 2005
2 Number of institutions offering doctoral programmes	409	In 2005
3 Number of different doctoral awards (e.g. including professional doctorates)	2	Officially, there are only two kinds of doctoral award in Japan, 'doctor' (equivalent to a Ph.D.) and 'doctor in professional law'

(Continued overleaf)

Table 15.1 (Continued)

Question	Number	Comment
4 Number of years over which doctorates have been offered in the country	Approximately 120	Since the Imperial University was established in 1887
5 Proportion of full-time to part-time students	80/20	Japan has had no part-time student system until recently. This figure is the proportion of non-adult students to adult students in 2004
6 Average time to completion (in years)	3–5	
7 Success rates	30–80%	There is a lot of diversity between science and humanities
8 Typical age range of doctoral candidates	27–30	
9 Proportion of male/female students	70/30	In 2005
10 Proportion of doctoral students studying who are nationals of other countries	18%	In 2004

Data sources

MEXT survey and Shinichi Yamamoto.

The place of doctoral study in the national/international context

Training future researchers

Doctoral study in Japan has been playing the important role of training future researchers who will work in academia and industry. The system was introduced in 1887 when the first modern university, called the 'Imperial University' was established in Tokyo. This university, which became the University of Tokyo after the Second World War, was composed of several colleges, including law, medicine, engineering, literature and science, and graduate schools. The graduate school at that time, however, was not like a college or school. There was no formal curriculum; students were trained individually by mentors within an apprenticeship mode. In addition, studying at graduate schools was not a prerequisite to become academics.

After the Second World War

Higher education in Japan was completely changed after the war. The main components of it were four-year undergraduate programmes and five-year graduate programmes, usually divided into two-year masters programmes and three-year doctoral programmes. Students must graduate from high school and be more than 18 years old to enrol in undergraduate programmes, although the government recently introduced a new rule that (exceptionally) admits talented 17-year-old students. To enrol in graduate programmes they must finish an undergraduate programme that will usually have taken four years. Thus, almost all the graduate students in Japan are over 22.

Graduate programmes in Japan are divided into three categories: masters programmes, doctoral programmes and professional programmes. The last were introduced in 2003. Masters programmes aim to train various kinds of professionals who will work for industry and others, and also include preparatory training for doctoral programmes. It usually takes two years to get a masters degree but in some programmes it takes only one.

Doctoral programmes mainly aim at training future researchers who will work for academia and industry. It takes five years to get a doctoral degree if students directly enrol from an undergraduate programme and three years if they finish a masters programme. However, in some cases, it is possible to get a doctoral degree in three years in five-year programmes and in one year in three-year programmes. The aim of professional programmes is to train highly skilled professionals in a specific field. The typical ones are law, business and technology management. However, in medical and dental training, Japan has no professional schools. Instead, we train such people in six-year undergraduate programmes that are followed by four-year doctoral programmes. Doctoral programmes in the medical and dental fields are mixtures of academic and professional training for those who already have medical or dental doctors' licences from the government. In other words, we have no distinction between Ph.D.s and professional doctoral degrees such as a doctor of education or doctor of medicine (for an overview of the Japanese system, see Figure 15.1).

In the 1990s, the driving force toward promoting science and technology caused graduate (doctoral) programmes to grow. This was followed by a new government initiative placing a priority on the research agenda, the selective allocation of resources, university–industry collaboration and global-scale competition for research outcomes. One of the most epoch-making facts that should be noted is the Science and Technology Basic Plan that started in 1996. In that plan, universities are regarded as important players for the promotion of science and technology through their research at graduate schools. Today, doctoral education is regarded as an engine for the

15   16   17   18   19   20   21   22   23   24   25   26   27 years old

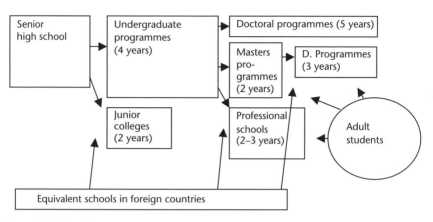

Figure 15.1 Graduate programmes in Japan.

promotion of science and technology by training students to be future researchers and by performing research in various fields including the most advanced scientific research (Yamamoto 1999; MEXT 2005a).

Funding issues

The funding of candidates

There are various kinds of financial support implemented in Japan. For graduate students, a scholarship loan (basically with no interest) provided by the Japan Student Services Organization (this was called the Japan Scholarship Foundation until 2004) has played the biggest role, enabling competent students who lack financial resources to attend graduate schools. More than 40 per cent of masters programme students and more than 60 per cent of doctoral programme students took advantage of these loans in the 1970s. Although the growth of the scholarship does not follow the expansion of student population (the figures have declined to 20 per cent and 50 per cent respectively), the loans provide basic financial support. The amount of this scholarship is 88,000 yen monthly for masters programme students and 122,000 yen (about US$1,100) for doctoral students. Additional support is available if the students pay interest. Students who, after graduation, serve as researchers for universities or related institutions for a certain period had not needed to repay this scholarship loan until the governmental revision in 2004 that abolished this privilege.

In 1985 the Ministry of Education, Culture, Sports, Science and Technology (MEXT) established a new, more competitive fellowship programme for young researchers, called 'Fellowships for Young Japanese Scientists'. With the aim of supporting young researchers who will conduct innovative and trail-blazing research, this programme provides a limited number of fellowships and research grants so as to allow students to concentrate on their research for two to three years. This new fellowship, managed by the Japan Society for the Promotion of Sciences (JSPS), is provided for graduate students and postdoctoral researchers on a highly competitive basis.

If funded, a Ph.D. student is paid 200,000 yen (about US$1,800) monthly and postdoctoral students are paid 364,000 to 446,000 yen monthly. In addition, students are given 1,500,000 yen (about US$14,000) or less as a research grant every year. Along with the promotion of the 'Programme to Support 10,000 Doctoral Students and Postdoctorates', which is included in the Science and Technology Basic Plan, these new competitive support devices are enhanced not only by the MEXT but also by other ministries.

In addition to the scholarship loan and the fellowship, research assistantships and teaching assistantships are also available. Table 15.2 gives a summary of the various schemes of financial support for graduate students drawn up by the MEXT.

The funding of institutions

Institutions that offer graduate programmes are mostly funded by the government, if they are national universities. Private universities are funded mainly from tuition fees. For the national universities, before incorporation in 2004 (which separated universities from the main body of the government and gave them autonomy for management), the government used to provide general university funds each fiscal year. The general university fund was

Table 15.2 Financial support for graduate students in Japan

	Fellowship by JSPS	TA		RA		Scholarship loan
		National universities	Private universities	National universities	Private universities	
Budget million yen	7,559	4,414	1,400	1,843	600	104,100
Eligible doctoral students	3,220	9,281	7,271	4,267	469	27,444
Eligible master's students		4,384	1,213			61,936
	fiscal 2004	fiscal 2003	fiscal 2003	fiscal 2003	fiscal 2003	fiscal 2004

Source: MEXT (2005b)

divided into many elements (e.g. salary for faculty members, equipment, travel, research and administrative costs, miscellaneous costs for students and so on). This system was quite rigid because the universities could not spend more than the limit of each item, nor transfer funds from one item to another. After the incorporation of national universities in 2004, the system of general university funding continued but with greater flexibility.

Kinds of institution

Authorization by MEXT

Doctoral degrees in Japan are granted only if the granting institutions are authorized by the minister of the MEXT. An institution that wants to grant doctoral degrees must be authorized as a graduate school with doctoral programmes. The authorization process for a graduate school starts with the submission of an application for setting up a new school or new graduate programme to the MEXT. The application must satisfy the requirements of the Graduate School Standard (by order of the minister) in terms of teaching staff, curriculum, equipment and facilities, and so on. The minister examines the application in consultation with the Council of University Establishment, which is composed of prominent professors in various fields, and decides whether to authorize it or not. The most important criterion is the quality and number of teaching staff; more than half of the staff must be professors who can supervise doctoral candidates. The professors who are recognized by the Council as eligible to supervise students are called '*Maru-Go* professors' in Japanese, which means that they are authorized by the minister to supervise candidates. This application process takes about a year.

Once authorized, the institution starts a new doctoral programme at its graduate school. A graduate school is a formal entity that provides one to several, and in large universities many, different doctoral programmes. An example of the organization of doctoral programmes is where a university has several graduate schools, i.e., graduate school of literature, a graduate school of engineering, a graduate school of medicine and so on. The graduate school of engineering, for example, provides several different programmes, such as doctoral programmes in civil engineering, mechanical engineering and electronic engineering.

Within each programme

In each programme, there are several teaching members of staff, including associate professors, research associates and the *Maru-Go* professors. Along with teaching staff, there are other kinds of staff, such as technical and clerical. A graduate school accepts new students into its programmes every year. Thus a doctoral programme has dozens of doctoral students or more. Recently the MEXT has required national universities to accept specific numbers of students. This requirement has made universities compete to accept students not only from their undergraduate or masters degree programmes but also those of other universities.

Expansion post-1990

We have observed a large expansion of graduate education in Japan, especially in 1990s, for which there are various explanations. For academics, the expansion was desirable for the status of their institution. For a single professor who teaches and performs research at a graduate school, the increase of graduate students means an increase in their ability to do active research. For the people at the ministry, the graduate school policy is desirable because there is a good possibility of increasing their budget as well as showing how they can respond to the promotion of science and technology.

'Intensive Graduate Programmes' or *Jutenka* in Japanese, which were initiated in the early 1990s by the government as a policy aimed at promoting graduate (doctoral) programmes at major national universities, made every national university think seriously about graduate programmes. The policy gave national universities additional resources when they expanded their doctoral programmes. Most national universities shifted their priority of management from undergraduate programmes toward graduate programmes. They submitted budget requests to the MEXT every year to create new programmes and/or to expand existing programmes. They claimed their graduate programmes would be useful for training human resources that would work not only in academia but also in industry and regional society.

Professorial status

Professors at universities that achieved the *Jutenka* were called graduate professors rather than just professors. A graduate professor became a symbol of high status. In addition to the symbolic merit, they enjoyed higher salaries and more resources. In science and engineering, professors needed manpower to assist with their research activities. Academics in science and engineering prefer research associates and research assistants to money. Their preference is very different from those in the humanities and social sciences, who prefer time and books to manpower (Yamamoto 2004a).

Forms of doctoral study

Doctoral study in Japan is performed under a single system, which leads students being granted Ph.D.s in various fields. Until 1991, Japanese universities granted Ph.D. degrees with various titles, such as doctor of law, doctor of literature, doctor of engineering, doctor of science, doctor of medicine. The MEXT strictly listed these types of doctorate in the Degree Order. Universities in Japan could not grant a doctorate in a new field unless it was listed in the Order. Then, the 1991 reforms made the doctoral degree into a Ph.D. Today, according to the Degree Order of the minister of MEXT, universities can grant Ph.D.s in various fields by identifying their specialty, such as Ph.D. in law, Ph.D. in physics and Ph.D. in engineering.

Japan does not have professional doctorates. In addition there was no notion of a professional dimension within the concept of a doctorate until the 1990s. The definition of doctoral degrees was such that by doing original research the doctoral candidates should add to existing knowledge. In the fields of science, engineering and medical research, however, this definition was somewhat modified according to the international standard so that the doctoral degree was like a 'driver's licence' to perform academic research and professional business. In the humanities and social sciences, the genera-tion of additional knowledge was strictly adhered to as a criterion and thus there were very few who were granted doctorates in those fields. Instead of studying within doctoral programmes, many doctoral degrees were granted in the form of 'thesis doctorates' as the evidence of major research with a long period of self-study.

The MEXT has reformed doctoral study and the degree-granting system several times since then. There remains a time-to-degree problem in Japan. Only 27 per cent of doctoral students were granted degrees in humanities in 2004 and 80.2 per cent in science. In 1991, it was only 4.7 per cent in humanities. Such low completion rates are explained by the fact that some people still believe, especially in humanities and social sciences, that Ph.D.s should be given only to established scholars who have produced great work and should not be given to young students even when they show sufficient enough ability to become researchers.

Fortunately, Japanese graduate students in humanities and social sciences used to be able to find jobs in Japanese academia without Ph.D.s. However, the globalization of higher education does not allow such a situ-ation and Japanese students now need a Ph.D. if they wish to secure posts internationally.

Students and their programmes of study

Students who intend to study at doctoral level must finish an undergraduate programme, if they enter a five-year doctoral programme, and must finish a masters degree if they enter a three-year doctoral programme. Most doctoral programmes in Japan fall into the latter category. Graduate schools provide a two-year masters degree programme followed by three-year doctoral pro-gramme. Thus, it is usual that students who study in doctoral programmes will have finished a masters programmes at the same institution.

In medical and clinical research fields, the doctoral programmes take four years and are directly connected to the six-year undergraduate programmes. It is required by law that medical and dental education is provided as a six-year undergraduate programme. Many students then go to graduate schools of medical and dental research, while they take the national examination for the licences (to practise) for medical and dental doctors.

Supervision

Generally speaking, a student who enrols in a doctoral programme has a supervisor (or more than one) who will supervise them from the beginning of study to the degree-granting. It is often the case that students request by whom they are to be supervised at their entrance examination.

To be doctoral candidates students must attend coursework and gain 30 credits. To get one credit, they must attend 15 hours of lectures or perform 45 hours of laboratory work. This means that students get four credits when they attend a two-hour lecture. Most Japanese graduate schools deliver their coursework for 30 weeks a year.

Supervision is very different between experimental and non-experimental research. Most science and engineering research areas are in the former category and most of the social sciences and humanities are in the latter. In engineering, for example, a student usually has a strong relationship with a professor as soon as they become a graduate student of the masters programme. The professor will have a laboratory and a research team, composed of the professor, a research associate, postdoctoral researchers and graduate students. Students work together every day at the laboratory and are supervised by the senior researchers and the professor. Students perform their research using shared data and information that are found at the laboratory. Their research topics are closely related to the research concern of the professor.

In humanities and social sciences, the student–professor relationship is different. Research is usually done alone although students attend seminars chaired by the professor and can exchange information and views about their research there. However, it is not unusual for students not to meet with their professor every day. Research activity is heavily based on reading books and other material and the research topic is sometimes very different from that of the professor.

Examination

The final examination for a doctoral degree is the critical point for a candidate because it determines whether the candidate will be granted a degree or not. Before the final examination, candidates must finish their coursework and must complete their doctoral thesis. This does not mean that candidates are examined only once during their doctoral programme. First, the results of their coursework are examined by rating and granting credits. The candidates must get more than 30 credits. Then they must write an intermediate paper or masters degree thesis before starting doctoral study. In some universities this stage is quite critical and some students are forced to leave the programme at this point. The role of supervisors increases when the students start writing their doctoral thesis. It is the supervisor that decides whether the doctoral thesis is strong enough to defend. If so, a small committee is organized by agreement with the graduate school. Then, the final examination is carried out by the examination team composed of the supervisor and other professors. Some professors are invited from outside the immediate programme. Following a successful defence, the Ph.D. is granted.

Other issues

The University Council, which has been the advisory body to the minister of the MEXT since 2001, made various recommendations on higher education policy in the 1990s. Among those, in 1998, was *Universities in the 21st Century and their Reform*. In this recommendation, the expansion of the role of graduate education was mentioned. As background information, the recommendation made a projection on the supply of and demands for graduate students, both in masters programmes and doctoral programmes. The result was a forecast as follows: in 2010, demand for graduate students with masters degrees will exceed supply, while supply of doctoral students will exceed demand. This projection was based on the past 10–15 years' data of growing graduate enrolment and growing demand for graduate students.

The MEXT asked a research group composed of several scholars of higher education research and economists to study the future demand and supply of graduate students. This study was done in 1997–8. The main concerns of the study were (i) enrolment on graduate programmes, (ii) the job market for the graduate students, (iii) future enrolment in graduate programmes in 2010, and (iv) the demand for graduate students in 2010. The year of 2010 was regarded as important because the 18-year-old population would continue to decline until that year and therefore enrolment would, in turn, continue to decline. The decline would cause serious problems for higher education management and its systems. Thus various kinds of systemic change will have to be achieved by that year and the graduate education system is no exception.

The study forecast the future demand and supply of graduate students, and the main figures are shown in Table 15.3. The analysis revealed first that it would not be easy, in 2010, for students to find a job at universities and colleges. The forecast was that the number of academic staff (professors and other full-time staff) would be 153,000 in 2010, while it was 158,000 in 1995. There would only be 2300 to 2500 new positions annually. Second, the job market within the industrial sector would be key in terms of demand and supply of human resources. In manufacturing industry, the demand for

Table 15.3 Expected supply and demand of students

	Supply of Students		Demand for Students	
	Case A	Case B	Case A	Case B
Masters course	171,928	168,141	181,298	164,989
Doctoral course	82,009	81,446	60,108	55,786
Total	**253,937**	**249,587**	**241,406**	**220,775**

Source: Ushiogi *et al.* (1988)
Case A is based on past 10 years' trend and Case B is based on past 15 years' trend.

masters students would grow 1.5 to 1.7 times compared with 1997. In service industries, demand would also increase. Demand for doctoral students would also increase by 2010 but supply would increase also.

However, the forecast was based mainly on the past 10 to 15 years' trend observations and did not necessarily include elements such as technology innovation and big educational reform for graduate schools, important factors that would determine the future supply and demand of graduate students. Actually the growth of doctoral enrolment has been larger than forecast. In 2004, enrolment in doctoral programmes was 73,446 and is likely to be larger than the 82,000 estimate for 2010 (Yamamoto 2004b).

These figures strongly indicate that universities are important stakeholders in the development of science, and policy-makers should examine and consider carefully the next step(s) toward better science systems in Japan.

Critical comment

In June 2005, the National Council on Education (*Chu-kyo-shin* in Japanese) published an interim report on graduate education policy titled *Graduate Education in a New Age: Toward the Formation of an Internationally Attractive System* (MEXT 2005b) to enrich graduate programmes in Japan. The Council listed four major functions of graduate education and suggested various reforms in order to train:

• researchers for R&D who are rich in creativity and imagination;
• professionals with highly sophisticated skills;
• academics with good teaching and research skills;
• highly talented people who can play an active role in a knowledge-based society.

Among these, training researchers and academics mainly fall to doctoral programmes, while professionals and highly talented people mainly fall to masters programmes (MEXT 2005b).

Until the late 1980s, the main direction of the reform of graduate education was to secure professional education in the masters programmes rather than to enrich research training in the doctoral programmes. This was partly explained by the fact that masters programmes had tended to be regarded as a preparatory stage for doctoral programmes and thus, in spite of growing demand for professionals, the main aim of the masters programmes tended to be academic research training. Additionally, most academics had been trained at graduate schools and secured employment at universities and thus did not know a great deal about training people for industry. They therefore were not interested in teaching practical and professional matters.

To improve this situation, the MEXT revised 'The Graduate School Standard' and each university must now follow this standard when they plan to establish and expand their graduate programmes. Graduate schools today can open their programmes in the evening, can enrol part-time students, can set their main aim to be professional education rather than research training, and can employ people from the non-academic sector who have special and practical knowledge and skills.

The 1990s witnessed a decade of university reform in Japan. Various kinds of reform, such as governance, management, funding, student services and curriculum, were intended to make the university more accountable to the students, the funding agencies and the general public, in contradiction of the traditional notion of university or faculty autonomy. It has been realized that expanded, broadened higher education and the progress of scientific research have made the Japanese university system unfit for the new requirements of the people. University reform has therefore continued into the early 2000s.

The role of doctoral programmes should be discussed in terms of human resource development not only for academia but also for industry and other sectors of society. There are various kinds of demand for professionals due to the recent fundamental change of industrial structure and the advancement of globalization. One of the problems is that existing graduate programmes do not respond fully to these needs. If there are mismatches between supply of and demand for Ph.D. students, the gap should be filled by improving the quality and system of graduate education as well as making people in industry become aware of the recent reform of graduate education in Japan.

In Japan, outside academia, someone with a Ph.D. is still regarded as a special kind of person that employers find difficult to manage because they believe that Ph.D. graduates tend to care only about their specialty and are thus not flexible within the changing environment of business. Overcoming this belief and giving graduates important roles are the solutions that will fit the new environment of globalization. To do so, there is a large agenda remaining that the government and universities need to address.

References

MEXT (2005a) *Higher Education in Japan – Reports of the Central Council for Education* (digest). Tokyo: MEXT.

MEXT (2005b) *Graduate Education in a New Age: Toward the Formation of an Internationally Attractive System.* Interim report by the Central Council on Education. Tokyo: MEXT.

Ushiogi, M. *et al.* (1998) *Report of the Study on Graduate Education from the Perspective of Quantitative Development.* Tokyo: Japanese Ministry of Education.

Yamamoto, S. (1999) The growing sophistication of research at a time of broadened participation in higher education, in L. Branscomb, F. Kodama and R. Florida (eds) *University–Industry Linkages in Japan and The United States.* Cambridge, MA: MIT Press.

Yamamoto, S. (2004a) An analysis of resource allocation for research, *The Journal of Science Policy and Research Management,* 19(1/2): 68–9.

Yamamoto, S. (2004b) Mismatches in supply and demand for S&T graduates at PhD level, in S. Avveduto (ed.) *Fostering the Development of Human Resources for Science and Technology.* Rome: Biblink Editori.

16

Doctoral education in Mexico

Salvador Malo

Introduction

In terms of research publications, Mexico is ranked twenty-first among Organization for Economic Cooperation and Development (OCDE) countries and second in the Latin American region, after Brazil. Yet it has only 0.5 persons per 1000 of the labour force devoted to research and development, and a total annual graduation of about 1200 Ph.D.s. There are 148 institutions of higher education offering doctoral programmes, however there is some concentration among this number with only 10 per cent of these institutions offering doctoral programmes in ten or more fields of study. As with some other countries at a similar stage of development, Mexico faces the difficulty of creating more synergy between the output of doctoral candidates and the national research and development agenda. At present such candidates tend to remain in the university sector.

The questionnaire

Table 16.1 The questionnaire

Question	Number	Comment
1 Total number of doctoral students studying	10,825	Equivalent to 7.7% of the total of 139,669 graduate students[1]
2 Number of institutions offering doctoral programmes	148	66.2% public and 33.8% private[1]
3 Number of different doctoral awards	525	This is the total number of different doctoral programmes offered.[2] There are no different doctoral awards[1]

4 Number of years over which doctorates have been offered	77	In 1929, doctoral programmes were initiated at the School of Philosophy and Literature at the National University of Mexico[3]
5 Proportion of full-time to part-time students		No reliable data is available on this issue
6 Average time to completion (in years)	5	This is the specified average time to completion; the factual average time is longer
7 Success rates	56%	Estimated by computing first-time enrolment in 1999 (2058 students) and total degree completion in 2003 (995 students). A more precise longitudinal analysis that traces cohorts – not included in official data – would produce somewhat lower completion rates[4]
8 Typical age range of doctoral candidates	24 to 32	The average admission age shows a wide variation since many candidates do not apply to masters and doctoral programmes immediately after earning their first degree
9 Proportion of male/female students	60/40	At UNAM in 2003,[3] the ratio was 55/45[5]
10 Proportion of doctoral students studying who are nationals of other countries	0.8%	See[3]

Note: numbers refer to the sources listed under 'Data sources' in the chapter

Data sources

1 ANUIES, *Anuario Estadístico 2003, Población Escolar de Posgrado*, www.anuies.mx/servicios/e_educacion/docs/pep_rsh03.pdf.
2 By area of study, the enrolment is 25 per cent in social science and administration, 21 per cent in natural and exact sciences, 19 per cent in education and humanities, 18 per cent in engineering and technology, 10 per cent in health sciences and 6 per cent in agricultural sciences.
3 *Diagnóstico y perspectivas de los estudios de posgrado en México*, www. iesalc.unesco.org.ve; Urquidi, V.L. and Lajous-Vargas, A. (1969) *Educación Superior, Ciencia y Tecnología en el Desarrollo de México*. Mexico: El Colegio de México.
4 ANUIES, *Anuario Estadístico 2002*.
5 UNAM, *Agenda Estadística 2004*, www.planeacion.unam.mx.

The place of doctoral study in the national/international context

The development of doctoral study

The introduction of doctoral programmes in Mexico took place around the middle of the twentieth century. These programmes evolved both as an outgrowth of the existing scholarly tradition within the humanities (philosophy), and through the influence of the new research-oriented faculty, in the form of several scientists who had returned from abroad after having obtained their training mostly in Europe and the USA. As with many other aspects of higher education in the country, these programmes were initiated at the Universidad Nacional Autónoma de México (UNAM), spreading out later to other universities.

Doctoral studies in Mexico continue to be affected by international forces and the growing internationalization of higher education. In addition to the steady number of scientists who join the academic staff of Mexican universities after earning their doctoral degrees in other countries, there has been a number of contributory factors in relation to the development of doctoral education in Mexico, notably: (a) the negotiation of trade agreements within large geographical regions; (b) the availability of scholarships and financial aid programmes attracting graduate students to American, Canadian and some European universities; and (c) the trend toward an increment in the mobility of students and academic staff, such as the Erasmus and Socrates programmes of the European Union (EU).

The role of doctoral studies in relation to research and development

Doctoral studies play a central role in Mexican research policy due to the importance Ph.D. graduates have in the overall national research and development (R&D) effort, as well as the fact that most of the research activities of the country takes place within higher education institutions. Not withstanding this, personnel in science and technology in Mexico are extremely scarce. As already mentioned, there are only some 0.5 persons devoted to research and development per 1000 individuals in the labour force, and a total annual graduation of about 1200 Ph.D.s. There are some 148 institutions of higher education offering doctoral programmes, only 10 per cent of which offer programmes in ten or more fields of study. Table 16.2 identifies those having programmes in the highest number of fields of study (COMEPO 2004).

Table 16.2 Institutions with the highest number of doctoral programmes in Mexico

Institution	Programmes
Universidad Nacional Autónoma de México	32
Universidad Autónoma de Nuevo León	23
Centro de Investigación y de Estudios Avanzados	22
Universidad de Guadalajara	20
Colegio de Graduados: Universidad Autónoma de Chapingo	19
Instituto Politécnico Nacional	18
Universidad Autónoma Metropolitana	15
Instituto Tecnológico de Estudios Superiores de Monterrey	13
Universidad Autónoma del Estado de México	11
Universidad Autónoma de Puebla	11
Universidad Iberoamericana	10

Funding issues

The National Council for Science and Technology (CONACYT) and the Ministry of Education (SEP) engage in different activities and programmes to promote graduate studies throughout the country, and to plan their growth in order to satisfy the increasing demand for quality in higher educatio and R&D. In 1976, CONACYT produced the first long-term plan for Mexico's scientific and technological development (CONACYT 1976a) and established the first major programme for human resources development that was soon able to receive international financial support (CONACYT 1976b). This programme focused on the policies needed to increase the limited number of doctoral graduates in the country.

Recently, these two federal government agencies have promoted various initiatives, many of which relate to doctoral studies. SEP operates several programmes that provide universities with grants to increase the number of their academic staff holding Ph.D. degrees, promote their doctoral cycles or support institutional development through competitive funding mechanisms that favour research activities and quality in academia. In addition, it has been instrumental in the establishment, operation and development of several non-governmental quality assurance, testing, accreditation and certification agencies (see www.sep.gob.mx/wb2/sep/sep_Educacion_Superior). CONACYT provides scholarships to students who pursue masters and doctoral studies in recognized graduate programmes, in Mexico as well as abroad. In 2003, Mexico's federal agencies awarded 23,804 students with scholarships to pursue graduate studies (CONACYT 2004). Finally, several of the large research universities, such as the UNAM and the Centro de Investigación y Estudios Avanzados (CINVESTAV), operate their own scholarship and financial aid schemes for students admitted to their programmes. It should also be noted that the great majority of public institutions offering doctoral programmes do not charge tuition fees.

CONACYT operates the *Sistema Nacional de Investigadores* (SNI) (see www.conacyt.mx/sni), which provides fellowships to academics and faculty who are active in research, as revealed by their yearly publications in peer-reviewed journals or in the writing of books. An individual agreement is established and renewed every three or four years that, in addition to providing substantial pecuniary rewards, allows the researcher to award a stipend to some of their students pursuing a doctoral degree. The number of researchers in a particular department or institution that belong to the SNI has a strong correlation with the quality and efficiency of the doctoral programmes administered by that institution. Therefore, SNI membership and level (there are four levels ranging from the equivalent of an entry-level faculty to the full professor position) is a good indicator of the quality of a given programme.

CONACYT also manages the *Padrón Nacional de Posgrado* (Graduate Programme Registry (see www.conacyt.mx/forma_cientif_tecno/prog_pos_nal/padron_nal_pos.htm), an assessment exercise that recognizes the best master and doctoral programmes in the country. It also manages the operation of the largest scholarship programme for students wishing to pursue graduate studies in research related areas, and competitive grant systems for R&D in basic and applied sciences, as well as in social sciences and the humanities.

Kinds of institution

Some of the large public research universities in Mexico are organized into professional schools, where most of the teaching activities are carried out, together with institutes and centres, where the most significant amount of research activity takes place. In these universities, doctoral programmes are organized through a 'graduate studies' office which coordinates the schools and the research centres. The separation between the main objectives of schools and institutes has created a two-class system within institutions, where different assessment and reward programmes coexist to address the needs of 'teaching' professors and those of the 'research' professors. An additional inconvenience, arising as a result of the separation between schools and institutes, is the lack of everyday contact between undergraduates attending schools to take courses and the research faculty at the institutes. Among this type of institution UNAM constitutes the leading research institution in Mexico, granting 427 doctoral degrees in 2003 and 478 in 2004 (UNAM 2004, 2005).

The majority of universities, however, follow a more direct route, having doctoral students attend their different professional schools or departments to undertake the study programmes associated with their particular area or field of activity. Among the public universities, the Universidad Autónoma

Metropolitana (UAM), the Universidad de Guadalajara (UG) and the Universidad Autónoma de Nuevo León (UANL) also have significant numbers of researchers (UAM, www.uam.mx; UG, www.udg.mx; UANL, www.uanl.mx). By contrast, research constitutes a substantial activity in only a handful of the numerous private universities in Mexico, the Instituto Tecnológico y de Estudios Superiores de Monterrey (ITESM) and the Universidad Iberoamericana (UIA) are two examples (ITESM 2005; UIA 2005).

Finally there is a significant number of higher education institutions that do not have undergraduate study programmes and offer only masters and doctoral degrees. CINVESTAV, the second most important research centre in the country is an 'only-graduates' institution, granting 151 doctoral degrees in 2003 in natural and exact sciences, biological and health disciplines, technology and engineering, social sciences and humanities (CINVESTAV, www.cinvestav.mx/publicaciones/anuario03/introduccion.pdf). Today, it employs more than 500 researchers in its eight departments, located in Mexico City, Guadalajara, Irapuato, Mérida, Querétaro and Saltillo.

According to CONACYT's 2001–3 report, of the total number of doctoral students enrolled in the year 2000 (8385), those who earned their degree accounted for 1220 (CONACYT 2004). Distribution of enrolment, by field of doctoral studies, shows that the highest concentration was in the natural and exact sciences (29.7 per cent), followed by the social sciences and administration (20.7 per cent), engineering and technology (16.5 per cent), education and humanities (16.2 per cent), health sciences (11.3 per cent) and agriculture (5.6 per cent).

Forms of doctoral study

Common form of doctoral study

The most accepted form of doctoral studies, in Mexico, requires that students be enrolled in accredited doctoral programmes, and complete their degree through a Ph.D. thesis that is complemented with at least one – usually several – publications in reputable international research journals. These programmes share similar operational procedures, both among themselves and with the doctoral programmes of US universities, such as assigning each student admitted into the programme a mentor, whose main responsibility is to assist the student in planning academic activities, according to the study programme, as well as supervising the different stages of the student's dissertation. In addition, advanced institutions, such as the UNAM, require the appointment of a tutorial committee that must approve both the dissertation project and the student's academic plan. This committee also supervises the student's progress, and assigns a basic course schedule covering the first four or five semesters (UNAM 2001). The tutorial system at the UNAM has been developed most successfully in programmes related to the natural sciences and, to a lesser extent, in the humanities and social sciences.

This may be due to the fact that full-time students are more numerous in the former. Despite the sizeable increase in the number of full-time students in the humanities and social sciences, there still exists a significant number of part-time students.

Other institutions, mostly the private universities, offer more rigid doctoral programmes, incorporating a heavy course load and a very structured path towards the completion of the degree. The absence of a research tradition within the departments is usually offset by the establishment of joint agreements with reputable universities in Europe, Canada or the USA.

Public and private institutions

Since the 1980s, the three main, doctoral-granting institutions in Mexico, the UNAM, the CINVESTAV and the UAM, together with three or four of the largest universities in the country, have produced a steady supply of new doctoral graduates. A distinct characteristic of these graduates is that almost all of them have come from public institutions and have mostly received their Ph.D. degrees on basic research areas in the natural sciences, health sciences and humanities. Faculty personnel at large public institutions have competed successfully for government and institutional grants to set up laboratory and infrastructure facilities. Private universities, in contrast, have enjoyed very limited experimental infrastructure and have therefore focused most of their doctoral programmes on areas of knowledge that do not require expensive investments in modern laboratories, libraries and information facilities.

When groups of scientists decide to embark on ambitious research projects involving graduate students and considerable subsidies (the so-called 'Big Science' projects), they rely on international collaboration agreements and networks for access to specialized resources abroad, such as particle accelerators, telescopes or historical archives, to name but a few examples. This practice enhances graduate student and academic international mobility but it contrasts sharply with the almost non-existent student exchanges within the country, except for the intense flow of graduate students towards the leading institutions in the Mexico City metropolitan area.

International collaboration

International collaboration in graduate programmes and research departments is evident from the number of publications they produce that include authors from foreign institutions. Graduate students are encouraged to be ever aware of new developments in their field of specialty, regardless of origin. In fact, to avoid endogamous faculty growth, most graduate programmes refrain from hiring their own former students into tenure-track positions, or at least persuade them to do postgraduate work at other institutions overseas for a minimum of a year before presenting a job application. At the UNAM this practice is mandatory in the exact and natural sciences areas, but infrequent in the social sciences and humanities graduate programmes.

Doctoral programmes recognized by CONACYT as being of high quality are equivalent to those found in the best universities in the USA or Europe and, therefore, one may conclude that individuals who have received their training in these programmes have the skills to make an independent contribution to the advancement of knowledge through original scholarly research. However, it is a fact that most Ph.D. graduates are involved in high-level research work in academic centres, leaving a negligible fraction stationed at the very few industries that boast advanced research facilities. Thus, the increase in doctoral graduates is not reflected in the country's overall productivity growth.

In Mexico, the staff at research universities is still almost *completely* free to select and explore any subject that stimulates their intellect, without external pressures to modify their research or adapt their methodology to accord with departmental or institutional overall planning guidelines.

The traditional sense of scholarship

Doctoral candidates are exposed to a very competent academic base, especially those who pursue their degrees at the main research universities. Graduate students receive a thorough training in their particular or specialized field of knowledge but want for the traditional sense of *scholarship*, as the number of true scholars in the country has diminished below what one might consider the minimum critical mass. Intellectuals and academics who sought refuge in Mexico from the various European calamities during the first half of the twentieth century, pioneered the scientific and humanistic tradition in the country. They cultivated an integrated and multidimensional manner of knowledge production, on a broad spectrum of fields that contrasts with the current over-specialized approach to research in almost any given field.

Doctoral programmes and technology transfer

The other side of the coin is related to the question: what measures has the productive sector adopted to attract young high-level researchers? Small and medium enterprises comprise the core of Mexican industry and they seldom need to invest in R&D activities in order to increase productivity. Larger enterprises that do have the potential to benefit from innovation derived from in-house research groups prefer to rely on technological transfer and acquisition activities rather than invest in those groups. The net result is the practical divide between doctoral programmes and the lack of demand for high-level researchers from the productive sector. Recently, CONACYT launched a strategy aimed at linking researchers and firms, which includes 30 consortium projects, each with 70 researchers (www.conacyt.mx, link to *redes y consorcios*). Most of the projects consist of partnerships that involve enterprises and research centres sharing efforts, with a view to improving competitiveness in Mexican industry. As a result of this initiative, in May 2005, the World Bank granted a US$250 million loan to fund the long-term project (2006–15) 'Innovation for competitiveness'.

Students and their programmes of study

There is an ample spectrum of options regarding the qualifications of candidates as well as the formal periods of study. In general, students are required to have a first cycle or *licenciatura* degree (i.e. professional) in any of the compatible professions to be admitted into a graduate programme which, in general, has a two-stage structure: masters and doctoral training. For example, a candidate on a Ph.D. programme in astronomy is required to have a first cycle degree in physics, engineering or chemistry. Humanities and social sciences require a more intense course load of about six to eight semesters during the masters phase before the candidate elaborates their dissertation project which must be approved by an ad hoc tutorial committee. Therefore, the periods of completion in these disciplines are usually very long, in some cases exceeding ten years. In the sciences, the course loads are usually shorter, from four to six semesters, and students are encouraged to engage in research early on in their programmes. Most doctoral programmes have a formal four- to six-year duration including the masters stage and are mainly devoted to research and scholarship. As mentioned above, the demand for doctorates in the productive sector is still negligible.

Supervision

Students are supervised by professors who have previously been selected by the student as a potential mentor. In some institutions like the CINVESTAV, students are required to take brief summer admission courses and tests before they are interviewed by the department faculty that in turn assigns a particular mentor. The larger institutions like the UNAM and UAM enjoy the very favourable status of having an almost one-to-one ratio of full professors to doctoral students and therefore the latter are encouraged to make a free choice based on personal interviews with the department's research faculty.

Examination

Most doctoral programmes require the approval of a set of qualifying examinations administered at the end of the masters cycle in order to become a Ph.D. candidate. The completion of the Ph.D. degree involves the preparation of a dissertation based on original research work and the successful presentation to a jury of between five and seven professors appointed by the department. This public, oral examination explores the candidate's ability to define a research project and their ability to explore the solutions, consequences and ramifications derived from the original project. The oral examination is, in fact, the culmination of challenging discussions with the jury members in what is called 'the defence of the thesis'.

Other issues

According to the Institute for Scientific Information (ISI), in 2003 Mexico produced 5783 papers representing about 0.72 per cent of world publications. About a fifth of these publications were concerned with physics, followed by health sciences (12.5 per cent), plants and animals (12 per cent) and chemistry (11.5 per cent). Each of the other disciplines represents less than 8 per cent of the country's scientific contribution. The *impact factor* provides a more detailed indicator of the publication data, being proportional to the number of citations a particular paper receives in the five-year period after its publication. This indicator shows that the disciplines that represent the largest fraction of the country's publications, and also those that receive more citations – physics, chemistry and plants and animals – have an overall *below* average impact factor, whereas those having the largest impact factor are, in decreasing order: astrophysics (6.6), immunology (5.6), molecular biology (5.4), neurosciences (4.4) and microbiology (4.3) (CONACYT 2004).

During the five-year period 1999–2003, the UNAM published 12,667 articles in international journals, with an average impact factor of 3.1, the largest in the country. CINVESTAV follows, with 5029 articles producing an average impact factor of 2.8. The UAM is the third research institution, with 1922 articles averaging an impact factor of 2.4.

Critical comment

One of the main weaknesses of doctoral programmes in Mexico is their distinct propensity toward promoting *systematic inbreeding*, that is, to consolidating a system devoted to the advancement of knowledge that serves only itself. This system has doctoral programmes of good – even high – quality, that enjoy ample international recognition, and that provide first-class training for graduate students. Nevertheless, it has not yet developed a relationship with the country's productive sector and, in some cases, has even failed to do so with respect to the undergraduate programmes offered by the same institution. One may argue that a doctoral programme should, as one of its main objectives, produce individuals with particular skills for original research, however, there is no regulation that compels Ph.D.s to work *only* at academic institutions, and no effective actions have been implemented to create a more meaningful and synergistic relationship between doctoral programmes and industry. Of course, there are some individual exceptions, however it is a fact that many doctoral programmes do not contemplate a wider horizon beyond that presented by the academic environment itself. One can say that another important weakness is low productivity. The number of Ph.D.s graduating every year is rather small compared to the overall undergraduate population and also in comparison with the total Mexican population.

References

COMEPO (Consejo Mexicano de Estudios de Posgrado) (2004) *Plan de Desarrollo del Posgrado Nacional*, www.comepo.org.mx.

CONACYT (Consejo Nacional de Ciencia y Tecnología) (1976a) *Plan Nacional Indicativo de Ciencia y Tecnología*. México, DF: CONACYT.

CONACYT (1976b) *Programa Nacional Controlado de Becas*. México, DF: CONACYT.

CONACYT (2004) *Informe 2001–2003 y Perspectivas para el 2004*, www.conacyt.mx. Mexico, DF: CONACYT.

ITESM (2005) *La Investigación y el Posgrado 2003–2004*. Tecnológico de Monterrey, México.

UIA (2005) *Primer Informe del Rector 2004–2005*. Mexico: Universidad Iberoamericana.

UNAM (Universidad Nacional Autónoma de México) (2001) *Reglamento General de Estudios de Posgrado*. México: Dirección de General de Estudios de Legislación Universitaria.

UNAM (Universidad Nacional Autónoma de México) (2004) *Agenda Estadística 2004*. México: UNAM.

UNAM (Universidad Nacional Autónoma de México) (2005) *Agenda Estadística 2005*. México: UNAM.

17

Doctoral education in South Africa: the challenge for development

Ahmed Bawa

Introduction

South Africa has adopted a macro-economic plan that sees it as becoming more integrated into the global knowledge economy. One of its major challenges is to understand how to increase its innovation capacity and there are many components to a strategy that is aimed at achieving this. An indispensable aspect of such a strategy is a substantial improvement in the system's capacity to produce a significantly larger number of Ph.D.s. The major crisis facing higher education in South Africa is the sluggishness with which it is producing a new generation of academics. It is not at all clear that the conditions exist for an effective approach to this. This chapter explores the growth of doctoral study in a higher education system that is operating in a post-apartheid era and where some issues of identity and legitimacy remain unresolved.

The questionnaire

Table 17.1 The questionnaire

Question	Number	Comment
1 Total number of doctoral students studying	8,112	These are figures for 2003
2 Number of institutions offering doctoral programmes	23	This is the number of public higher education institutions in South Africa
3 Number of different doctoral awards (e.g. including professional doctorates)	2	Ph.D. and D. Tech at the moment. The latter are offered at universities of technology. There are discussions underway for 'professional' doctorates at other institutions

(Continued overleaf)

Table 17.1 (Continued)

Question	Number	Comment
4 Number of years over which doctorates have been offered in the country		To be determined
5 Proportion of full-time to part-time students		This data is not available at the current time
6 Average time to completion (in years)	3.5 4.5	In natural sciences In human sciences
7 Success rates	Less than 12%	There is currently deep concern relating to the throughput rates
8 Typical age range of doctoral candidates	25–30	Most candidates come directly from the masters degrees. In education and medicine students come later in their careers
9 Proportion of male/female students	1:5	A more detailed analysis is given in the text
10 Proportion of doctoral students studying who are nationals of other countries	23%	These students are mainly from other African countries

Data sources

The data sources are mainly from the HEMIS (Higher Education Management Information System) site that is managed by the Department of Education. Some of the data has been drawn from the Human Resources for Knowledge Production Conference held in Cape Town on the 23–4 June 2005.

The place of doctoral study in the national/international context

The pressures of the post-apartheid era

The higher education system in South Africa has responded to the pressures of transformation and change in a post-apartheid era (see Cloete *et al.* 2002). Three days in late April 1994 saw South Africans stand in long winding queues to vote in the first ever fully democratic election. The African National Congress, which was to emerge as the governing party, went into the election on the basis of a programme of action that was captured in a manifesto called *The Reconstruction and Development Programme* (*RDP*). It defined three pillars on which the new government was to base a large, integrated and an all-encompassing policy development process. The first was the need for reconstruction in a society that is characterized by deeply racialized inequalities. The second relates to the need for economic growth within a globalization framework, to move towards global competitiveness and to enter the terrain of what Castells has described as the rise of the network society or the knowledge economy (1996: 1). The third of the pillars relates to the need for the entrenchment of democracy and social justice.

Prior to 1994, the national higher education system was subjected to a variety of very substantial investigations that included local and international experts, such as that funded by the International Development Research Centre (IDRC 1992). The findings relevant to the issues discussed in this chapter may be summarized as follows.

- The first was that the system was deeply fragmented. The strong, better-funded research institutions were historically white, while the historically black institutions had poor research and graduate education profiles. The universities and 'technikons' occupied very different conceptual spaces within the higher education system and were hopelessly disarticulated in terms of student mobility.
- The second was a similar disarticulation of the higher education system from the needs of the South African context in two respects: first its disarticulation with the reconstruction needs of the new South Africa and second its disconnection from the challenges that face South African industry. While the South African research system (which has approximately 0.5 per cent of the world's researchers) produced about 0.5 per cent of the published research in internationally recognized journals, its output of patents and commercializable intellectual property was much smaller than those of other comparable science systems.
- The third was the identification of the deep structural imbalances that permeated the system in terms of race and gender.

The post-1994 era in South African higher education

The *RDP* acted as a backdrop for the policy processes that unfolded. In short, in terms of the policy processes that took place in the post-1994 period the former uncomplicated, unquestioned place of higher education in apartheid society came under scrutiny. This was partly due to the high levels of contestation relating to the public purse (for housing, health etc.) and partly because there were strong perceptions that the existing system had been geared to meet the needs of white South Africa. The Treasury threatened further cuts for the sector unless clear indications of progressive transformation were achieved and measures of quality were instituted. The national Department of Education created the Higher Education Quality Committee. It subjected higher education to the 'rigours' of a new South African

Qualifications Authority as a means to tie higher education into a national education and training paradigm within a National Qualifications Framework. It also produced a Higher Education Act that opened the way for a much heavier 'steering' role for the government in higher education.

Of immediate relevance to the discussion on doctoral education in post-apartheid South Africa was the policy investigation into the science system more generally. This investigation gave rise to the establishment of a national system of innovation that brought together into a single framework the research systems of the higher education sector, the private industrial sector, the science councils and government laboratories. One of the major engines for the development of coherence, articulation, change of ethos etc. has been the institutionalization of large funding drivers such as the Innovation Fund.

Research and development as a part of GDP

More recently there has been a Department of Science and Technology decision to raise the resources to take up the national spend on research and development (R&D) from 0.7 to 1 per cent of gross domestic product (GDP) – one approach to enhance the capacity of the science system to compete globally. A report for a recent conference produced by the Human Sciences Research Council (HSRC 2005) indicates that to make good use of the increased resources for R&D there is a need to take up the spend on Ph.D. education by a factor of three or four. The reason for this is that according to this report the current annual output of Ph.D.s makes up just 0.002 per cent of the population. In India this figure is 0.01 per cent and in the USA it is 0.02 per cent. Of concern for the South African higher education system is the fact that the current throughput rate is of the order of 12 per cent of the registered cohort. There are currently about 8000 Ph.D. students registered and about 1000 graduate annually. (The data in this section is taken primarily from HSRC 2005.)

The question that is now being posed is whether there is capacity in the higher education system to take on the challenge of raising its output of Ph.D.s at an unprecedented level and to do this without eroding quality. Already there have been three or four significant steps taken to address this issue. The Department of Science and Technology has announced the 'South African Research Chairs Initiative', a massive programme of developing up to 210 research chairs as additional capacity in the national system. These chairs will be required to focus on graduate education.

The second initiative is a new higher education funding paradigm that targets higher levels of subsidy at graduate education. The problem with this approach is that while subsidy-based funding helps to nudge institutions in particular directions, these may not necessarily converge with the particular strategic challenges that are faced by the national system.

A third initiative was begun earlier on. Large funding drivers were put in place by the Department of Science and Technology and the Department of

Trade and Industry that bring together university–industry R&D partnerships on the basis that this would involve graduate students in industry-based research activities. This has had an influence on the diversification of the research base of higher education institutions and it provides much welcomed resources for masters and Ph.D. students.

Each of these influences doctoral education in complicated ways. It is however safe to say that there are other powerful de-cohering forces on higher education that help to undermine these initiatives.

Funding issues

Institutional funding

There has already been some indication of the national higher education funding system. The extent to which institutions are dependent on the public purse really depends on the nature of the institution and in particular whether or not it attracts sufficient numbers of fee-paying students, is able to generate large amounts of third-stream funding or funding from investments. Success in these areas is mainly a function of the history of the institution, whether or not the institution has a substantial research orientation and whether or not the institution has an endowment base or a historical asset base that permits it to generate significant amounts of third-stream income.

The national Department of Education runs a full-time equivalent (FTE) based subsidy system with categories that are clustered in terms of nominal assessments of the cost of programme delivery. There are also special funds aimed at projects deemed to be of national strategic consequence. Access to higher education for young South Africans who are academically underprepared due to the disastrous state of most South Africa schools would be an example of this. Another would be the research subsidy system based on the publications output. As was alluded to above, the subsidy for doctoral studies has been significantly increased in the recent past.

How Ph.D. candidates are funded

The state of funding for Ph.D. students depends heavily on the nature of the institution at which the student wishes to study and on the discipline in which the student wishes to work.

The National Research Foundation (NRF), which may be regarded as the South African equivalent of the National Science Foundation in the USA, has funding mechanisms for free-standing Ph.D. candidates. These are free-standing in the sense that they are not connected to a particular supervisor or a particular research programme. These scholarships are available to be deployed mainly in South Africa but with a few kept for international deployment. The value of these scholarships was R55,000 (approximately £5000) in 2006. Most supervisors of Ph.D. students will indicate that the value of these scholarships is hopelessly insufficient. The reason for this is that the labour market is quite severely distorted in the sense that individuals with a masters degree will be able to enter the labour market, both in the public and private sectors, at salary levels that may be at least four or five times the level of these scholarships.

The higher education institutions, depending on their funding capacity, may contribute to building packages that are more realistic. There is how-ever a structural challenge that faces the system. Academic salaries have slipped back disastrously in relation to other salaries in the public and private sectors. Consequently when suitable packages are built up for doctoral students these may actually compete with the salaries of younger academics (and thus supervisors). One of the outcomes of this funding situation is that a significant number of doctoral students are part-time. They work in full-time or part-time jobs and then spend way in excess of the minimum number of three years to obtain a doctoral degree.

Several institutions, as a means to address the unacceptable race imbal-ance in terms of their staff structures, are employing the best masters graduates from what in South Africa are called the 'designated groups' as lecturers. These appointments are made conditionally in the sense that these junior faculty members are guaranteed tenured appointments on the basis that they satisfy certain conditions such as having made significant progress towards a Ph.D. and having published at least one article in a 'recognized' peer-reviewed journal. This seems to work well where it has been tried.

Kinds of institution

Kinds of institutions offering the awards

South Africa has a unitary higher education system and what used to be called the 'technikons' are now called either 'universities of technology' or 'institutes of technology'. Alongside the diverse set of universities, these institutions may also offer doctoral studies. In the new higher education landscape there are 23 institutions and each has the necessary legal machinery to offer doctoral studies. Whether institutions do offer doctoral degrees or not in specific areas depends fundamentally on internal decisions that relate to capacity. The Higher Education Quality Committee (HEQC), which is the national quality assurance agency, lays out certain processes and benchmarks as a means to allow institutions to assess this capacity within a national framework.

The organization of awarding institutions

Most graduate programmes at South African universities are organized on a faculty-by-faculty basis, where faculty refers to, for example, the Faculty of Science or the Faculty of Education. Usually, outside of general university rules that relate mainly to quality control issues, faculties have the decision-making processes devolved to them to organize the way in which graduate studies are offered. Having said this, some graduate studies enterprises are organized within departments/schools in ways that mimic the way in which graduate schools organize graduate education. For instance the School of Development Studies at the University of KwaZulu-Natal has a programme of coursework for graduate studies in a range of areas and these take a modular form with a set of core courses and then a set of wrap-around courses depending on the area of specialization of each student. These are managed, administratively and academically, within the School.

Each faculty will have a postgraduate committee that is usually chaired by the dean or by a deputy dean. This committee manages the curriculum, the examination process, any challenges related to the process of supervision and other issues.

Forms of doctoral study

At the moment there are just three doctoral qualifications available to South African universities that are subsidized by the state: the Ph.D. (Doctor of Philosophy), D. Tech (Doctor of Technology) and the 'Senior Doctorate'. The last of these is aimed at senior individuals who have achieved a very substantial body of published research with findings that have caused change in the direction of the discipline.

Students and their programmes of study

The qualifications required of candidates

The degree structure at South African universities is fairly standard, though there is some flexibility. The National Qualifications Framework defines the relationship between the different qualifications that exist in the system. A masters degree is the usual entry requirement into doctoral education. The masters is nominally a one-year qualification but usually takes up to two years. It rests upon a one-year honours qualification, which is usually made up of a set of highly intensive, specialized courses with a research project. This in turn is built on the bachelors qualification that is a three-year under-graduate qualification and generally has two majors. Approximately 40 per cent of the students with a bachelors qualification continue into the honours.

There are cases where some structured two-year masters programmes accept students directly from the bachelors qualification but this is not the usual route.

Periods of study

The Ph.D. is nominally a three-year qualification, though a minimum time for a Ph.D. is set at two years. In the sciences the average completion time is slightly more than three years. In the humanities it is more like four and a half years.

Modes of study

It was mentioned earlier that financial circumstances often act to apply pressure on students to consider part-time study though it must be said that it is very rare that a Ph.D. in the natural, biomedical and engineering sciences is done in this mode. There are particular faculties, especially education and management studies, in which there is a preponderance for doctoral studies to be done in the part-time mode. Students may formally register for part-time study.

Employment destinations

The South African labour market is for the most part rigid but it is evolving. The traditional trajectory for doctoral graduates was either into academic positions at universities or into the research positions in what we might call the performing science councils and in private sector laboratories. In recent years there are new trajectories that have opened up. Many of the senior officials in the civil service who took up positions in the post-1994 era hold Ph.D.s.

Gender and doctoral studies

The gender profile of Ph.D. enrolments is complex and needs to be looked at in terms of what are called the CESM (Classification of Educational Study Matter) categories if a thorough analysis is to be made. An aggregation analysis of the 2003 national enrolments indicates that the participation of men is approximately 50 per cent higher than that for women. This is a reversal of a trend at the undergraduate level where the participation rates of women is approximately 4–6 per cent higher than those of men. This ratio in terms of doctoral *graduation* rates in 2003 is very much the same, about 1:1.5.

It is also instructive to look at the doctoral enrolments in the human and natural sciences as a lens to analyse gender differences. Aggregate figures (again referring to the data for 2003) indicate that the enrolments in the human sciences are approximately 40 per cent higher than those in the natural sciences. In the human sciences the participation of men is 40 per cent higher than that of women and in the natural sciences this ratio heads up to 60 per cent.

In the South African context it is important to perform an analysis of the participation of women relative to men in terms of the old apartheid race categories since these are still used as a means to measure the transformation of the system. It is interesting to note that the participation rate of African South African women in doctoral education is about 9 per cent of the total enrolments while that of African men is about 21 per cent, producing a ratio of about 2.3:1. For Indian and white South Africans this is about 1.3:1 and it is about 15:1 for 'coloured' South Africans.

In summary, the total number of doctoral students registered in 2003 numbered 8112 and the participation rate of men at this level is approximately 50 per cent higher than that of women.

(Note that all the data in this section are drawn from the Higher Education Management Information System of the national Department of Education.)

Race and doctoral studies

In the South African context it is important to understand the way in which its racialized past plays itself out in terms of participation rates in doctoral education. In the mid-1990s more than 80 per cent of South Africa's science system was white and more importantly about 80 per cent of the under-graduate and graduate students in the sciences at that time were white. Drawing once again from the cohort data of 2003, of the 8112 registered doctoral students, some 30 per cent were African South Africans, 5 per cent were 'coloured' South Africans, 9 per cent were Indian South Africans and 56 per cent were white South Africans. This refers to the overall system in terms of the CESM categories.

This has to be seen in the context of a population of 46.5 million in 2003 wherein the racial categorization was: Africans 80 per cent, 'coloureds' 9 per cent, Indians 2 per cent and whites 9 per cent. This indicates that there is still a very substantial under-representation of Africans and 'coloureds' and an over-representation of whites and Indians in these cohorts. But what has the trajectory been? In 1993, African students made up only 7 per cent of the total Ph.D. enrolment and whites made up 87 per cent of the cohort. These changes occurred through a fairly substantial increase in participation from 4933 in 1993 to 8112 in 2003.

It is also interesting to observe that the ratio of the human science/natural science enrolments is 1.6:1 for Africans, 1.4:1 for 'coloureds', 1.5:1 for

Indians and 1.3:1 for whites. This implies that there is substantial participation in all the race groups in both areas without any large imbalances.

Issues of religion

As far as it is possible to assess there are no clear and discernable enrolment characterizations relating to the impact of religion. There are, however, the obvious ones in the sense that most universities will have fairly substantial schools of theology and these would have a preponderance of Christian students.

Supervision

The predominant mode of supervision continues to be the traditional apprenticeship model that connects students to single supervisors in relationships that are often tight and close. This traditional model has worked well although, from time to time there are tensions and challenges brought to bear on these. For instance:

- there are often misunderstandings of the mutual roles of the supervisors and students in these relationships which give rise to a breakdown of trust; many universities are now developing legal or semi-legal contracts that make clear what is expected of each party in these, often complex, relationships;
- from time to time clashes occur between student and supervisor that relate to matters of academic freedom and often these are corrected through some sort of mediation;
- in the South African context conflicts sometimes come into being on the basis of perceived or real concerns over the power configurations that arise from the race and gender imbalances that continue to plague the system.

In addition to the above, there are very interesting experiments going on in terms of the creation of groups of students who are team-supervised, though the usual requirements of having a clearly defined supervisor tends to persist. These approaches are mainly a result of situations where there is a substantial increase in the number of students but is also a recognition that in areas in which there are substantial interdisciplinary overlays, the traditional model may not work that well.

Examination

The examination process is determined on an institution-by-institution basis and within institutions on a faculty-by-faculty basis. But there are some general trends. Usually the supervisor(s) and student agree on the date of submission of the thesis for examination and the supervisor(s) will then formally write to the faculty postgraduate committee indicating that they are in agreement that the thesis be subjected to an examination process. When there is conflict in this regard it is the right of the student to require the thesis to be examined, whether the supervisor agrees or not. In most institutions, the relevant postgraduate committee will appoint one local, internal examiner and at least one external (usually international) examiner. The postgraduate committee constructs the final assessment on the basis of the two or more examiners' reports.

Any other issues

This chapter opened with a note that the major crisis facing higher education in South Africa is the slow rate at which it is producing a new generation of academics. The key issue here has been alluded to earlier and this is that South African higher education is experiencing a crisis of identity and a crisis of legitimacy. Both are tied to history and both apply enormous strains on the future of the institutions and the knowledge projects of these institutions. More importantly, as a result of this, there are clear indications that there is severe state under-funding of higher education with the consequence that academic salaries have fallen behind comparable occupations. It is therefore not at all clear that this system will be able address the issue of increasing its output of Ph.D.s. Perhaps it is necessary to pose a more fundamental question: 'is South African higher education more generally on a sustainable footing'?

One of the key indicators of this is what has been called the static employment profile of the higher education sector in terms of qualified and research-active academics. A recent study indicates that, between 2000 and 2003, the sector increased the number of academics by a mere 34 while student enrolments have grown by approximately 127,000. An analysis reported in HSRC (2005) has been done of the full-time equivalents (or FTEs) of the R&D workforce science system (the higher education system together with the science councils). This indicates that between 1991 and 2001 the FTEs fell from 15,983 to 9213. This is made much more serious if one takes into account the ageing of the professoriate. In 1990, 18 per cent of the journal articles were written by researchers who were 50 years old or older. In 2002 this percentage had increased to a staggering 48 per cent.

There are therefore deeply systemic problems that militate against a simple workable solution to the issue of taking up the production of Ph.D.s by a factor of three or four in a sustainable fashion. These problems involve a number of issues but paramount among them are: the legitimacy of higher education, its funding and the funding of students and the conditions of service of academics.

References

Castells, M. (1996) *The Rise of the Network Society*. Oxford: Blackwell.

Cloete, N. *et al.* (2002) *Transformation in Higher Education: Global Pressures and Local Realities in South Africa*. Cape Town: Juta and Company.

HSRC (2005) *Human Resources for Knowledge Production in South Africa*. Cape Town: HSRC.

IDRC (1992) *Towards a Science and Technology Policy*. Ottowa: IDRC.

18

Doctoral education in Thailand

Soottiporn Chittmittrapap and Sudaporn Luksaneeyanawin

Introduction

As knowledge becomes recognized as one of the important factors in the development of the economic status of a country, so too does the higher education. In Thailand, doctoral graduates are recognized as one of the key success factors for increasing the potential and the competitiveness of the country. For the past three years there has been a massive increase in the number of higher education institutes and doctoral programmes in Thailand. The number of universities has increased from 24 public and 28 private to 76 public, 59 private and 2 open universities (as of January 2006). The importance of all this is reflected in the UNESCO and the World Bank statement, 'As knowledge becomes more important, so does higher education. Countries need to educate more of their young people to a high standard – a degree is now a basic qualification for many skilled jobs. The quality of knowledge generated within higher education institutions is becoming increasingly critical to national competitiveness' (see www.tfhe.net/report/overview.htm).

The questionnaire

Table 18.1 The questionnaire

Question	Number	Comment
1 Total number of doctoral students studying	10,516	9944 in public universities 572 in private universities
2 Number of institutions offering doctoral programmes	37	25 public universities 12 private universities
3 Number of different doctoral awards	15	

(Continued overleaf)

Table 18.1 (Continued)

Question	Number	Comment
4 Number of years over which doctorates have been offered	36	
5 Proportion of full-time to part-time students	95:5	Approximately
6 Average time to completion (in years)	4.38	
7 Success rates	15–100%	Depending on the programme No summative statistics
8 Typical age range of doctoral candidates	26–30	Mean 31.8 years
9 Proportion of male/female students	1:1.034	
10 Proportion of doctoral students studying who are nationals of other countries	1.07%	Doctoral students = 2.6%

Data sources

The above-mentioned data refers to the academic year 2005. The academic year in Thailand (of most curricula) runs from June to March in most programmes that are reported by the Commission on Higher Education of the Ministry of Education. This annual report about doctoral students in higher education institutes can be accessed from the website: www.mua.go.th (mostly in the Thai language). Most of the doctoral students in Thai universities are full-time but a few institutes also have part-time students. However, the number of part-time students reported is not accurate. The success rates are also reported according to the programmes and specialization. These are cumulative data of the last five-year period that is the maximum time the students can take to complete a Ph.D. degree after their masters degree. It is very difficult to report with summative statistics on the cumulative time. However, the lowest success rate is reported in the field of biomedicine while 100 per cent success rates are reported in the fields of mass communication, dentistry and veterinary medicine (in 2004). The data about the doctoral students and other graduate and undergraduate students who are nationals of other countries can also be accessed from the web-based data at www.inter.mua.go.th or asking via email at intcoop@mua.go.th.

The place of doctoral study in the national context/the role of the doctorates in relation to national research policy

Within the scenario outlined above it can be seen that the doctoral element in higher education has a critical role to play in creating knowledge, nurturing talent and spearheading the shift from an industrial-based society to a knowledge-based and information-intensive society. The number of doctoral graduate students enrolled each year in Thailand has increased significantly from 851 in 2000 to 1993 in 2004. The number of doctoral graduates has also increased from 571 in 2000 to 1216 in 2004. The outstanding universities also aim to increase the ratio of graduate students to up to 50 per cent of their total enrolment.

The introduction of university reform and the policy on autonomous universities have, in practice, led to very limited resources. Undertaking this educational reform has meant that an autonomous university needs more funds to strengthen the doctoral programmes. Thailand higher education institutes have to create initiatives and strategies to re-engineer the university administration to move towards excellence and towards an attainment of their maximum benefits.

The place of doctoral study in the Thai context

As Thailand is developing at a rapid pace it is clear to most observers that we need more doctorates to aid the process of development in every sector (e.g. in education, government, industry, business and so on). Indeed, we suggest that the growth of doctoral programmes in Thai universities is essential at present. Most universities have to do a 'needs analysis' before they will start a graduate, masters and Ph.D. programme. They have to take into consideration the related factors in the provision of good programmes, for example, their strength in the area, the infrastructure of the university, the collaborative research network or their strategic partners both within and outside the university. These factors will help them towards the goal of academic excellence. Actually the goal of academic excellence for a university is not determined purely by the quality of its academic staff and the related factors aforementioned. Another significant factor is the quality of the students that attend the university. Many universities provide grants to recruit students with successful academic histories and research potential. Graduate students are, in many senses, the research 'arms' in research-intensive universities.

In our view research is both a means and an end in itself. It is used as a 'means' within the education process and yet its outcomes represent the kinds of new knowledge that can be used for the continuing development of the country. Research agencies in Thailand now provide research grants that will help to answer the problems of the country, mainly in what are called agenda-based, functional-based and area- or regional-based research. In other words, this is a very top-down research policy that will be productive *if* the implementation of research granting process is well defined and operated. As well as the grants from research agencies in and outside Thailand, universities also need to provide the grants for a bottom-up research policy to support the kinds of research that cannot answer the immediate needs of the country and yet are necessary to maintain the fundamental development of ideas that is needed for future applications. This latter policy can be sustained by allowing staff to recruit potential students to help them carry the torch towards research excellence.

We hope that we would be able to convince every sector that the social and economic development of Thailand in this information age is related to education that is research based. We suggest that students with high research capabilities should be fully supported by the sectors involved, as well as by the universities.

Funding issues

Seventy per cent of Thai doctoral students work in government sectors. Out of this group 40 per cent are from the higher education institutions and 30 per cent are from the other public sectors. Such students are supported by their organizations, while the remaining 30 per cent are self-supporting. At present the tuition fees are quite reasonable. Most Thai universities also set up financial support systems for their doctoral students due to an awareness of the need for the development of the country, as discussed formerly. The teaching assistantship (TA), research assistantship (RA) and the research funding to support students' research are basically planned to share the doctoral students' expenses as well as to initiate the teamwork concept. The funding that supports foreign students in Thailand is quite different. Some 70.9 per cent of the foreign students are self-supporting, whereas 6.7 per cent are sponsored by international agencies or their own countries.

According to the Thailand budgeting system, there is no specific funding system provided for doctoral study. Most of the budget allocated to the universities is allocated for personnel salaries. At present the Thai government implements the students' Income Contingent Loan system (ICL) to support any potential students to get through their higher education.

Another initiative that started in 1996 is the Royal Golden Jubilee (RGJ) doctoral project. This aims to increase the number of highly qualified doctoral graduates. The Thailand Research Fund (TRF) introduced the project. The RGJ funding system is allocated to the highly qualified and research outstanding professors through the institutions to mentor their best students so that they may continue their education to Ph.D. level. In the past few years, the Commission on Higher Education of the Ministry of Education decided to co-fund this project if the students have already been recruited to be staff members of the universities. The number of grants allocated is quite high each year, especially in some specific areas that are perceived as necessary for the development of the country.

Higher education institutions and doctoral degree awards

A centralized quality control strategy

There is no limitation on the higher education institutions in terms of the number of doctoral degrees awarded. However, there are rules and regulations that any university has to fulfil if it wants to start a study programme. The Ministry of Education has an academic committee to examine whether the universities applying to award doctoral degrees have met the standard requirement that will guarantee the delivery of high-quality education.

In recent years there has been a massive growth of higher education institutions and the process of setting conditions and rules and regulations about the graduate programmes has become somewhat more concrete to ensure quality. In 2005, new ordinances and regulations were announced regarding the standard of operation in each institution. This announcement raised awareness in the institutions of the need to try to attain and then sustain the standards necessary to guarantee that the programmes adhere to these ordinances. With this newly-introduced centralized quality control strategy, only 25 out of 78 public universities (32.05 per cent) and 12 out of 59 private universities (20.33 per cent) are now able to provide doctoral graduate study.

Graduate schools

The graduate school of Chulalongkorn University was the first established organization within Thai higher education designated to the administration of all the graduate studies within a university. It has operated successfully now for more than 20 years. In 1996 there was a concept that doctoral education should be carried out continuously from the bachelor degree stage onwards and graduate programmes were regarded as a continuation of undergraduate studies. This concept was well accepted in Thailand. Undergraduate programmes looked after by faculties have to come to play an important role in graduate programmes as well. When the number of graduate programmes and the number of graduate students increased and faculties became more familiar with the rules and regulations, the academic and administrative management shifted from the graduate school to the faculties. The graduate school became a centre for quality control and liaises between all the graduate programmes. Administration by the graduate school of the graduate programmes is now limited to the multidisciplinary or interdisciplinary cross-faculty programmes.

There are now three types of organizational structure of graduate schools: (i) graduate schools with full responsibility for all graduate programmes (e.g. King Mongkut Institute of Technology, North Bangkok; Prince of Songkhla University; Khonkaen University); (ii) graduate schools with a limited role for multidisciplinary and interdisciplinary graduate programmes (e.g. Chulalongkorn University; Chiangmai University; Mahidol University); and (iii) no graduate schools, all the programmes from bachelor degrees to doctoral degrees being taken care of by the faculties and universities (e.g. Suranaree University; Thaksin University; King Mongkut University of Technology, Thonburi; Ramkhamhaeng University).

International colleges

Where there are an increasing number of international doctoral programmes in many universities, some establish international colleges to organize such programmes at all levels from undergraduate to graduate. These institutes are separate from the graduate schools. Assumption University and Mahidol University, the top two popular institutions for foreign students at all levels of study in Thailand, are the examples of the last model, whereas Chulalongkorn University and Kasetsart University, the top two institutions with most foreign doctoral students, do not have any separate system for the international programmes.

Dominance of the Thai language

The language used in academic programmes is Thai except in some disciplines such as English language and literature. Since most of the programmes in Thai universities are conducted in the Thai language it is impossible for foreign students to enrol. However, during the past few years an increasing number of programmes have been conducted in English to accommodate foreign students. Clearly, these programmes help to enhance the number of foreign students in Thailand. In the academic year 2004, 4334 foreign students were enrolled in 55 higher education institutions (mostly private ones). Out of this number, 2939 (67.81 per cent) of the students studied at the bachelor degree level. Only 113 (2.6 per cent) foreign students studied at doctorate degree level. This number of foreign doctoral students was only 1.07 per cent of all the doctoral students (10,516) in Thai universities. The highest number of foreign students are Chinese, followed by Myanmar, Indian, Vietnamese, Laos and Japanese. The highest number of students from the western world are Americans. Most of these students are self-funding.

Forms of doctoral study

Differences in doctoral programme nomenclature

A survey in the academic year 2005 revealed that there were 225 doctoral degree programmes offered by 354 organizations in the Thai higher education system (faculties, colleges, schools or institutes). There were 37 universities that offered doctoral study. The names of the programmes were quite confusing. The same academic discipline operated by different organizations used different names. For example, the doctoral programmes in biotechnology were offered by ten organizations in nine universities under different names. One university offered this programme in the Faculty of Science but another university offered it in the Faculty of Agriculture. In another university, two different programmes were offered under the same discipline, one programme in biotechnology and another in agriculture biotechnology. There was another programme in biotechnology offered by the above-mentioned university. More than half of the programmes used different names even though the degree discipline was similar or might contain the same essence, such as the programme in public administration and the programme in public management.

Differences in nomenclature of awards

The names of the doctoral degree awarded also varied. However, this is not as confusing as the names of the programmes. Doctor of Philosophy (abbreviated to Ph.D.) is the most common doctoral qualification offered by Thai universities. There are various other qualifications offered by various universities in some specific fields or disciplines as follows:

- Education: Ed.D. (Doctor of Education) (Chulalongkorn University, Prince of Songkhla University, Srinakarindhwirote University). Ed.D. (Doctor of Environmental Education) (Mahidol University). Tech.Ed.D. (Doctor of Technical Education) (King Mongkut University of Technology, Thonburi).
- Engineering: D.Eng. (Doctor of Engineering) (Chulalongkorn University, Prince of Songkhla University, Thammasat University, Mahidol University, Ubolratchathani University). Ph.D. (King Mongkut Institute of Technology, North Bangkok).
- Science: D.Sc. (Doctor of Science) (King Mongkut University of Technology, Thonburi, in energy technology, Mahidol University in nutrition and technology of environmental management). Ph.D. is mostly used for the doctoral degrees in science.
- Business admin: DBA (Doctor of Business Administration) (Chulalongkorn University, Thammasat University).

- Public admin: D.P.A. (Doctor of Public Administration) (Burapa University, Maefahluang University).
- Public health: Dr.P.H. (Doctor of Public Health) (Mahidol University).
- Law: JSD (Doctor of Juridical Science) (Chulalongkorn University). LLD (Doctor of Law) (Thammasat University).
- Nursing   D.N.S. (Doctor of Nursing Science) (Songkhla University).

There are also some qualifications that are misleading, mostly in the field of biomedical sciences. These are called 'doctor' in their disciplines but are in fact qualifications obtained in undergraduate programmes, for example:

- MD   (Doctor of Medicine);
- DDS   (Doctor of Dentistry);
- DVM   (Doctor of Veterinary Medicine);
- PharmD.   (Doctor of Pharmacy).

Doctoral students and their programmes of study

Qualification required

Most of the doctoral programmes in Thailand are offered to graduates with a masters degree. Only some programmes accept applicants with bachelor degrees. The programmes that accept bachelor degree graduates usually structure their programmes in such a way as to require a longer period of study for these students. At present, some outstanding universities, such as Chulalongkorn University and Mahidol University, launch doctoral programmes with straight-through studies from bachelor to masters to doctoral to attract outstanding students with high research potential. These programmes are carried out through honours programmes offered to undergraduate students.

There are no identifiable issues of gender, race, or religion related to the enrolment of doctoral students. In the past, male students were the majority in doctoral study because the social perception of Thai society in the past put a lot more emphasis on the education of males. However, at present the number of female students is higher than male students at the bachelor and masters degree levels. The proportion of male to female students at the doctoral level is nearly the same (1:1.034). All universities allow students of any religion to be enrolled, including monks.

In some institutions such as Chulalongkorn University, English proficiency (TOEFL score at 500, at least) is also required to ensure that the standard of English is satisfactory enough to access the knowledge from international resources.

Periods of study

Most doctoral programmes have a maximum five-year period of study, starting from masters degrees. Research-intensive programmes where coursework is not needed are also offered, especially in science and technology. At least one publication in a recognized international journal is required before the completion of study in all the doctoral programmes in Thailand.

Due to the five-year time constraint, most doctoral programmes are full-time. However, students may take leave for good reasons, such as to collect fieldwork data or to go abroad to other well-equipped institutions.

Funding and destinations of doctoral graduates

One of the major factors in improving academic quality is the qualification of the faculty members. The increase in the number of higher education institutions has helped to open up the chance of employment for qualified doctoral graduates. A recent survey revealed that 40 per cent of doctoral students are employed at the universities before they come to study. Most of them get scholarships from their universities or from the government to further their study. Since the government is well aware of the need for doctoral graduates in the government sectors, 30 per cent of the doctoral students are sponsored by the government. The remaining 30 per cent are self-supporting. There are very few scholarships from the private sector to support doctoral students.

In Thailand, people with degrees from higher education institutes are well recognized and respected. A degree is socially valued and most people would like to acquire one – there is very much a notion of 'value added' about higher education. In the past there was no special budget allocated to support students' higher education whereas the 12 years of basic education is compulsory and is fully supported by the government. In 2006, the government started a new loan scheme to support low-income students. This scheme aims to help students who cannot afford higher education, both in the public and the private universities. This policy will facilitate self-support students to pass through their studies with less difficulty.

An employment survey of doctoral graduates reported that nearly 100 per cent of doctorates with scholarships go back to work in their institutions and government sectors. About 20 per cent without scholarships get a job in the private industrial or business sectors.

The supervision and evaluation of the candidates

In order to maintain the standards of programmes and to meet the key performance indices, the Ministry of Education through the Commission on

Higher Education announced the 'Standards of Operation – SOP for Graduate Programmes, 2005' to control and evaluate the programmes offered by the universities. This SOP gives guidelines with regard to many aspects such as the semester/trimester structures, the credits offered and the programme structures.

Two different types of doctoral programme have been introduced, one based upon research (48 credits are required for the masters degree candidates, 72 credits for the bachelor graduate candidates), the other combining coursework and research. The standards specify that at least three qualified faculty members must be responsible for the programme. The main responsible persons must be staff members with either doctoral degrees or associate professors in that discipline. The main thesis adviser/supervisor and co-adviser must be a staff member with doctoral degrees or associate professors with strong research experience. A qualifying examination is taken before the submission of the dissertation proposal. Appropriate research training courses should be provided to all students.

The examination committee must consist of at least three faculty members and one external examiner. All of them must possess doctoral degrees in that field or in a related field or must be an associate professor with teaching and research expertise. The student must submit their dissertation for examination and in all cases students must undergo the viva examination chaired by the head of the department or a person appointed by the department. Before the doctoral qualification is granted, at least one paper from the dissertation/research findings must be accepted for publication in a recognized, peer-reviewed international journal.

The quality assurance system

In Thailand, the Office for National Education Standards and Quality Assessment under the Ministry of Education is legitimately designated to accredit the academic institutions at every level from primary to higher education. Nevertheless, the quality framework is aimed only for institutional review in the first phase (started in 2001). The committee of the Deans of Graduate Schools in Public Universities (DGPU) has launched the 'GSA – Graduate Studies Quality Development and Assurance System' to add subject review to the existing system focused on graduate programmes. Most of the public universities use this system as an outline and guideline for their internal quality control. This system is now modified and is called the 'Curriculum Quality Assurance – CQA'. It covers all levels of offered courses at Chulalongkorn University including the Ph.D. programmes. The quality system comprises of context, resource and resource management, and enhancement of quality. Both conformance and performance indicators are set up to assess the quality of the courses.

References

Bureau of Higher Education Strategic Planning, Commission on Higher Education. (2005) *The analysis of the academic performance of higher education institutions of Thailand.* Published by the Commission on Higher Education, Bangkok, Thailand.

The Bureau of International Cooperation, the Commission on Higher Education (2004) *Foreign Students in Thai Higher Education Institutions in 2004.* Thai Higher Education Review 2004: 30–31. Bangkok Block Printing House. Bangkok, Thailand.

Ministry of Education Announcement (2005) *The Standard of Operation for the Graduate Programmes.* Published by the Ministry of Education. Bangkok, Thailand.

Ministry of Education (2005) *Programmes and Curriculum, Thai Higher Education Institutions.* Ministry of Education. Bangkok, Thailand.

Task Force on Higher Education and Society (for the World Bank and UNESCO) (2000). Higher Education in developing countries: Peril and Promise. Washington World Bank Press 2000: 9.

Soottiporn Chittmittrapap. (2002) Graduate Studies Quality Development and Assurance System , Series No. 1: Quality Framework and Code of Practice. Medipress DPLC. Bangkok, Thailand.

Soottiporn Chittmittrapap. (2002) Graduate Studies Quality Development and Assurance System , Series No. 2: GSA Requirements. Medipress DPLC. Bangkok, Thailand.

www.mua.go.th\\Pplan\Date13\NumAllUni.xls\NumAllUni
http://www.grad.chula.ac.th
http://www.inter.mua.go.th

Part 5

In Part Five of this book some of the issues that have arisen within the country chapters are drawn together to set out an agenda for further discussion both in and between countries. For example, discussions include:

- the purposes of doctoral education, specifically in relation to the criteria for the award and the relationships between those criteria and skills, purpose and assessment;
- the demarcation of doctoral study by distinctive nomenclature;
- the dangers that may be identified where the current interest in generic skills training shifts the focus of doctoral education to a functionalist, skills led perspective;
- the way in which doctoral education is organised and delivered at a national level, including the effects of concentrating PGR in fewer institutions;
- the quality of the doctoral product, completion rates and the overall contribution the doctorate makes to societies and in particular the close link of doctorates to national economic performance and hence the question of what subjects may best support national economies.

19

Conclusions

Stuart Powell and Howard Green

Introduction

We have suggested that our purpose in this book was to support the current debates and future challenges for ourselves in the UK and for others world-wide through a better understanding of developments and approaches in doctoral education in other countries. In so doing we did not suggest that we have been able to define clear themes that run through principles and practices of postgraduate education worldwide and from which we can learn transferable lessons – in the first instance our sample is too small for such a claim and in any case to draw themes in such a way would be to run the risk of creating an artifice from what is essentially a number of disparate contextual-ized situations. Each country has its own history with regard to postgraduate research and each has its own sets of pressures and drivers for change (even when part of a wider organization such as the EU). What can be discerned, however, are common issues facing many countries. What is interesting perhaps is to see how different countries go about addressing those issues – recognizing the contextualized nature of their responses and actions.

We did not, therefore, argue that our survey would lead to the adoption by any one country of the approaches of others (*policy transfer*). However, we do argue that countries are better able to understand their own approaches and develop new strategies by understanding how others operate (*systems under-standing*), and reflecting on these approaches (*policy learning*).

Purpose of the doctorate

Assumptions about the purpose of the doctorate

The purpose of the doctorate remains a fundamental question both within higher education itself, within government departments that are con-cerned with the provision of postgraduate degrees and within industries and

professions that are the 'users' of some postgraduate 'products' (i.e. employers of successful candidates). Yet as we have seen in earlier chapters it is a
topic that is rarely discussed explicitly within any of these organizations, let
alone between them. There are of course assumptions made about purpose
and indeed further assumptions that other parties may be identifying the
same purposes as oneself. Our argument here is that without a clear understanding of purpose it is impossible to develop a rational argument about
approach, funding, delivery mechanisms and all the other paraphernalia
that go with the doctorate.

Identifying the purpose of the doctoral award

There are examples in earlier chapters of where the purpose of the award, in
terms of where it leads the successful candidate, is clearly recognized. In
Poland, for example, we learn that the doctoral award is primarily a gateway
to academia that links to the habilitation, which in turn provides the licence
to practise as an academic. A contention of the doctorate as primarily
linked to an academic career and continuation of the discipline is part of
the current debates in the USA, where a substantial majority of successful
candidates do *not* follow an academic career path. Of course, within any one
country different institutions may have differing views on purpose in this
respect – at least in terms of destinations of successful candidates. It has been
noted anecdotally by a senior member of staff at Oxford University in the UK
that it is recognized there that the vast majority of doctoral candidates are
intent on a career in academia ('that is why they come to us in the first
place'). Yet clearly, other universities in the UK see the doctorate as a high-
level award that may lead to one of many possible careers.

The most recent survey of Ph.D. 'destinations' in the UK, at the time of
going to press, is UK Grad Programme (2006). This survey does not directly
break down the number of Ph.D.s going into academia as such but it does
note the proportion going into 'education' (of course this may involve all
levels of schooling). Nevertheless it is perhaps worth noting here that:

- of those UK-domiciled Ph.D. graduates who entered employment in the
  UK in 2004 and who responded to the survey, 47.8 per cent entered the
  education sector as against 16.3 per cent in manufacturing industries,
  15.5 per cent in health, 9.1 per cent in business, finance and IT and 5.7
  per cent in public administration;
- of those UK-domiciled Ph.D. graduates who left the UK for work or for
  work and study abroad, 59.1 per cent were employed in the education
  sector, 'predominantly in higher education' as against 25.7 per cent in
  manufacturing, 6.7 per cent in health, with the other employment sectors
  accounting for the remaining 8.5 per cent.

Indications are, therefore, that somewhere around half of successful
students in the UK are likely to enter education in one of its levels and

we can surmise (although the survey does not help us in our purpose here) that these will predominantly be going into university teaching and research.

In some cases the national purpose that underpins the doctoral award is the identified need for technological advance and subsequent economic growth. Indeed, there is a strong explicit relationship in several countries between doctoral awards made and economic growth. Perhaps in contrast to the somewhat vague references to the relationship with economic growth and technological change in the UK, several countries are far more emphatic about the importance of doctorates to economic growth and technological change. While it would be convenient to locate such a view only in the emerging economies, this is not the case. Certainly, countries such as Brazil, India and Thailand talk explicitly about expenditure on doctoral education and their economy, and South Africa notes that, in the context of the policy objective of increasing spending on research and development from 0.7 to 1 per cent of gross domestic product (GDP), there is a need to increase the spend on doctoral education by three of four times. However, increasing the number of doctoral awards made is also an explicit objective of policy in other countries such as Canada, Denmark and Finland. This overt objective leads to a more planned approach to all aspects of doctoral education that we note below.

Employment destinations

In the UK there have been recent surveys that indicate not only what kinds of job candidates find but where those jobs are located. The latest survey has already been cited above. An earlier survey in 2005, where academia was differentiated, indicated that, 'The data also challenge the view that a PhD leads only to a career in academia or research. In fact less than half of this cohort are employed in the education sector, fairly equally divided between teaching and postdoctoral research. Significant numbers are found in all sectors of the economy' (UKGrad 2005).

The output of doctorates is seen by many as synonymous with meeting national objectives relating to advancements in research and development – in short, related to a country's technological edge on its competitors. In this context it matters where successful candidates go, and what they do when they get there, in the sense of a national investment in doctoral study yielding dividends or not. Countries are seeing a need to require the students that they fund to 'repay' that debt in terms of a commitment to work in the country for at least a certain period of time. Such a view implies an interventionist approach to doctoral study on the part of public agencies that does not always appear overtly to be the case. It underlines the tensions in the development of doctoral programmes in the EU between the high level rhetoric of doctoral programmes for the European knowledge society (EUA 2005) and the policy and practice of member states.

Box 19.1 Editors' comment

It is necessary to distinguish between doctoral education and the doctoral award when discussing purpose. The former is about ways in which candidates can be brought to a situation where they can be successful in attaining the latter. In turn, it is important to retain an understanding that the latter is an academic award – indeed, the highest attainable by a programme of study (this is one of the few universal givens) – and one that indicates through the production of an original research programme that the holder has the ability to undertake research effectively in an independent, continuing way. The purpose of study then must be to attain the award and the purpose of the award is to signify that the holder has the abilities that we describe above – is, in essence, qualified as a 'doctor' (in the Ph.D. sense rather than the medical). There is of course then a second level of purpose that relates to the point of having people in society with the doctoral qualification at all. Here is the dilemma with the doctorate. With some exceptions (and setting aside the medical doctorate) a doctorate is not a qualification to *do* anything – rather it is a signifier of a level of ability. When we talk about the purpose of the doctorate we therefore need to be clear whether we are talking about (i) purpose in terms of the process of getting a doctorate, (ii) the purpose of having an award defined in the way that it is or, finally, (iii) the purpose of having people in society in general who are 'qualified' at that level. Of course all of these purposes are interrelated. The danger is that national debates will lead to actions driven by perceptions of the purposes under the last of these three categories (the most general) without thinking through what this means for the processes of study and for the way in which the award is designed, as is made manifest in its criteria.

A current example of this in the UK and in Australia is the focus on so-called 'generic skills', which relate to the general purpose of what doctoral level people should be able to do. Whether or not such skills are actually necessary for the wide range of people who study at doctoral level is a largely unanswered question but the focus itself – right or wrong – leads to real difficulties if it operates in isolation of any changes to the criteria for the award (purpose (ii) above).

'Production levels' for doctorates

Variation of production levels between countries

The production of doctorates shows considerable variation between the countries we sampled as we can see in Table 19.1. Clearly this reflects, to a

Table 19.1 Doctorates awarded and students registered

Country	Population 2005 (000s)	Number awarded[1]	% population	Numbers registered[2,3]	% population
Australia	20,400			37,511	0.184
Brazil	184,200			38,948	0.021
Canada	32,200			32,066	0.1
Denmark	5,400	1,000	0.018	4,815	0.09
Finland	5,200	1,385	0.026		
France	60,700			70,000	0.115
Germany	82,500	23,043	0.027		
Japan	127,700			74,907	0.059
Mexico	107,000	1,200	0.01	10,825	0.01
Netherlands	16,300			19,000	0.117
Poland	38,200	6,144	0.016	33,040	0.086
South Africa	46,900	1,000	0.002	8,112	0.017
Thailand	65,000	1,216	0.0019	10,516	0.016
United Kingdom	60,100	15,780	0.0262	111,990	0.186
United States	301,041	42,155	0.014	837,640	0.228
China	1,303,700			165,000	0.012
India	1,103,600	13,733	0.001	65,491	0.006
	3,560,141				

Notes:
1 Numbers refer to various years 2003–5 and include overseas students
2 Numbers refer to various years 2003–5
3 US figures include masters, exclude nationals studying abroad but include overseas students

major extent, simple country characteristics such as population and level of development. We noted in the introduction that this can be standardized to reflect investment in research and development in relation to gross national product (GNP). In Table 19.1, we look at production in relation to country population.

One might expect that there would be a simple correlation between research and development spend and the number of doctorates produced or registered in relation to population. The relationship is however not simple. Finland and Germany, both in the top group for research and development, are joined by the UK in terms of doctorates awarded in relation to population. The middle group are represented a little unexpectedly by the USA and Poland. The third group, not surprisingly, includes the developing economies of Mexico, South Africa, Thailand and India.

If we turn to the numbers enrolled in doctoral programmes, we find a slightly different picture with Europe, North America and Australia having similar levels of activity. The figures for the USA are slightly problematic as they include masters students, which clearly inflate numbers. What the table and country chapters make clear is that the relationships are not as simple as we might expect and raise questions about the role of the doctorate in the research and development activity and spend in individual countries.

Planning numbers of doctoral candidates

We find similar contrast in the trends and targets for doctoral students in the countries sampled. Several countries, in both the developed and developing world, have seen growth and are planning additional growth in the next few years. In Denmark the number is planned to double in the next few years while in Finland, where there was a 50 per cent increase in the 1980s and 120 per cent in the 1990s, numbers are planned to increase to 1600 doctorates awarded per annum in 2008. In Brazil, which has witnessed a 10–15 per cent growth in the last five years, there are plans to increase the annual number of awards to 15,000 in 2010.

This planned growth contrasts vividly with the approach in several other countries including the USA, UK and Germany where there appears to be little, or no, planning of doctoral student numbers. We see from the German case that decision-making appears to be at the level of the individual supervisor while in the UK it is the institution which regulates numbers, hence planning numbers at a national level is currently impossible even if it were thought desirable. The approach to numbers of doctoral students is very different in Nordic countries in general and in Finland in particular, also in France and in some of the developing economies where intended doctoral numbers are clearly articulated and funded.

India and China stand out in terms of the number of doctoral students and the potential market for institutions to attract them. While the volume of undergraduates is large (though not in relation to total population) this is not the case when it comes to doctoral study. If participation rates are to rise in the long-term to those of the western European countries, the demand for an infrastructure to deliver doctoral programmes will be enormous.

In short, decision-making concerning the numbers of doctorates produced varies significantly between those countries in which higher education and research is centrally managed, such as China at one extreme, but including the Nordic countries and France, and those at the other extreme in which, for constitutional or ideological reasons, there is little if any planning, such as the UK, USA and Germany.

If we consider these last three countries we can see that in the UK there has been observable growth overall but this has been achieved largely in an unplanned way, driven in part by games-playing with the research funding model (RAE) rather than by notions of supply and demand or indeed (national) need. The cases of the UK and Germany highlight the difficulties of any central planning because, as is the case of the UK, all universities have the right to offer doctorates, even if they are not funded to so do, and in the case of Germany all professors have similar rights. Whether this approach is sustainable in the future is questionable, particularly as the EU begins to set research targets for the Union as a whole. Change will, however, be very difficult as institutions and staff regard doctoral work and their ability to engage in it as defining elements of university life.

Box 19.2 Editors' comment

In the sample of countries chosen there is a continuum in respect of national planning of doctoral numbers from high central control to unplanned local determination. Yet across this continuum, growth is a common feature – there is no discernible bias towards more or less growth at either end. Neither is there any simple correlation between research and development spend and the number of doctorates produced in relation to population.

Diversity in the doctoral award

As the complexity of the workplace has increased and the need for highly qualified postgraduates has developed so the demand for more increasingly diverse doctoral-level work has arisen. Several of the country chapters have noted such trends and that the kinds of knowledge and skills displayed by successful Ph.D. candidates are not necessarily readily usable in the workplace contexts they sought to enter. Some countries seem to have responded positively to such changing demands – others have responded little or not at all. And as a consequence we can recognize two broad groupings: countries which have a broad range of doctoral awards, in terms of both title and nature of the award and those who have retained the Ph.D. in its traditional form.

Countries such as China, South Africa, the Netherlands, Mexico, Japan, Denmark, Germany and India retain the tradition of the Ph.D. as the single award at doctoral level. Although some differentiate when it comes to the precise naming of the award, making specific reference to the subject of the award, the award itself is essentially a Ph.D. Some countries such as Finland appear to be in a period of transition as the new graduate school based doctorates vie with the traditional Humboldtian dissertation-based model.

Other countries, notably the USA, UK and Australia, have begun to adapt their doctoral systems to better reflect the changing nature of demand and have introduced a series of awards which are now described as professional doctorates. Such doctorates focus on developing candidates to make contributions within the specific area of their profession. Professional doctoral programmes may have some set components where students are gathered together for learning experiences that have predetermined outcomes. In short, it is decided that there are certain key aspects of existing knowledge that they must understand and key skills they must learn if they are to be able to operate at the doctoral level within their professions (see Green and Powell 2005 for a fuller discussion of professional doctorates in the UK and Powell and Long 2005 for the results of a survey of professional doctorates in the UK).

The tension between these two paths (diversion and traditional) comes when there is misunderstanding as to the nature of any new forms of doctorate. For example, a perception that professional doctorates are 'taught' and therefore somehow 'less than' the traditional form may lead to a diminishing of those awards in the eyes of some. In fact, professional doctorates may contain some elements that are delivered in taught sessions but then students undertaking traditional Ph.D.s often attend taught sessions as well (as is evident in many of the country chapters). The significant differences come, of course, in the assessing of such elements. Students who are undertaking a traditional Ph.D. may well attend taught sessions but are unlikely to be assessed on their learning in those sessions – typically, examination will be by final assessment of the dissertation alone. In contrast, a student undertaking a professional doctoral programme may be assessed on learning outcomes prior to the final assessment and some of these may involve attendance at taught sessions.

In our view the tensions noted above may be resolved if it can be made clear that all doctoral awards indicate achievement at the same (doctoral) level. As we have indicated above, where that level is defined in terms of contributing to knowledge and thus indicating an ability to continue to make such contributions independently, then parity of awards is achieved. What is required is the establishment of individual criteria – however disparate they may be – that can be used across disciplines and professions to act as indicators of achievement of (common) level.

The fact that we have read that some countries, such as Canada, are beginning to recast their professional doctorates as Ph.D.s, albeit focused on the professions, indicates that such commonality of level exists – what is changing is nomenclature.

Box 19.3 Editors' comment

It seems as if the doctorate is changing with some countries developing doctorates other than the traditional Ph.D. (e.g. professional doctorates). In reality, however, what is changing is the scope of doctoral-level work and to a lesser extent the way in which doctoral-level learning is managed. Scope is widening as universities begin to respond to the increasing complexity of the workplace and the need for cutting edge workers across a range of disciplines and particularly for those working across traditional disciplinary boundaries. At the risk of oversimplifying, Ph.D.s are not awarded only in the hard sciences but rather doctoral study ranges across all intellectual disciplines.

This phenomenon has created some difficulty of interpretation in part at least because some countries have changed nomenclature without necessarily changing the crucial criteria for the award (contributing to the discipline). What is needed is for clarity and transparency around the notion that all doctoral awards indicate achievement at the same (doctoral) level and the individual criteria for those awards – however disparate they may be – can be used across disciplines and professions to act as indicators of achievement of (common) level.

Issues of globality

Beyond globalization

We use the term 'globality' here to describe a worldwide, interconnected economy that ignores national boundaries. In the past, doctoral study has been part of the 'globalization' of world research and development and has been part of the general expansion of international trade and foreign investment, the mobility of labour and the integration of markets. But it seems to us that the doctorate is now becoming part of a reality that extends beyond such globalization; it is becoming part of a condition rather than a process, part of a world research environment in which traditional and familiar boundaries are being surmounted or made irrelevant (see Yergin and Stanislaw 2002 for a fuller discussion of globality).

Trans-national research and development

There is an increasing awareness of the global nature of much current research and many, if not all, of the contributors in this book make reference to it. Research and development has become a trans-national affair as pressures on researchers to deliver outcomes has extended the need for resources beyond the abilities of single countries and as advances in communications systems have increased exponentially the possibilities for effective collaboration at a distance. These changes are equally relevant to the doctorate and its development. The issue of globality however spans many aspects of doctoral production as we have seen in the country chapters, embracing as it does issues of competition, language, brain drain and collaboration, all of particular and vital importance to countries such as the UK that depend heavily on the international dimension of doctoral education.

International competition for doctoral students

International competition within the producer countries is growing as most of the developed world now recruits internationally for its students. From the UK perspective, where international students are particularly important in the sciences this will become increasingly problematic.

We have noted that many countries now deliver their programmes in English so as to have access to research which is predominantly in English. As far as the native English speaking world is concerned, such competition is increasingly important, particularly as its comparative advantage has up to now been guarded by the importance of language. There are however consequences for other major languages, not to mention the minority languages such as Dutch, Finnish and Danish, if the majority of the advanced work, particularly in science, is conducted in a second language.

International movement of doctoral candidates post-qualification

In several countries included in this book, there is concern about the impact of international movements of doctoral candidates. In several cases, there is concern about the so-called brain drain, as students move to, for example, Europe and North America to undertake their doctorates, only to be retained post-qualification and never return to the home country. Given the attraction of higher salaries, the most advanced economies are able to overcome their doctoral and postdoctoral deficits with overseas students, thus negating many aspects of the economic development policies of the developing world. Without overseas candidates, science and technology development in the USA and UK, for example, would be in serious difficulty.

Countries such as the USA, UK and Australia have always seen themselves as having a role in global education and research, supporting other countries in which infrastructure is still developing relative to demand. However, in recent years this role has begun to change towards a system (at least in the three countries used as exemplars here) that relies on overseas students to undertake research needs, with potential detrimental impacts on the sponsoring countries.

The Polish example is particularly concerning as the movement of successful doctoral candidates reflects the more general outward movement of young people observed since Poland joined the EU. With low academic salaries many doctoral candidates look abroad, and particularly to the USA, for employment.

Many countries encourage students themselves to be international in their outlook. In several the international mobility of students is noted as increasing, with the deliberate aim of facilitating the development in those students of global perspectives. In Mexico, students are encouraged to work or study abroad before applying for jobs; in Australia similarly there is an emphasis on international impact – including the use of examiners from overseas as a way of internationalizing the validation of the award being made. In Europe there are of course specific programmes of the EU directed at enhancing the possibilities for mobility of doctoral (among other) students.

Global capacity

One of the significant features of the chapters in this book is the vast potential of some countries in terms of both providing students and training programmes and in terms of advancing research and development. India and China are perhaps the most striking examples in this respect (though they are not alone, with countries such as Brazil and Thailand showing similar possibilities). India for example has one of the largest higher education sectors in the world with over 10 million enrolled students. At present only 0.65 per cent are engaged in doctoral study but clearly this proportion will increase as the newly qualified undergraduates move up through the professions and through academia. Indeed, the doctoral population in India is set to increase with a government agreement in 2005 to increase the number of doctoral students fivefold by 2015.

In China the background is different with the key historical feature being that the Chinese higher education system was completely disbanded during the Cultural Revolution (1966 to 1976). In a sense then Ph.D. education began from nothing in 1981. It may well be that the infrastructure to support postgraduate study is still in need of significant development in China. Nevertheless, the annual number of Ph.D. graduates jumped from 18 in 1983 to 188,000 in 2003. China has clearly achieved great momentum over this 20-year period albeit with some difficulties (described by Lee in his concluding remarks).

What is noteworthy here is that both India and China may have in the past been exporters of doctoral students, yet the signs are that the relationship is changing as both countries develop their infrastructure for postgraduate research. Those that were once suppliers (of students) will become competitors. The European, North American and Australian chapters make little if any reference to changes in these global flows. Such flows should however give cause for concern and consideration of strategic offshore investments in the production of doctorates, as is the emerging case in undergraduate education. In a country such as the UK, where international students now make up 46 per cent of the student population at postgraduate research level, and in which both the national science base and individual university's finances depend on these numbers, changes in global flows will have major impacts (UUK 2006).

Box 19.4 Editors' comment

Doctoral education is now part of a world research environment in which traditional and familiar boundaries are being surmounted or made irrelevant. The relationship between countries in terms of being suppliers of students or providers of doctoral education is likely to shift along with the changing strengths of economies and the degrees of dependence on technological advancement. In short, the ebb and flow of doctoral students across international borders is not likely to remain constant.

Funding

Direct involvement of the state in funding postgraduate research

In some countries there is direct involvement of the state to varying degrees in the funding of doctoral education, whether this is through some form of block grant to institutions or, as in the case of Poland, the several funding streams (direct or indirect) to both institution and/or student. The precise level of funds paid directly to institutions has depended to some extent on the importance placed on doctoral programmes and their contribution to the national science base. This has encouraged a more precise link between national planning targets on doctoral numbers and funds available. Several countries now have target numbers for doctoral students with allocation of appropriate funding.

Funding linked to the quality of the research degree process

In other cases, levels of funding are more closely linked to the quality of the research degree process as measured by completion rates. This retrospective approach is the one adopted by the RTS in Australia and is not dissimilar to the approach adopted by the UK research councils. Currently the UK funding councils are struggling with an approach that, if adopted, would follow completions rather than the number of students enrolled. Clearly such an approach emphasizes product rather than process, typical of national treasuries, and influences the notion of the doctorate as an award rather than as the beginnings of a research career.

Doctoral education as free to all students

Several countries provide doctoral education free to all students while others see the fee as an important component of funding for the institution. The social-democratic welfare model described in the Finnish case exemplifies the 'fee free' nature of the Nordic countries, which is also the case in Australia and Canada. In countries where fees are charged, there is a considerable diversity of fee sponsorship including the individual, employers, research councils and institutions themselves.

Funding via loans

There is little discussion in the chapters about the use of loans, formal or less formal, in the funding of doctoral work. Only in the cases of Japan and Thailand does the loan figure significantly in the discussion of funding. However, it is probable that in most countries where the student is responsible for funding their studies, loans are of some importance. In the UK for example, self-funding is not unusual, and much of this is in the form of loans from various sources, including parents.

Doctoral candidates as students or employees

In some countries students are students, in others they are employees and in others a hybrid. The case of the Netherlands highlights the tensions between the benefits to the student of a salaried approach and the benefits to the institution of a stipend.

The level of financial support for doctoral candidates, whether employees or students, is a concern for all countries if they are to attract and keep well-qualified candidates. This is highlighted in Canada where the recent significant increase in the stipend has occurred precisely to raise the profile and importance of doctoral candidates. It was noted in the French case that being paid relatively low salaries has raised recruitment challenges and there is now the prospect of significant increases.

South Africa illustrates another dilemma where stipends need to be raised to attract quality candidates in an environment where academic salaries have slipped relative to many other workers.

Supply, demand and cost

We can observe the different approaches to the way in which decisions are taken about student funding. Given that funding is finite in the majority of cases, some level of competition for funding is always present. However, the degree of competition will be driven by the supply and demand of the market-place. In the case of India, with its NETS competition, a large number of stipends are allocated following a national competition.

The chapters gave very little, if any, attention to the actual funding required for doctoral work, implicitly at least relating funding levels to the market and institutional behaviour. It is only recently that the UK has taken a closer look at the costs of providing doctoral programmes. The report by JM Consulting suggests that current funding is far below costs. We wait to see whether this valuable piece of costing research will result in changes to institutional allocations.

Box 19.5 Editors' comment

We need to consider costs in relation to benefits. There is an implicit assumption that doctoral education is worthy of funding, in whatever form, presumably to achieve the desired national outputs in science and technology. We might suggest that the complexity of the funding models reflects a pragmatic incremental approach to funding, rather than one which is based on sound cost–benefit arguments. It might be that funds could be spent very differently to achieve the same economic and technological gains.

The delivery of postgraduate education

Authority to deliver

In terms of the authority for institutions to deliver doctoral programmes we can recognize two groups of countries: those in which the structure of higher education gives autonomy to institutions to offer a full portfolio of awards and those in which higher education is more closely controlled and managed by the state. The former group is typified by those countries that have followed a British model of higher education in which all institutions of higher education[1] are able to award doctorates. In Australia for example, as the population of universities has increased, those newly-designated have been granted research degree awarding powers.

At the other end of a continuum are countries in which the research degree awarding powers are to varying degrees far from automatic. Here universities themselves are not semi-autonomous organizations. Suffice it to say at this stage that in Japan and China, for example, universities have to apply for authorization to run programmes and make research degree awards – in these countries such authorization becomes a matter of controlled status and inevitably creates a stratified system. In Germany and the Netherlands the divide is well defined (only universities can award doctorates), while the other institutions of higher education (in Germany the *Faculschule*) cannot.

Concentration in selected universities

Despite what is written above about autonomy with regard to provision of programmes, there is a considerable difference between having the authority to award research degrees and actually being involved in this market. Decisions on capacity, costs and markets influence institutional decisions. Concentration in the level of activity, for legal authority or for more pragmatic reasons, appears to be a trend across most countries at both institutional and disciplinary levels.

Notwithstanding the authority to award doctorates, the concentration of postgraduate research in selected institutions is present in many of the countries. There does appear to be a tendency for a concentration of activity, some examples of which are highlighted in Table 19.2. If this data is scaled for population size, similar patterns emerge across all countries sampled with the exception of the USA, which in terms of awards made has a significantly greater concentration of awarding activity.

There are further, subtle, aspects of concentration when we add disciplines to the mix. This is well illustrated by the Mexican case, as noted in Table 19.2, in which 148 universities offer doctoral programmes and yet only 10 per cent of these offer awards in ten or more fields of research. In the European case, many universities now specialize in specific disciplines, particularly as far as research and research degree awards are concerned, so that while such institutions may continue to have the authority to offer research awards, these may be in restricted fields of study.

Table 19.2 Examples of concentration of activity

Country	Doctorates awarded
Canada	6 institutions award 50% of doctorates
UK	13 institutions award 50% of doctorates
USA	49 institutions award 50% + of doctorates
Brazil	3 institutions award 43% of doctorates
Mexico	Only 10% of universities offer doctoral programmes in 10 or more fields of study

---

Box 19.6 Editors' comment

The situation with regard to the degree to which individual institutions within a country are autonomous in terms of postgraduate recruitment and ability to make doctoral awards can be characterized as comprising two groups of countries: those in which the structure of higher education gives autonomy to institutions to offer a full portfolio of awards and those in which higher education is more closely controlled and managed by the state. Whichever grouping a country falls into it seems that increasing concentration of research within a certain grouping of (high status) universities is commonplace across our sample. In one sense this is perhaps inevitable as the costs of doing research rise and the need for critical mass, at least in some areas of science and technology, becomes ever more evident. There is a danger however that universities that do not have, or lose over a period of time, the right and the ability to run programmes and make awards will become universities not driven by the demands of cutting edge research. We would question the sense in which an institution that does not engage in research at all, and hence has no postgraduate provision, can truly be termed a 'university'. To us one of the key purposes of a university is to be operating at the edge where knowledge is created rather than merely operating at a subsequent point where it is disseminated. Lack of research necessarily diminishes an institution in this respect. The same applies to disciplines within a university where research withers or has never taken root. However, as we note below with respect to graduate schools, a little creative thinking around collaboration can obviate the inter-institutional tensions which research degree awarding powers seem to create.

Graduate schools

Doctoral programmes associated with graduate schools

The trend across most countries described in this book has been for doctoral programmes to be associated with graduate school development, which itself has led to concentration on focus of activity within institutions. There are, as we might expect, a wide range of different organizational structures which come under the heading 'graduate school'. We have noted this to be the case in the UK (see Woodward and Denicolo 2004). However a global review of the graduate school provides even greater diversity of structure, purpose, funding and authority.

Different models of graduate school

There are differing models of the notion of graduate school in terms of location and focus. At one end of a continuum are those institutions in which the graduate school cuts across all the disciplines, schools, departments or faculties and thus operates at an institution-wide level. At the other end of this continuum are countries where, typically if not entirely, graduate schools within universities manage their affairs at a disciplinary level. For example, in Japanese universities one can find graduate schools in several disciplinary areas. In a further twist to this dimension of discipline specificity, the Finnish case highlights the development of discipline-based graduate schools operating at a national level. In this latter case the research expertise in a particular discipline is pulled together to the intended benefit of the nation. All of the variations may have their own advantages: (i) university-wide systems offer possibilities of unifying the quality expectations of students and regularizing procedures between disciplines; (ii) discipline-specific graduate schools on the other hand enable differentiation according to the particular needs and demands of the relative disciplines; (iii) yet again, nationwide discipline-specific graduate schools such as are found in Finland might seem to offer advantages present in both other models described here in as much as such schools increase uniformity of student expectation and yet allow discipline-specific issues to be addressed.

Different approval processes for graduate schools

In many countries the establishment of a graduate school is a matter for government or for a government agency such as a research council. The graduate school or research school becomes reified into a regulatory structure at a national level. This approach allows the state to influence not only the numbers but also the quality criteria that must be achieved before students are admitted to programmes. We saw in Finland and France that the state is very much involved in the designation of graduate schools through the agency of research councils. In the Netherlands, driven by increasing doctoral student numbers and the demands for more structured training, the Dutch government stimulated the growth of a system of research schools. The Japanese case illustrates a highly centralized process in which institutions must apply for authorization from the state to set up a graduate school and hence have doctoral programmes and there is a standard set of criteria set down by the state which all such applications must meet. These are not unlike those demanded in the Netherlands: a thorough research training programme, a well defined scientific mission, autonomy as far as finance and administration is concerned, opportunities for cooperation and a critical mass within the research environment. In Japan, the entire process of application and approval normally takes about 12 months.

> **Box 19.7 Editors' comment**
>
> The place and functions of graduate schools within universities and in relation to the provision of postgraduate studies varies considerably across our sample. The existence of so many kinds of graduate school performing so many different functions points up the perceived need for research work to be given specific recognition within university management systems but also indicates the uncertainty that surrounds just what form that recognition needs to take to ensure the most effective delivery. In our view a graduate school is most likely to succeed where it addresses the specific needs of an individual institution. Each institution must first ascertain those features that mark out its particular identity and then pursue a model of graduate school that will serve its specific needs; there is no one model that fits all – no one model that is inherently the most effective. Particular national or institutional circumstances should drive the kind of graduate school that is put into operation. Of course it may be that the notion of a defined graduate school is not appropriate at all; what we would suggest however is that an institution needs to have some way of recognizing the specific needs of the postgraduate population and some strategic approach to dealing with those needs.

Programmes of study

Length of programmes

Some countries such as the USA tend to include what would be termed elsewhere a masters stage within their doctoral programmes. It is also the case in the USA and in other countries such as Germany that doctoral students are typically treated as members of staff of the university in which they are registered; their studies are therefore combined with teaching duties. These factors lengthen the apparent 'time to completion' but do not necessarily increase the amount of actual time spent studying. To further confuse the situation, some of the reported times appear to be based on the length of bursary or other funding rather than being based on the actual rates (see for example the chapter on India).

Average stated times to completion in our sample vary considerably, from three to eight years but, as noted above, these times depend on the system for counting study time. It is noteworthy that study periods often vary between disciplines within country norms; in particular, where arts and humanities disciplines are mentioned by contributors it is regularly reported that students in these disciplines take longer to complete than do students in other disciplines. The other factor that is regularly reported as significant is the mode within which study is undertaken. Clearly part-time students take longer – and not just twice as long. But again what counts as part-time is ill-defined and in many cases (again the USA and Germany are good examples) students may be registered as full-time but carry out part-time functions as members of staff or are employed in part-time jobs, in addition to their full-time registration, in order to fund their studies or their living costs. In short, full-time registration does not necessarily mean full-time study.

Age on completion

Some of the variability noted in relation to age on completion is a function of the undergraduate and taught postgraduate structures and the age at which candidates enter the doctoral process. Germany is particularly concerned about the age of candidates on completion, which averages at 32.7 years. The figure quoted for Canada is 36 years. Of course the key variable we should consider is age at the start of the programme. In the UK for example, where an increasing number of candidates are over 30 at the outset of their studies, an average age of completion of 32 years is unsurprising. So again we must look to more subtle explanations before making judgements about doctoral processes from data such as 'age at completion'.

Attrition rates

The issue of attrition rates is one where international comparison would benefit significantly from the development of a common set of definitions. There does appear to be significant variation between countries in terms of attrition (sometimes referred to as 'completion') rates from countries where the figure is very low, such as South Africa and India (12 and 22 per cent completing successfully, respectively) and those where the figure is high such as the Netherlands (70 per cent). Within that range there is considerable variability, with many countries highlighting the difference between the sciences, social science and the humanities.

Box 19.8 Editors' comment

In our view it is unwise to equate period of registration for a research degree with quality of work undertaken. Here is one of the crucial distinctions between taught courses and research degree programmes. It cannot be the case that someone doing research for a shorter period of time will necessarily be producing research of any lesser quality or indeed be learning any less about researching as an activity more generally. Conversely, just because someone takes longer than the norm to complete their research programme does not mean that their research or, again, their learning is any the less because of that longer period. When it comes to research degrees, time on task is not the relevant issue when it comes to judging the quality of outcomes.

It follows from this that national governments or their agencies that begin to use time to submission as a tool to judge quality of an institution's work are running the risk of making erroneous judgements. Of course, time to completion may be a matter of concern when it comes to the cost effectiveness of training programmes. However, research councils and governments that use this as a way of judging quality need to be aware of just what they are about, in part at least because if the same criteria that are used to judge cost effectiveness are also used to make judgements when this is not an issue (e.g. for a self-funding student) then we have a situation where criteria that are reasonable in one context (cost effectiveness) are not so in another (quality of work produced and student learning accomplished).

The length of programmes of study and the age of successful candidates relate to a whole range of issues outside of the research programme itself (e.g. age of commencement, length of time from enrolment of student to registration of project and status of the student in terms of attendant teaching commitments). It is overly simplistic and hence dangerous to begin, as is evident in some countries, to use crude measures of such periods of 'study' time as markers of quality of student experience. Attrition rates are, however, useful in judging how effective the relationship is between prior training, recruitment and support given.

Quality assurance

National quality frameworks

Some of the countries sampled are moving or have moved to a national system of quality frameworks and auditing. For example, in Australia a broad-based national quality audit of higher education institutions is conducted through the Australian Universities Quality Agency (AUQA). Established early in 2000, AUQA is responsible for auditing the quality of Australian universities, including assessment of research and research training. It measures performance and outcomes and its audit reports are publicly available on the AUQA website. This mirrors in broad terms the situation in the UK with the Quality Assurance Agency (QAA) fulfilling a similar function and also making public its findings.

Guardians of the doctoral standard

Organizations such as the AUQA in Australia and the QAA in the UK also act as the guardians of the standards of the award in the sense that broad standards are set out at national level with universities interpreting those standards at local level through their own criteria for the award. So, for example, the Australian Qualifications Framework (AQF) and the UK's Framework of Higher Education Qualifications (FHEQ) are unifying systems of national higher educational qualifications (the AQF includes qualifications across all sectors – schools, vocational education and training as well as the higher education sector whereas the FHEQ is restricted to higher education).

Both these national frameworks have similar words to describe what is meant by the doctorate. Indeed, the words used in both documents are replicated with minor variations of emphasis across most of the countries sampled. The AUQA serves here as an example. It states that, 'the Doctoral degree recognises a substantial original contribution to knowledge in the form of new knowledge or significant and original adaptation, application and interpretation of existing knowledge'. It goes on to specify the format of doctoral outcomes – intended presumably to open out the notion of what a thesis might contain beyond the notion of an empirically based series of studies: 'Doctoral programme outcomes may take the form of a comprehensive critical review of literature, empirical research, creative work or other systematic approach embedded in a field or discipline, and/or they may be based on advanced and sustained critical reflection and analysis of professional theory and practice'.

Box 19.9 Editors' comment

National level bodies that set out the parameters of what counts as quality of provision (in terms of both processes of training and its products) and monitor how well individual institutions perform within these parameters, offer the potential to ensure some notion of the minimum standards that a student may expect within a country. The same might apply within a federal system – though clearly at a federal rather than national level. The danger may arise however that what is laid down becomes a series of targets that institutions expend energy in reaching, rather than a minimum standard for the student experience. An edict that is laid down from 'above' – in this case at a national/federal level – may prove sterile if there is no sense of ownership from universities themselves. It seems then that what is crucial in any national quality-setting and auditing process is that there should be real consultation between the quality agency and the universities as the various standards and the descriptions of how to meet them are devised and implemented. By 'real' here we mean consultation that is transparent to all and which

> contains the crucial elements of negotiation – cycles of proposition and
> response with evidence of mutual recognition of the various inputs and
> the actions upon them (or reasoned rejection of action).

Supervision

Formal and informal approaches to the appointment of supervisors

Both France and Japan have developed approaches to supervision that are
worthy of comment. In France (and similarly in Poland) supervisors must
gain the 'habilitation' in order to supervise, a diploma awarded after
approximately five years of research work following the award of the doctorate. Interestingly, the habilitation, which in France at least involves presentations to a panel of three peers and a board, is concerned more with the
research projects than with the pedagogic issues of supervision. In Japan
supervision appears to be far more regulated than in the other countries in
our sample (with the possible exception of China). Academics wishing to
supervise research students must be formally approved by MEXT (see the
chapter on Japan) and receive the title of *Maru-Go* professor. The process,
which takes around a year to complete, gives the academic a special stamp of
approval by the ministry to supervise doctoral candidates.

At the other end of the spectrum from this highly regulated structure, the
case in Germany appears to be far more relaxed with academic staff not only
free to supervise but apparently to manage the entire process single-handed.

The UK and the majority of the remaining countries appear to occupy a
middle ground in which competence in the area of research and previous
experience are the key criteria in the appointment of supervisors. Increasingly training is advocated in addition to meeting the criteria and there is an
emphasis placed on increasing the quality of supervision even though there
is, again, little direct evidence of poor supervision. In the UK, training of
supervisors has become a key feature of the revised *Code of Practice* (QAA
2004), and similarly it is an accepted part of the doctoral scene in Australia
where the relevant government department requires each university to 'sign
off' the number of supervisors who undertook formal supervisor training.

Workload of supervisors

The workload of supervisors is an issue that concerns many countries and
which links implicitly to the quality of the student experience. There are
examples, such as France, of a regulation around student numbers and workload; here supervisors should not have more than two students at any one
time – but it appears that in reality numbers are much higher, particularly in

the social sciences and humanities. It seems that where regulation is in place it is usually more in terms of appropriate loads and in the context of overall workloads rather than specific set 'allowable' numbers.

Box 19.10 Editors' comment

We have noted in this section the example of the 'habilitation' in France and have suggested that it is concerned more with the research projects than with the pedagogic issues of supervision. We have also noted that the training of supervisors is now a feature of many countries.

In the light of this, it seems to us important to consider just what it is that supervisors are being trained for and, again, this comes full circle to questions about the nature of the doctoral award to which the student aspires. As we have stressed elsewhere in this book, our view is that the student is engaged in acts of learning about how to do research, is studying for an academic award that has criteria that the student needs to demonstrate that they have met. Supervision is, therefore, primarily an act of pedagogy – not of research. Hence it follows that research degree supervision should be about how the supervisor can most effectively engage with the learner in the latter's attempts to provide evidence to meet the criteria for the award.

In one sense it might seem that the art and the science of teaching should readily transfer to the research degree context from the other kinds of university teaching that the academic member of staff is engaged in. However, what makes research degree supervision different is the expectation that the student will attain a kind of mastery that is on a par with the supervisor's and that in respect of the specifics of knowledge the student will exceed that of the supervisor. The 'curriculum' is about extending knowledge not merely transferring it. The essentials of the teacher/pupil (or master/novice) relationship are different from that which pertains at all other levels of learning and therefore the pedagogy is new.

The changing nature of the student population

Gender

The indications are that the student market for doctorates has changed considerably over the past 20 years in the majority of the countries in our sample. For example, in most countries the gender balance has shifted, reflecting positively in favour of women. In the USA, over 45 per cent of doctorates awarded in 2004 were to women candidates; that said, gender is still an issue in several countries as far as academic staffing is concerned. It was noted for example that in the Netherlands only 8 per cent of the full-time professoriate is made up of women (despite a much more favourable ratio of male/female at doctoral level).

Ethnicity

In the UK, considerable discussion is devoted to access and equal opportunities at the undergraduate level, but little if anything is said about these issues at doctoral level. In direct contrast, there is for example considerable concern in Australia that the indigenous population is significantly under-represented in doctoral study and steps are being taken to redress the imbalance. In the Netherlands specific policy, manifest in the Mozaiek Programme, seeks to attract minorities into doctoral study. In the UK data on such matters tends to reside at the institutional level and hence in most institutions, where student numbers are dominated by undergraduates, the contribution which doctoral numbers could make to the overall figures is insignificant.

Perhaps the most interesting discussion of ethnic imbalance is found in the case of South Africa where there has been significant change in the post-apartheid period. In 1993 only 7 per cent of doctoral enrolments, in a racially segregated university system, were 'African' (the term used to describe black Africans as opposed to those of Asian or European extraction). This had risen to 30 per cent by 2003, although the African population at that time represented 80 per cent of the total.

Status of students

Nowhere is status of the student more confused than in the UK, where a doctoral candidate may be a student or a member of staff, may be funded by a bursary or from a variety of other sources (including self-funding), or may be salaried. Canada, the USA and Australia have similar varied structures. These differentials in status give rise to significantly different rights for the doctoral candidate. Arguably, the EU in its adoption of the terminology 'early stage researcher' has added further confusion to the designation by implication, failing to recognize that the early stages of being an 'early stage researcher' often involve being a research student.

The use of posts which combine doctoral research and teaching, often referred to as 'graduate teaching assistants' (GTAs), is common in the USA and increasingly so in the UK and Australia. Such GTAs may be one way to approach bridging the divide between student and employee. This hybrid has the benefit of providing many of the employment rights and privileges of 'staff' without undermining the essentially 'student nature' of the process.

Pressures within Europe to move to employee status will create difficulties for several countries. The issue of status takes us to our fundamental question concerning the doctorate – is it an academic award or a mechanism by which to undertake high-level research? If it is the former then the status of student would appear to be logical. If the latter, employee status may be more appropriate, but only following a serious review of what the doctorate entails.

Box 19.11 Editors' comment

The nature of the doctoral student population has changed in the context of wider social changes in the countries sampled in this book. It is also the case that it has changed as the nature of the doctorate itself has changed. For example, the introduction of doctoral study in the professions (manifest in the growth of professional doctorates in the UK and elsewhere) has meant a new kind of doctoral student who may have significant professional commitments, a particular kind of relationship with the university in terms of attendance, 'supervision' (which may involve supervision of practice in the workplace) and with funding regimes. Systems have to be flexible enough in their design and in their operations to accommodate the broad range of students who are now studying at doctoral level. While this may be accepted at the general level of statements of policy, there is a danger that at the level of the detail what governments and institutions have in mind when they implement policies on the ground is the full-time, male, science-based student direct from an undergraduate or masters programme. In short, the rhetoric of inclusivity and lifelong learning is sometimes at odds with the practices of the providers of postgraduate education where the model of 'Ph.D. student' that is acted upon is much narrower than the reality.

Doctoral outputs

The dissertation or thesis

Across the countries sampled it is a commonplace, though not universal, expectation that the research programme will lead to a single final piece of submitted work upon which the candidate will be assessed in terms of its contribution to knowledge. The lack of universality relates to situations where there are subsidiary pieces of work that are assessed prior to (or in some cases simultaneously with) the examination of the final piece. In essence, the usual practice is to require a doctoral candidate to develop an intellectual position (sometimes referred to as their 'thesis') from which they can sustain an argument and defend it publicly. What is submitted as a bound volume is referred to either as the 'thesis' or the 'dissertation' (i.e. the dissertation that the candidate writes in defence of their 'thesis').

Defining the form of doctoral submissions

The form of this submitted work is defined, across our sample, with greater or lesser degrees of precision. The Australian example embedded in the AUQA, as noted earlier in this chapter, lists the forms that the submission may take and includes, in addition to the traditional notion of empirical research, critical review, creative work and 'other systematic approach[es] embedded in a field or discipline, and/or they [the submissions] may be based on advanced and sustained critical reflection and analysis of professional theory and practice'. This would seem to be – particularly in the latter phrases – an attempt to open up the whole notion of what the 'products' of doctoral study might be. The notion of what counts as a 'contribution' is here being refined by the inclusive way in which the form of the submission is described and in this sense substance is being defined by form. Nevertheless, this move to open up the notion of what may count as a doctoral contribution is a feature of more than one country sampled. It may well be, though we do not have the evidence here to substantiate it, that this move is indicative of a general trend towards a more liberal interpretation of doctoral contribution.

Publication of research outcomes

In many of the countries cited in this book the publication of research results is a precursor, necessary in some cases, to the examination of a candidate's work. The countries most consistently concerned to see work published are those in Scandinavia, while the UK presents a more confused picture (see Powell 2004 for a review), with many universities offering a separate award (the 'Ph.D. by published work') for work that has been published prior to examination.

Examination

In the countries sampled in this book the notion of peer review of the outcomes of the doctoral study programmes invariably underpins the various national systems. It is also noteworthy that, universally, the participation of one examiner who is external to the university is taken as necessary. In some countries (e.g. Australia) the notion of 'external' may be interpreted to mean external to the country.

In many countries the overall concept of the examination of a doctoral candidate also contains the notion that the defence of the submission should be undertaken in a way that is open to public scrutiny. For example, in France the defence takes place in front of a jury composed of two referees, the supervisor and other experts. After the applicant has described their research findings to the assembly there will be a discussion with the jury about the results and the candidate will be asked to justify the research strategies that were employed as well as being subjected to questions about the 'scientific context and the literature' and so on. It is noted in the French chapter that the quality of the discussion varies greatly from one jury to another and that there are no formal guidelines for the organization of the defence. In the USA the written dissertation is required to be approved by at least three committee members and is most often 'defended' publicly. So, the extent to which the examination is held in public or in private varies across countries and indeed varies within countries across institutions. It seems to us likely that in this age of increasing public accountability the trend in the future will be towards more openness and thus situations where the process of examination takes place in private and is cloaked in secrecy will become increasingly rare.

The examination of complementary studies

It is a feature of the country chapters that doctoral training is regularly seen to contain some training that is complementary to, or supportive of, the main thrust of the research programme. The way in which such training components are treated in terms of assessment within the overall examination of doctoral achievement however is not clear. Perhaps the most typical approach is exemplified in France where no examination or assessment of complementary training is planned at the current time, such training being regarded as an opportunity for students to gain 'extra knowledge on scientific matter'. In this model, attendance may be required but there is not seen to be any need for formal assessment at the doctoral level.

Box 19.12 Editors' comment

We identify two key current issues in the assessment of work at doctoral level that apply in most if not all of the countries sampled. First, there is the issue of just what is to be assessed and how 'complementary' studies are related to the overall package of assessment. In our view, doctoral assessment ought to be solely about judging whether or not a candidate has produced evidence sufficient to indicate that they have met the stated criteria for the award – no more and no less. It follows that attainment of 'generic' skills is either a part of those criteria or it is not – and if it is then it must be subject to examination. Referring back to the programmes of study and any

---

attendant supplementary elements, it must be the case that if such attainment is not part of the criteria then it should not be part of the *necessary* teaching and learning process. In the UK at present it seems to us that the situation is confused and the relationship between skills learning, assessment and the criteria for the award is opaque rather than transparent.

Second is the issue of openness to public scrutiny. It seems to us that situations wherein the doctoral submission is treated as a document in confidence, where the examination of the doctorate itself takes place behind closed doors and where even the examiners' reports are kept confidential to the awarding boards within universities in perpetuity are lacking in the necessary public transparency. We describe here the situation in many UK universities. Both the publication of results as part of the learning process and the examination of it and the designation of the viva as a private as opposed to public affair are ways forward that merit consideration. There is no doubt that moving away from the existing model, which is predominant in the UK and to a lesser extent in some other countries, would involve fundamental changes to the whole of the process and product of doctoral education.

Conclusion

Objectives of the book

At the outset of this book we suggested that much of the development of doctoral work in the UK was being undertaken without an understanding of doctoral activity in other countries and this observation led us to set out objectives relating, in part, to the making of international comparisons and drawing together issues of common concern.

In this conclusion it is perhaps appropriate to focus on some of these issues in the spirit of setting out an agenda for further discussion in and between countries.

The purposes of doctoral education

There are discussions to be had about the purposes of doctoral education, specifically in relation to the criteria for the award, relationships between skills, purpose, criteria and assessment, and demarcation of doctoral study by distinctive nomenclature.

Generic skills training

We suggest that the current interest in generic skills training is in danger of shifting the focus of doctoral education to a functionalist, skills-led perspective. The emphasis is typically on a business or team skills approach. But as we have noted elsewhere (Powell and Green forthcoming) the doctorate's purpose is to do with learning about research through the advancement of knowledge not with the building of rafts and playing management games.

The organization and delivery of doctorates

There are issues to do with the way in which doctoral education is organized and delivered at a national level, including the effects of concentrating it in fewer institutions.

The quality of the product

There are questions relating to success, including the quality of the product, completion rates and the overall contribution the doctorate makes.

The doctorate in the context of national economic development

We have seen that for many countries the doctorate is treated as a fundamental element of research and development policy and, ultimately, national economic growth and success. While the relationship between research and development spend and numbers of doctorates is not a simple one, much doctoral investment is predicated on economic growth and technological advancement. This places considerable emphasis on the need to attract well-qualified students into the system and retain them once trained. We have seen that several countries are concerned about brain drain and that the return on their investment frequently benefits others, often competitor or more advanced economies. This is well illustrated in the current recruitment of students to the so-called STEM subjects (science, technology, engineering and maths), where large numbers remain in the UK to undertake post-doc work, many of whom never return to their home country.

The content and disciplinary spread of the doctorate is equally challenged by this close link to national economic performance. The key questions that arise relate to what the subjects are that may best support the national economy and whether or not the award should be fashioned more specifically to that end.

Note

1 The most recently designated universities in the UK following the 2004 White paper have to apply for research degree awarding powers.

References

EUA (European Universities Association) (2005) *Doctoral Programmes for the European Knowledge Society.* Brussels: EUA.

Green, H. and Powell, S.D. (2005) *Doctoral Study in Contemporary Higher Education.* Buckingham: Open University Press.

Powell, S.D. (2004) *The Award of PhD by Published Work in the UK.* Lichfield: UK Council for Graduate Education.

Powell, S.D. and Green, H. (forthcoming) A framework for the future of doctoral study: resolving inconsistent practices and incorporating innovative possibilities, in R. Hinchcliffe, T. Bromley and S. Hutchinson (eds) *Skills Training in Research Degree Programmes: Politics & Practice.* Maidenhead: McGraw-Hill.

Powell, S.D. and Long, E. (2005) *Professional Doctorate Awards in the UK.* Lichfield: Council for Graduate Education.

QAA (Quality Assurance Agency) (2004) *Code of Practice for the Assurance of Academic Quality and Standards in Higher Education: Section 1: Postgraduate Research Programmes,* 2nd edn). Gloucester: QAA.

UKGrad (2005) *What do PhDs do?* UK Grad Programme, available at www.grad.ac.uk/cms/ShowPage/Home_page/Publications/p!edceaFj, accessed 15 September 2006.

UK Grad Programme (2006) *What do PhDs Do?* UK Grad Programme, available at www.grad.ac.uk/cms/ShowPage/Home_page/Publications/p!edceaFj, accessed 21 September 2006.

UUK (Universities UK) (2006) *Patterns of Higher Education Institutions in the UK.* London: UUK.

Woodward, D. and Denicolo, P. (2004) *Review of Graduate Schools in the UK.* Lichfield: Council for Graduate Education.

Yergin, D. and Stanislaw, J.A. (2002) *The Commanding Heights: The Battle for the World Economy.* New York: Free Press.

Index

The Society for Research into Higher Education

The Society for Research into Higher Education (SRHE), an international body, exists to stimulate and coordinate research into all aspects of higher education. It aims to improve the quality of higher education through the encouragement of debate and publication on issues of policy, on the organization and management of higher education institutions, and on the curriculum, teaching and learning methods.

The Society is entirely independent and receives no subsidies, although individual events often receive sponsorship from business or industry. The Society is financed through corporate and individual subscriptions and has members from many parts of the world. It is an NGO of UNESCO.

Under the imprint *SRHE & Open University Press*, the Society is a specialist publisher of research, having over 80 titles in print. In addition to *SRHE News*, the Society's newsletter, the Society publishes three journals: *Studies in Higher Education* (three issues a year), *Higher Education Quarterly* and *Research into Higher Education Abstracts* (three issues a year).

The Society runs frequent conferences, consultations, seminars and other events. The annual conference in December is organized at and with a higher education institution. There are a growing number of networks which focus on particular areas of interest, including:

Access	FE/HE
Assessment	Graduate Employment
Consultants	New Technology for Learning
Curriculum Development	Postgraduate Issues
Eastern European	Quantitative Studies
Educational Development Research	Student Development

Benefits to members

Individual

- The opportunity to participate in the Society's networks
- Reduced rates for the annual conferences
- Free copies of *Research into Higher Education Abstracts*
- Reduced rates for *Studies in Higher Education*

- Reduced rates for *Higher Education Quarterly*
- Free online access to *Register of Members' Research Interests* – includes valuable reference material on research being pursued by the Society's members
- Free copy of occasional in-house publications, e.g. *The Thirtieth Anniversary Seminars Presented by the Vice-Presidents*
- Free copies of *SRHE News* and *International News* which inform members of the Society's activities and provides a calendar of events, with additional material provided in regular mailings
- A 35 per cent discount on all SRHE/Open University Press books
- The opportunity for you to apply for the annual research grants
- Inclusion of your research in the *Register of Members' Research Interests*

Corporate

- Reduced rates for the annual conference
- The opportunity for members of the Institution to attend SRHE's network events at reduced rates
- Free copies of *Research into Higher Education Abstracts*
- Free copies of *Studies in Higher Education*
- Free online access to *Register of Members' Research Interests* – includes valuable reference material on research being pursued by the Society's members
- Free copy of occasional in-house publications
- Free copies of *SRHE News* and *International News*
- A 35 per cent discount on all SRHE/Open University Press books
- The opportunity for members of the Institution to submit applications for the Society's research grants
- The opportunity to work with the Society and co-host conferences
- The opportunity to include in the *Register of Members' Research Interests* your Institution's research into aspects of higher education

Membership details: SRHE, 76 Portland Place, London W1B 1NT, UK Tel: 020 7637 2766. Fax: 020 7637 2781. email: srheoffice@srhe.ac.uk
world wide web: http://www.srhe.ac.uk./srhe/
Catalogue: SRHE & Open University Press, McGraw-Hill Education, McGraw-Hill House, Shoppenhangers Road, Maidenhead, Berkshire SL6 2QL. Tel: 01628 502500. Fax: 01628 770224. email: enquiries@openup.co.uk – web: www.openup.co.uk

Related books from Open University Press
Purchase from www.openup.co.uk or order through your local bookseller

DOCTORAL STUDY IN CONTEMPORARY HIGHER EDUCATION

Howard Green and Stuart Powell

- How can the full range of doctoral study in the UK be best described?
- What are the key features that are driving change to the system?
- What are the implications of current initiatives and the increasingly international context of research degree study?

This book covers the differing kinds of doctorate award that exist currently and discusses critically issues that arise from the ways in which related forms of doctoral study are organized and assessed. It focuses on doctoral study, in all its forms, in the higher education sector in the United Kingdom, while being contextualized within an international dimension.

Drawing on both quantitative and qualitative data, the book focuses on the diversity in doctoral study. It examines the current state of the full range of doctoral awards, describes them, and then critically analyses tensions that exist. For example, it assesses the definitions and relations between different kinds of doctoral award, the pedagogy that surrounds them and the examination phases of each. The book also offers suggestions of ways to resolve the tensions associated with different forms of study and indicates possible future directions.

Doctoral Study in Contemporary Higher Education is an essential text for those who manage, fund and deliver education at doctoral level.

Contents
*Foreword – Preface – Acknowledgements – List of abbreviations – **Part 1: Context** – The origins, issues and recent development of doctoral study in the UK – Doctoral study, Government and the workplace – **Part 2: Range of doctoral awards in the UK** – The PhD and the diversity of doctoral study – The PhD by published work – Professional doctorates – Practice-based doctorates – **Part 3: Issues surrounding the development of doctoral study** – Funding of doctoral programmes – Length of doctoral training programmes – **Part 4: Managing doctoral study** – The nature of doctoral supervision – Monitoring and assessment – Principles and purposes of doctoral examination – Processes of examining the doctorate – **Part 5: The future of the doctorate** – Future directions – References – Index.*

288pp   0 335 21473 8 (Paperback)   0 335 21474 6 (Hardback)

PROFESSIONAL DOCTORATES
INTEGRATING PROFESSIONAL AND ACADEMIC KNOWLEDGE

David Scott, Andrew Brown, Ingrid Lunt and Lucy Thorne

- What are professional doctorates?
- How do they change professional knowledge and improve practice?
- How can universities organise doctoral programmes to facilitate professional learning and development?
- What is the most appropriate relationship between professional and academic knowledge?

This book examines the relationship between advanced study on professional doctorate courses and professional practice. In particular, it examines issues that relate to:

- recruitment
- aims and purposes
- selection of content and focus
- assessment procedures
- curricular structures
- pedagogy
- teaching strategies
- conditions for learning
- support for professionals
- relations with interested bodies and stakeholders.

The book develops in-depth case studies of three professional doctorates: the doctorate in business administration (DBA), the engineering doctorate (DEng) and the education doctorate (EdD).

Professional Doctorates: Integrating Professional and Academic Knowledge makes an important contribution to this neglected area of research. It provides essential reading for policy makers in higher education and those interested in professional doctorate study.

Contents

March 2004 184pp 0 335 21332 4 Paperback £22.99
0 335 21333 2 Hardback £65.00

THE DOCTORAL EXAMINATION PROCESS
A HANDBOOK FOR STUDENTS, EXAMINERS AND SUPERVISORS

Penny Tinkler and Carolyn Jackson

- What is the viva and how can students prepare for it?
- What should supervisors consider when selecting PhD examiners?
- How should examiners assess a doctoral thesis and conduct the viva?

The doctoral examination process has been shrouded in mystery and has been a frequent source of anxiety and concern for students, supervisors and examiners alike. But now help is at hand. This book sheds new light on the process, providing constructive ways of understanding the doctoral examination, preparing for it and undertaking it.

This book stands alone in the field due to the extensive research undertaken by the authors. During a four year project, interviews were conducted with candidates and academics from a wide range of disciplines through the United Kingdom. Outcomes and ideas from the research have been united to provide the most comprehensive information available.

Real life accounts and case studies are combined with useful advice, tasks and checklists to create an illuminating handbook. This user-friendly book is a vital resource for anyone involved in the doctoral process. No doctoral candidate, examiner or supervisor should be without it.

Contents
Acknowledgements – Introduction to the PhD examination process – Understanding the doctoral viva: what is it for? – Understanding the doctoral viva: how does it work? – Viva preparation: long term – Selecting examiners – Who attends the viva? roles and obligations – Examiners: should you examine? – Examiners: assessing a PhD thesis – Viva preparation: short term – Viva preparation: final stage – In the viva: candidates' perspectives – The viva: tips and issues for examiners – Post viva – References.

192pp   0 335 21305 7 (Paperback)   0 335 21306 5 (Hardback)